SHAKESPEARE AND THE REASON

SHAKESPEARE AND THE REASON

*A Study of the Tragedies
and the Problem Plays*

by

TERENCE HAWKES

Routledge & Kegan Paul

LONDON

First published in 1964
by Routledge & Kegan Paul Limited
Broadway House, 68-74 Carter Lane
London, E.C.4

Printed in Great Britain
by Compton Printing Limited
London and Aylesbury

Second impression 1968

SBN 7100   1502   X

To
ANN

CONTENTS

vii

PREFACE

WHEN OPHELIA turns aside Hamlet's remarks about *The Mousetrap* with

> You are naught, you are naught.
> I'll mark the play.
>
> (III, ii, 142–3)

she makes a very proper comment on dramatic criticism. The first object of any writing about Shakespeare should be to send the reader back to the plays. Such a stark statement perhaps does injustice to a great deal of modern criticism and the proposition on which it rests, that the critic's interpretation can never claim primacy over Shakespeare's own words, may not be wholly valid. If it were, it would deny the critic his undoubted advantage of hindsight. By its means he may argue quite without vanity that he can discern the larger significance of the plays more clearly than could Shakespeare himself. And as a result he can claim that his comments may be necessary to a proper understanding of them. Nevertheless, to assert this should not be to deny that the purpose of Shakespearean criticism properly extends beyond itself. The question is not one of primacy so much as of direction; criticism which is self-regarding is also self-defeating.

I hope, therefore, that the reader will 'mark the play' as much as anything which he reads in this book. In fact its nature requires that this be done, for it tries to suggest a new way of looking at some of the plays, and the validity of its argument will depend to a great extent on a close reading of them.

An attempt has been made first of all to place the plays in a context of concomitant ideas in order that certain of their elements may be thrown into relief. The ideas are those which concern the human faculty of reason, and this has meant that I have had to speak of matters of medieval and renaissance philosophy and theology as well as of other related areas of human thought in order properly to state my case. Because this

ix

constitutes an invasion of the territory of specialists of all kinds, my conclusions are advanced with diffidence and in the hope that my indebtedness to those writers has been fully recorded.

The plays which will be discussed are those seven, *Hamlet*, *Troilus and Cressida*, *All's Well That Ends Well*, *Measure for Measure*, *Othello*, *Macbeth* and *King Lear* which are generally spoken of as the 'tragedies' and the 'problem plays'. Whilst they are, naturally, inseparable from the rest of the canon, they have been considered as a 'group' both because of their intrinsic interest as such and because it has seemed unprofitable to destroy the pattern of thinking about the problems of the human reason which they seem to contain. They have been treated in what appears to be their most likely chronological order for this reason. The date of *Macbeth* is not certain but in making the assumption that it was written before *King Lear* I have argued implicitly that it represents part of a developing pattern of thought which requires that play as its conclusion.

As far as possible the plays have been allowed to speak for themselves and their structure encouraged to impose itself on what is said about them rather than the reverse. Whilst an attempt has been made to direct the reader's attention in a certain way, any otherwise unwarranted intrusion between him and the text has been avoided.

The view of life, and of the role of the reason in it which emerges from such a study, should not necessarily recommend itself to us simply because Shakespeare upholds it. The nature of Shakespearean idolatry is such that his opinions on most matters have been invested with the kind of authority which implies their uncritical acceptance by everyone. Yet an abundance of evidence exists to show that Shakespeare was not a pleasantly liberal thinker, that improbable product of so many of our flattering projections of ourselves. Rather, he could be said to have approved of a number of extreme positions in political, social and economic matters which should be as abhorrent to a modern democracy (I speak from what I hope is a generally acceptable twentieth-century standpoint) as those of the period which they reflect. Even if we grant that Shakespeare's opinions are eclectic and 'de-personalised', they exhibit nonetheless an antipathy towards much that we might in other circumstances find admirable in his own period. A good deal of the argument of these plays could be considered, if shallowly, to embody a protest against the 'new-fangled' notions of the English renaissance. It is as well to remember that many of those notions nevertheless brought a large amount of good into the world. On the other hand it need hardly be said that beneath Shakespeare's views of particular matters there runs a deep concern with the universal problems of the human condition, which has a proper claim to be of abiding interest.

The reader is not, therefore, invited to approve or disapprove of what Shakespeare says; my concern is simply that he should be heard to say it. In this way I hope that his words will be allowed the kind of primacy which they warrant both as great art and as part of our experience of a past age. The relationship between that age and our own has been assessed in different ways, and to call it that of a beginning to an end perhaps misrepresents a complex situation. But to say that in the tragedies and problem plays we are confronted with an attempt to deal with an immediately recognizable, because modern, problem is hopefully both permissible and indicative of their significance. The seeds of our world are in Shakespeare's as much as they are in any, and much of the interest which these plays have for us lies in their formulation of an older predicament which we have inherited. The solution which they offer to it may not be acceptable to us, but they force us to recognize that a dilemma existed and exists in human affairs which requires a solution. As a result they provide us with much more than mere information about the past; they force us to re-live and re-think our culture's past in the company of a mind whose commitments make us appraise our own. In order to capture that experience it is necessary to exercise the special kind of attention which Ophelia rightly recognized should be afforded to momentous drama. If this book helps to inculcate that in its readers, then its purpose will be amply fulfilled.

ACKNOWLEDGEMENTS

MANY PEOPLE have helped and encouraged me and will know that I am grateful to them. I am particularly indebted to Professor E. C. Llewellyn, my colleagues of the English Department of University College, Cardiff, and especially to Miss E. M. Brown and Mr. G. Ingli James. Special mention must be made of the extent to which Mr. H. M. Quinn made available to me his specialized knowledge and his unflagging goodwill. He cheerfully read and re-read a very trying manuscript, and his advice kept me from making many mistakes. Those which remain are my own responsibility. I am also grateful to Professor the Reverend W. M. Merchant of the University of Exeter for maintaining the kindly and stimulating interest in my work so characteristic of him.

Parts of Chapter 4 were originally published in a different form in *Studies in Philology*, and I am grateful to the Editor of that journal for permission to reprint them.

Some of the material of Chapters 2–6 formed the basis of a series of lectures given at the State University of New York, Buffalo, N.Y., during the summer of 1963, and I am grateful to Professor O. A. Silverman who has made my visits to the United States both possible and comfortable.

My thanks must also go to my students on both sides of the Atlantic who have borne the burden of my views with tolerance and good humour. Their observations, invariably perceptive and often chastening, are incorporated into the body of what I have written to such a degree that it is impossible to single them out and give them the credit they warrant. It can only be said that I am sure I have learned more from them than they have from me, and that they deserve a better book.

Anybody who writes about Shakespeare will incur an obligation to two major critics, Professor G. Wilson Knight and Professor L. C. Knights. My own is so great that detailed acknowledgement of it is impossible, and it must simply be said

Acknowledgements

that the seeds of most of what I have to say will be found in their writings. In this respect, I share the company of many others to great profit, and count myself fortunate to do so.

My greatest debt of gratitude is to my wife.

T. H.

University College,
Cardiff.

Note: All Shakespearean quotations and references are taken from *The Complete Works* (Tudor Edn.), ed. Peter Alexander, (London, 1951).

Reason, in itself confounded,
Saw division grow together,
To themselves yet either neither,
Simple were so well compounded,

That it cried 'How true a twain
Seemeth this concordant one!
Love hath reason, reason none,
If what parts can so remain'.

Whereupon it made this threne
To the phoenix and the dove,
Co-supremes and stars of love,
As chorus to their tragic scene.
  (*The Phoenix and Turtle*, ll. 41–52)

REASON AND INTUITION:
APPEARANCE AND REALITY

Yit Mynde, I sey to yow, be-thynke
In what perell ye be now! take hede!
(*Wisdom*, ll. 903–4)

IN HIS ESSAY on *Troilus and Cressida* G. Wilson Knight speaks of a 'dynamic opposition' between two faculties of the human mind and makes this the basis of a brilliant analysis of the fundamental philosophical oppositions with which the play itself is concerned.[1] He admits nevertheless that the terms he has used to describe them, 'intellect' on the one hand and 'intuition' on the other, '. . . cannot be ultimately justified as exact labels for the two faculties under discussion . . .' although he finds that the faculties themselves are clearly embodied in the play.

Many critics have since disagreed with this view and have supported their arguments against it by pointing to the same lack of 'ultimate justification' for the terms, and by denying the existence amongst the Elizabethans of the concepts to which they refer. As J. C. Maxwell puts it, '. . . the notion of a supra-rational intuition has no place in the thought of Shakespeare or of his age.'[2]

The purpose of this chapter is in part to show that not only did the thought of Shakespeare and his age contain a clear-cut notion of the existence of a mental faculty of 'supra-rational intuition', but also that far from having 'no place' it might be said to have occupied a crucial position in that culture. In

[1] G. Wilson Knight, 'The Philosophy of *Troilus and Cressida*' in *The Wheel of Fire* (Oxford, 1930), pp. 47 ff.

[2] J. C. Maxwell, 'Shakespeare: the middle plays' in *The Pelican Guide to English Literature* Vol. 2, *The Age of Shakespeare* (London, 1955), p. 215.

addition, it will be argued that some fairly 'exact labels' may be found which can legitimately be used to describe the opposition in the mind with which Professor Knight was concerned.

The 'labels' which will be suggested are 'reason' (in place of Knight's 'intellect') and 'intuition' (in a sense rather different from that implied by his use of the same word). In order to complete a full contemporary picture of the end and purpose of the faculties in question two other terms will be needed and 'appearance' and 'reality' will be used for these. In what follows, an attempt will be made to justify their choice, to define their use, to demonstrate the existence of the ideas about the human mind to which they refer, and to place these in an Elizabethan context.

Certain difficulties are immediately raised by such a project. First, Shakespeare did not use these terms himself in any exact way, nor would we expect him to have done so. He was primarily a dramatist, and so was concerned to make a dramatic use of ideas; to exhibit them in action on the stage rather than to discuss them with the kind of regard for precise definition that we would expect had he written philosophical dialogues and not plays. Therefore, if an understanding of these ideas (even a recognition that they existed) can illuminate without limiting the plays which contain them, it will be necessary to try to put into words, to 'define' matters which Shakespeare was able, much more satisfyingly, simply to enact.

Any discussion of those matters must raise another difficulty, for whatever the actual framework of ideas in a culture may be, it is not necessarily the same as that held to and acted on by the culture in practice. An age can be mistaken about itself (most are) and can be as unaware as any of its individual members of the nature of its own motivations. The same applies equally to one culture's view of another. Little 'objective' truth exists in this respect, and much that we discern in Elizabethan and Jacobean civilization would have been unrecognized and possibly denied by an Elizabethan or Jacobean person. There is nothing unreasonable in this: whatever a culture believes to be true is true for that culture. But this in itself cannot deny the existence of whatever later cultures perceive in an earlier one. No civilization has any absolute claim on veracity and we need to find what we are looking for in the past as part of a process of self-identification; hence we place our own truth *a fortiori* over the truths of previous ages and we believe in it in order to believe in ourselves. The ultimate difficulty lies in deciding how much and to what extent ideas which seem to us to have been important in any period were in fact significant and formative in their effect on the way people lived and thought at that time. The simplest method of dealing with the problem in this case is to relieve the present chapter of half of the burden and to place that on the rest of the book. Thus, if Shakespeare's interest in the matters discussed here can be illustrated in succeeding chapters, then that will provide a reasonable case for arguing that they were significant both for him and for his audience.

Moreover, the way in which the plays deal with these concepts may also illuminate them; a 'two-way' interchange takes place in such matters which considerations of the relationship between literature and society too often discount. 'Popular' forms of communication like the drama can determine as well as reflect human thinking. For example, in our own time not only may television claim to be 'like' life, but it can also be the means of causing life to become disturbingly like itself. The same applies, to an admittedly lesser extent, to Shakespeare's plays in their period, so that whilst all great drama must invariably be congruent with its own culture, to designate particular 'causes' and 'effects' in what amounts to an extremely complex *rapport* can be misleading.

It is particularly so when the less concrete manifestations of human activity in any period are relegated to the limbo of 'background'. Drama makes use of a 'conversational' method of communication both in itself and between itself and the civilization which constitutes its audience. To think of it as making 'statements' before a back-cloth of historical events and ideas creates a quite improper distinction between modes of human self-consciousness which in fact co-exist and inter-act 'conversationally' as parts of a whole greater than themselves. The notion of 'congruency' necessitates those of equality and interdependence and the designation of the elements involved in it as 'back'- or 'fore'-ground destroys such balance. Those distinctions may perhaps be avoided in the present case by giving some indication of the way in which the ideas in question formed part of the totality of the age's experience and pervaded it on the levels both of thought and of action; they will be seen, it is hoped, through the minds of those who thought about them and heard, however variously and amorphously expressed, in the many voices which spoke of them. If they, and the problems they created, can be discerned in a conspectus of this kind, then it will be possible to approach Shakespeare's own particular and powerful formulation of them in a manner both appropriate to its status and indicative of it.

The result will not be to set up a Procrustean bed and to fit Shakespeare's plays to it so much as to sketch out a small part of the Procrustean bed which his own age (like all ages) had constructed for itself, and to which his own plays (like all great plays) are well fitted perhaps because they themselves had helped in the construction.

Of course, any modern critic who considers issues of this nature will find himself faced with the problem of talking about the ideas of one culture in the language of another. For whatever the extent to which our own civilization may be a development of the earlier one and may use a language which springs from a common source, it nevertheless differs from it in many ways, and different preoccupations of all kinds surround the words it uses. Shakespeare's civilization is so unlike that of modern Britain that it may by now be almost less misleading to treat it as an alien culture than to attempt to cope with the difficulties which arise from the presumption of an identity which no longer exists. Neither course is completely satisfactory, and for this reason it has seemed easier to try to give some sort of historical perspective to these notions in order to by-pass some of the confusion which surrounds them in the modern world.

Most human ideas have a long and complex history which resists codification, but it seems reasonable in this instance to suggest two focal points; that is, points in time at which their form was crystallized and given new significance by notable thinkers who had, for their own purposes, gathered together and unified most of the disparate accretions of thought which such concepts usually attract to themselves. In the case of the notion of a human mind which had two major faculties, one rational and the other intuitive, its two most important formulations prior to Shakespeare's time seem to have been those of Aquinas and Ficino. And in so far as the juxtaposition of these names, one of a medieval Scholastic, the other of a renaissance Neo-platonist, both great writers of 'summations' of human thought, evokes so powerfully the intellectual climate of the Elizabethan period, it gives support in itself to the judgement that these represent points at which any account should be fuller than at others. Accordingly an attempt has been made to correlate the work of these two thinkers, and thus to demonstrate the kind of fusion between their conclusions which the Elizabethans were able for many reasons to make. The history of the concepts of reason and intuition and of appearance and reality at points other than these will in consequence be only slightly treated, and in a manner intended simply to show the means by which a connection between these two became possible.

It must of course be said that the terms which will be used are not easily defined for our own culture, although this will have to be briefly attempted. Questions which concern the human mind, and the nature of its reason or of its perception of reality are of an order of complexity in the twentieth century which would have surprised a man of Shakespeare's sensibility in the seventeenth. So many different issues are involved in each case that it is difficult even to think of them as the same questions. The world was smaller then, if no less complicated, and much that could be safely labelled 'rational' or 'real' has for us passed out of those realms into others of a psychological or sociological nature.

We should remember nevertheless that however diffracted such ideas may be in our own time, the culture of the Elizabethan and Jacobean period had a firm hold on them; so firm, that it did not feel the need to talk about them with the kind of precision which we would require of our modern spokesmen. That in itself is one of the major differences between our civilization and theirs, and it lies behind some of the difficulties mentioned above whilst raising a final one which concerns succeeding chapters.

An age not yet wholly committed to an analytical mode of thinking about the world can speak to itself by means of art; it can use metaphor where we would require argument; it can watch a play where we would look for facts and figures. Because Shakespearean drama depends so heavily on language of a metaphorical kind, because it is poetic drama, the modern critic who talks about it has in effect to discourse about something whose nature is non-discursive. More simply, he has to write in prose and in modern English about plays written in verse and in

5

renaissance English. This of course presents an aspect of a problem which has already been stated in another way. A culture which, like our own, experiences the disquietude which comes of a compulsion to define and analyse runs the risk of losing sight of that which it seeks thereby to understand. If it can be said that the mode of our thinking is an 'explaining' one, then the danger arises that not only will the critic find himself talking about one culture in the language of another, but that by such 'explanation' of it, he will eventually explain it away.

It may be possible to avoid that by means of leaving sufficient room within the subsequent discussion for the complexity with which their own culture surrounded these ideas to be hinted at wherever it cannot be stated. This has been attempted on the larger ground that Shakespeare's civilization, and his plays, have, of course, much more to them than appears here and it would be foolish to think otherwise. Nevertheless, even so qualified a purpose forces an odd role on the arguments which follow for they constitute in themselves an act of analysis, of 'reasoning', of a sort that Shakespeare himself would perhaps condemn. Paradoxically, their shortcomings will perhaps prove his point about the shortcomings of this kind of activity.

Reason and intuition are difficult words to use in a modern context, although we usually suppose that everyone understands what is meant by them. For instance, we sometimes assume that they refer to two different operations which the human mind performs, and yet it is clear enough that these activities, if they are such, are very closely related. Indeed, part of the difficulty lies in the fact that the words could be said to refer not so much to two different pursuits of the mind as to the mind's two different ways of pursuing the same end, namely truth. The difference between them is perhaps more one of means than of ends, and it may be less confusing to think of both words as the names of separate 'faculties' or powers said to exist within the mind, and on which it can draw in accordance with the kind of cognition required by a particular occasion.

A traditional view would see the faculty of reason as man's prime possession, that which most sharply distinguishes him from the animals. By means of it he is able to reach certain kinds of conclusions, to proceed from 'given' facts to others which are not given. Involved in this process are a number of other activities of the mind related to the reason as additional means by which its end is reached; the use of observation, experiment, and inferences made from these all constitute 'rational' activities because they help in the movement towards the reason's goal, the establishment of factual truth.

The faculty of intuition is also concerned with truth but uses an entirely different method of reaching it. Intuitive thinking is non-inferential; it omits all the successive stages of the reasoning process and reaches its conclusions instantaneously, in a single leap. Observation and experiment play no part in this process for it is quite alien to them. Intuition exercises a mode of mental activity which is distinctively *not* rational (though it may be given a higher status than that of the reason; it may be considered 'super-rational'). Its goal is a kind of 'fact' inaccessible to the reason because it cannot be reached in the reason's way. If we call reason 'discursive' in its method, intuition should be called 'non-discursive'.

These, usually, are the characteristics we imply when we use these words today. Whether they accurately describe any real aspect of experience or not, whether such a faculty as the 'intuition' exists in fact, raises philosophical or semantic difficulties best reserved for those qualified to deal with them. Professor A. J. Ayer has questioned the value of 'intuition' as a meaningful word, including it among those which '. . . are brought in just to disguise the fact that no explanation has been found (for certain mental phenomena),'[1] and if we accept the terms of his argument we must agree. Similarly, the concept of the reason, as it has been described, is vulnerable from many modern points of view. On the other hand, and in a larger sense, the concept that there are two modes of perception, one rational, one intuitive, has always provided a symmetrical configuration of human experience; it embraces the paradox of complementary-yet-opposed states of being: earthly and heavenly, physical and spiritual, even male and female. Our convictions in such matters however are not really in question here.[2] The present concern is to establish the

[1] A. J. Ayer, *The Problem of Knowledge* (Penguin edn. London, 1956), p. 33.

[2] An interesting and certainly valuable modern view of these issues is given by T. E. Hulme in 'The Philosophy of Intensive Manifolds', in *Speculations*, ed. Herbert Read (London, 1924). See also Frank Kermode, *The Romantic Image* (London, 1957), pp. 129 ff.

existence of certain concepts in a past age; the difficulty of giving names to them which may be used in critical discussion is perhaps best dealt with by making use of words which can, however generally, evoke the ideas of that age and suggest their complexity.

The notion that there were two faculties in the mind, one whose mode was 'rational' and another whose mode was of a higher 'intuitive' order was a very precise one amongst Shakespeare's contemporaries, and a brief glance at its history will perhaps enable us to understand the nature of the problem which it brought into being. Its roots are found ultimately in Greek thought. In his account of the human mind Aristotle makes a clear distinction between the faculty of intellect (*nous*) and that of the reason (*logos*). The reason, he says, achieves its end by discourse, by logical processes from first principles; its direction is towards factual truth, its movement discursive, its mode that which we would call 'rational'. The intellect, on the other hand, is considered to be a faculty above the level of discursive reasoning, beyond it and inaccessible to it.[1] Like Plato (whose division of the mind is similar to Aristotle's, though his terms are different),[2] he regards the discursive reason as a faculty sufficient in itself for the day-to-day operations of the mind, but inevitably superseded by the faculty of pure intellect which has access to higher regions of reality.

The full extent of Aristotle's influence on western thinking is incalculable, but elements of it are clearly discernible in the work of the Scholastic philosophers, and attention should be drawn to the greatest of these in order that his account of the difference between the mind's two modes of cognition may be examined; it was a formative one for succeeding ages.

St. Thomas Aquinas speaks of the human mind in a manner which recalls that of the Greek thinkers.[3] Like Aristotle, he

[1] *De Anima*, Bk. III. See D. J. Allan, *The Philosophy of Aristotle* (London, 1952), pp. 78 ff.
[2] Cf. *The Republic*, Bk. VI.
[3] It is obvious, of course, that in a very important way he differs from them. For pre-Christian philosophers, nothing is superior to man's reason. The *ratio* was capable of perfection (as *recta ratio*) and led directly to the highest virtue. For Aquinas, however, man is a created being, and he is as a result much more concerned with his limitations than with his perfections. To the Christian, reason is imperfect and fallible. This difference is well

divides it into two faculties, calling these the *ratio superior*, the higher reason, and the *ratio inferior*, the lower reason. The higher reason is said to be '. . . intent on the consideration and consultation of things eternal'; whereas the lower reason is '. . . intent on the disposal of temporal things'.[1] The difference between them is virtually the same as in Aristotle, and the higher reason seems to be a faculty which might be called 'intuitive'. Its method of knowing is like that of the Angels; for an Angel, all knowledge is infused into the mind in a moment, and no discursive thinking or any 'rational' process takes place; the Angel's thought reaches instantly to truth, without doubt, error or indecision:

> When an Angel apprehends the nature of anything, he at the same time understands whatever can be either attributed to it, or denied of it. Hence, in apprehending a nature, he by one simple perception grasps all that we can learn by composing and dividing.[2]

This intuitive power is discernible in Man as a vestige of an angelic capacity; the confines of time and place, and 'here and now' do not restrict it; it reaches its conclusions by dispensing with the successive and discursive movements of the reason towards fact; it perceives in a flash of immediate apprehension.[3]

The *ratio inferior*, on the other hand, is 'lower' only in the sense that it has a less exalted purpose. It depends on sense-data for its operation and must work its way by those means from premiss to conclusion until it reaches a limited goal of contingent truth. It is discursive in operation, confined to time and place, to a 'here' and a 'now'. This is the faculty by which we normally live, work and think; it is earth-bound, sub-lunar and so imperfect, and

[1] *Summa Theologica* I. Q.LXXIX., A. 9. All references are to the edition of the *Summa Theologica* translated by the English Dominican Fathers (London, 1922).
[2] *S.T.* I. Q.LVIII., A. 324.
[3] *S.T.* I. Q.LVII., A. 1. Cf. Frank Kermode, *op. cit.* pp. 9 ff.

illustrated by comparing, say, the view of Seneca that virtue lies in the 'right' use of reason alone: '*Virtus non aliud quam recta ratio est*' (*Epistulae Morales* LXVI, 33. Cf. also LXXVI, 22 and LXXI, 17), with that of St. Augustine who counsels almost the reverse; man must believe in order that he may understand.

(presumably, though this is only implied) is so as a result of the Fall.

It should be noticed that these two aspects of the human *ratio* have complementary functions which are not mutually exclusive. This is to say that they are both conceived to be parts of the same whole, that of the *ratio*; the intuitive faculty is just as rational, though of a higher *genre* of reason, as the faculty of reason itself, and the two are interdependent. As Aquinas says, quite firmly, (he is essentially a 'rationalist' thinker in this way), '. . . the higher and lower reasons are one and the same power . . .'[1] The difference lies in function and object, rather than kind.[2]

Elsewhere, Aquinas relates this intuitive faculty to the idea of the intellect as Aristotle had done, and regards it in the same light, as existing in a realm above the senses, and independent of them. It is a faculty which never deceives, and is '. . . always true as regards what a thing is.'[3] Able to know the absolute nature of a thing, it does so independently of what the senses tell it.[4] Seated in the soul, as part of it, it therefore has freedom from all mundane restriction.[5] Its scope rises above nature, and the earth; although in Man, it is supernatural.[6]

Whilst Man possesses this divine faculty his total being is nevertheless rational, and as such earthly in its mode. His mind fundamentally requires the 'many and various operations', the 'composing and dividing' which typifies the discursive motion of the faculty of reason, in order to acquire a certain necessary kind of knowledge. By this he remains tied to the earth, and to the senses through which he perceives the earth. But his senses are unfortunately neither acute nor accurate; they know only the 'outward accidents' of things, and the 'images of bodies', not true reality. Only through his intuition can Man attain the ultimate reality, and perceive, like the Angels, the 'essences of things'.[7] Aquinas even goes so far as to hint that the *ratio inferior* is a defect of the mind, although a necessary one in view of Man's fallen condition; it should not, however, be despised, for it is man's

[1] *S.T.* I. Q.LXXIX., A. 9.
[2] *S.T.* I. Q.LXXIX., A. 8.
[3] *S.T.* I. Q.LVIII., A. 5.
[4] *S.T.* I. Q. LXXV., A. 2 and A. 5.
[5] *S.T.* I. Q. LXXV., A. 6.
[6] *S.T.* I. Q.LXXVI., A. 6.
[7] *S.T.* I. Q.LVII., A. 1.

proper function to live virtuously in accordance with its dictates. Because of it the mind remains essentially mundane, although potentially, because of the *ratio superior*, it has a God-like capacity. The meanest, as St. Augustine allows, is *capax dei*. Nevertheless, Man's specific characteristic is ratiocination, or *discursus*.

In his picture of Man's mind, Aquinas takes an impartial view. He calls one aspect of *ratio* 'higher', one 'lower', but he does not imply that one is better than the other, merely that one is more concerned with 'higher things' than the other. Both 'reasons' are essential to the complete man, and properly employed, will reach the same truth, not two opposed versions of it; the one, in effect, becomes a means of knowing the other. The major distinction he makes is that '... wisdom is attributed to the Higher Reason, Science to the Lower.'[1] By this, the contemplation of the spiritual lies within the province of the intuition; the study of the natural world constitutes the province of the reason. Both provinces are part of a greater whole, the divine plan of the universe as a single and indivisible unity.

Aquinas and the other Scholastics are undoubtedly the source of many Elizabethan ideas, not the least of them this one, and it is from his account of the faculties of a 'lower' and a 'higher' reason, so firmly imprinted on the Middle Ages by the *Summa Theologica* and other works, that the Elizabethan concept of a similar division in the mind seems in part to spring.[2] However, that later age had experienced some significant changes of emphasis in the matter, involving a different notion of the 'lower' reason's role in human affairs which was to have far-reaching results.

---

[1] *S.T.* I. Q. LXXIX., A. 9. The difference here is that between *scientia*, the knowledge of external facts proper to the *ratio inferior*, and the higher beatific knowledge of *sapientia*, the wisdom which lies beyond mere facts, and which is accessible only to the *ratio superior*. This latter knowledge leads ultimately to the love of God and is, in short, piety: *ecce pietas est sapientia*. See Fr. Kenelm Foster, *St. Thomas, Petrarch, and the Renascence* (Aquinas Society of London, paper no. 12, Oxford, 1949), pp. 8 ff. Cf. C. N. Cochrane, *Christianity and Classical Culture* (New York, 1940), pp. 470 ff., in which this distinction is more fully described in respect of St. Augustine, whom Aquinas appears to follow here.

[2] Another major source is of course Boethius' *De Consolatione Philosphiæ*, Bk v, Prose v.

A distinctive feature of Scholastic thought might be said to be its capacity to be all-embracing. If its aim was to see a unity in all things then this was superbly (if by some modern standards mistakenly) achieved; it saw no disparity (or did not allow itself to see any) between the evident truths of Theology and those of other disciplines. The study of God and the study of nature revealed the same unchanging truth, for this was God's world and He was discernible in it.

However, by Shakespeare's time this view was held much less securely in practice than it was in principle. The study of God might still reveal the truth about Man and the world, but the facts which the study of nature revealed seemed to be increasingly incapable of supporting that truth and even capable of revealing 'counter-truths' which could be said, with some daring, to deny it. God's world was beginning to exhibit the disturbing possibility that it might become Man's, and whilst there is no doubt that all societies in all ages tend to detect similar processes within themselves and feel obliged to accuse some of their members of defection from a commonly-held ideology, the evidence suggests that such disruptive forces were at work in a more positive way during this period than in others. The beginning of the end of what has been called the 'honeymoon of philosophy and theology'[1] is of course discernible both before and after Aquinas and the divorce was delayed until much later. Nobody can be sure when it took place,[2] but it might be said that by the time Elizabeth came to the throne, the only question which remained to be settled was that of the custody of the children. Some indication of the situation's extent can be detected in the way in which Aquinas's ascription of interdependent roles to the two aspects of *ratio* had been subtly replaced over the years by a view of their relationship which was very different in its implications.

One of the most persuasive of Shakespeare's contemporaries who wrote about the human reason was Francis Bacon. His account has been said to owe a good deal to the ideas of those Nominalist thinkers of the Middle Ages who have, perhaps unfairly, been credited with undermining the unified concept of

[1] Etienne Gilson, *A History of Christian Philosophy in the Middle Ages* (London, 1955), pp. 489–545.
[2] Cf. Frank Kermode, *op. cit.*, pp. 138 ff.

Man and the world so forcefully upheld by Aquinas.[1] This may or may not be so, but there is little doubt that the Nominalist inclination to concern itself more with the 'lower' reason and less with its 'higher' counterpart[2] would have been enthusiastically supported by Bacon if he had known of it.

In fact, his view of the reason and its function is a modern one; it strikes chords in most of us which Aquinas's does not. Reason, Bacon claimed, was the most powerful means of advancing man's learning, a point on which Aquinas would have agreed with him; but he also claimed that reason was a means of making 'progress' in a world which measured such activity by material results, and Aquinas would not have agreed with that. There was of course nothing new in such a notion and the idea of the discursive reason as more than a mere necessity (or even a liability) in fallen Man was not uncommon both before and after the Middle Ages. One result of such a notion had been that Man was enabled to use his reason to enquire into the mysteries of nature for purposes other than the simple need to keep alive. The process of 'advancing' learning (and thus Man) might be broadly labelled 'scientific' in its leanings, and Bacon must be considered an important figure for the present argument partly because his own contributions as a theorist in that direction were regarded, not least by himself, as significant.

Not surprisingly, he is concerned (whatever his protestations to the contrary) that those parts of human experience which are not susceptible to the reason should be firmly separated from those which are.[3] We should not, he advises, engage overmuch in pursuits not capable of being turned to use; we should recognize our limitations and not seek '. . . to fly up to the secrets of the Deity by the waxen wings of the senses.' The proper area to which the senses and the reason should be confined is the study of the world around us. Since precise knowledge of spiritual matters lies beyond our limited vision, it is better to concern

---

[1] The extent of Bacon's debt to Nominalism is not clear, but see Basil Willey, *The Seventeenth Century Background* (London, 1934), pp. 29–43, and D. G. James, *The Dream of Learning* (Oxford, 1951), pp. 19 ff.

[2] See D. J. B. Hawkins, *A Sketch of Medieval Philosophy* (London, 1945) pp. 24 ff.; also Gordon Leff, *Medieval Thought* (London, 1958), pp. 104–14 and 279–94.

[3] *Advancement of Learning*, II, xxv, 1–25.

ourselves more fully in the employment of that faculty wherein positive certainty may be found. Reason was the only faculty whose claims Bacon was prepared to recognize in this respect, and it became therefore the only instrument of the mind in which he could feel unqualified confidence. A complicated world requires a utilitarian means of dealing with its complexities, and Bacon's view of the reason was that it fulfilled such requirements. Hence he argues that

> ... in the mind, whatsoever knowledge reason cannot at all work upon and convert is a mere intoxication, and endangereth a dissolution of the mind ...[1]

Like the Nominalists he would deny (as would Professor Ayer) any practical value to concepts or words not susceptible to the reason:

> ... Words are but the images of Matter; and except they have life of Reason and invention, to fall in love with them is all one as to fall in love with a picture ...[2]

In fact, the end of all knowledge is to give 'a true account of (the) gift of reason to the benefit and use of men.'[3] From this point of view, Bacon can go on to argue that Theology has therefore no real contact with natural philosophy, except to 'infect' it, and the two are best kept separate because of this; *Da fidei quae fidei sunt*, since '... we ought not to attempt to draw down or to submit the mysteries of God to our reason.'[4] The separation of the reason's functions implicit in this, and the suggestion that it should look up to God, or down to the earth because it cannot do both, commits Bacon to two related conclusions. First, that the study of nature is best pursued by itself without reference to a higher order of being; this involves what might be called a 'scientific' view of the world, as opposed to a more unified conception comprising both the physical and the spiritual within it.[5]

---

[1] *Advancement*, II, xxv, 15.
[2] *Ibid.*, I, iv, 3.
[3] *Ibid.*, I, v, 11.
[4] *Ibid.*, II, vi, 1.
[5] As Robert Hoopes says, *Right Reason in the English Renaissance* (Harvard, 1962), p. 162: 'Until the seventeenth century ... the reachings of reason are subordinated largely in the interests of preserving faith. With Bacon, what-

Second, and as a result, he is committed to a scheme of thinking which establishes the reason as a secular force with a function quite distinct from that of its former counterpart, faith.[1] The idea of a composite *ratio* with a dual aspect has been replaced by that of a mind which has two distinct halves, each with a separate job to do. Bacon is much more interested in one half than in the other for, as he says, '. . . to speak truly of things as they are in worth, rational knowledges are the keys of all other arts.'[2] Thus, where Aquinas might be said to be a rationalist in one way, Bacon is a rationalist in quite a different way. The difference involves much more than that between a saint and a lawyer; it is the difference between a medieval culture and a modern one.

Bacon may be taken with some justification as representative of a movement of ideas which was rapidly gaining ground at the time.[3] Its progress was swift and successful, beginning to gain momentum at the turn of the sixteenth century, and reaching a preliminary climax with the foundation of the Royal Society in 1660.[4] It constituted a movement towards science as we now know it, towards the conquest of nature by means of the kind of certainties that the reason could give. It has been said that a 'revolution' of sorts was taking place, and, having regard to the kind of thinking which characterized it, it was a revolution which had taken the old idea of a unified mind and divided it

---

[1] It is in this that Bacon may be said to inherit the tradition of Nominalism. Robert Hoopes, *op. cit.*, p. 92, puts the Nominalist Ockham's position succinctly; 'Ockham's severance of the traditional bond between reason and faith leads directly to the doctrine of the double truth, according to which a proposition may be at once philosophically true and theologically false.' Cf. my remarks on *Troilus and Cressida* below.

[2] *Advancement*, II, xii, 2.

[3] Bacon's relationship to the 'general' thought of his time is in fact unclear, and to consider him to be in any way 'typical' is possibly misleading. However, such a persuasive theorist might be said to be as capable of forming opinion as of reflecting it, and in that respect he must be accorded a position which could be called influential. Cf. Basil Willey, *op. cit.*, pp. 29 ff.

[4] See A. Wolf, *A History of Science, Technology and Philosophy in the Sixteenth and Seventeenth Centuries* (London, 1935), pp. 39 ff.

---

ever his pious protestations, the reverse is the case . . . (he) was far less concerned to keep religion uncontaminated by science than he was to keep science unadulterated by the superstitions and prejudices of theology.'

into two. As S. L. Bethell concludes, describing the end of the process in the latter part of the seventeenth century, but in a way which has significance for an earlier period:

> Reason was exalted; but 'reason' meant only those mental operations that the mathematician and the scientist employed or any operation analogous thereto. Intuition, feeling, 'imagination' . . . were at a discount.[1]

It will be recalled that Aquinas had said '. . . wisdom is attributed to the higher reason, science to the lower.' If we take Bacon's *dicta* concerning the reason as indicative of a general attitude towards the human mind on the part of the scientists who both preceded and followed him, it may be suggested that the Elizabethan scientist was in general terms 'committed' to the *ratio inferior* as the most important of the mind's faculties in much the same way as his modern successors. For many of them, then as now, to be 'rational' was to be progressive, and as a corollary, to be 'worldly' was not, as it was formerly, to be sinful, but to be a good scientist. Without paradox, the medieval axiom *ecce pietas est sapientia* could become *ecce scientia est sapientia*, and the growing tension between *scientia* and *pietas* not only forms part of the movement of ideas in the Elizabethan period, but is also a paradigm of the way in which Elizabethan culture was changing its course.[2]

Paul Kocher[3] has convincingly described what he calls a 'metaphysical dualism' in the culture which resulted from that tension. If science pulled the mind strongly in one direction, religion pulled it equally strongly in another. Thus, even though science was tentatively given the somewhat lowly status of 'hand-

---

[1] S. L. Bethell, *The Cutural Revolution of the Seventeenth Century* (London, 1951), pp. 57 and 63-4. See also V. Harris, *All Coherence Gone* (Chicago, 1949), pp. 82 ff. D. G. James, *op. cit.*, pp. 60 ff. A. N. Whitehead, *Science and the Modern World* (Cambridge, 1927), pp. 52 ff. For a modified view of the situation cf. Frank Kermode, *op. cit.*, pp. 141 ff.

[2] See W. C. Dampier, *A History of Science and its relations with Philosophy and Religion* (Cambridge, 1948), 3rd. edn., pp. 92 ff. Also A. C. Crombie, *Robert Grosseteste and the Origins of Experimental Science* (Oxford, 1953), pp. 138 ff.

[3] Paul H. Kocher, *Science and Religion in Elizabethan England* (San Marino, 1953), pp. 10 ff. See also W. Notestein, *The History of Witchcraft in England* (Washington, 1911), Martha Ornstein, *The Role of Scientific Societies in the Seventeenth Century* (Chicago, 1928), and F. R. Johnson, *Astronomical Thought in Renaissance England* (Baltimore, 1937), *passim*.

maid' of Theology, the Church frequently felt the need to place restrictions on its activities.[1] Innocent III's *De Contemptu Mundi* (translated as *The mirror of mans lyfe* by H. Kerton and published in 1576, 1577 and 1586) was often quoted in polemics whose purpose was to show the vanity of earthly studies, and of scientific study in particular, as were the works of Thomas a Kempis, translated many times between 1503 and 1640. Writers such as Caspar Loarte (*The Exercise of a Christian Life*, 1579) and Robert Parsons (*Christian Exercise*, 1582) form part of a community of anti-scientific opinion, and although the official *Homilies* of 1567 and later tended to accept scientific investigation as an unavoidable fact, they added a qualification to the effect that a study of the Scriptures was to be preferred.[2] In fact, whilst no church or group (other than the Fideists) was wholly against the scientists (the iconoclastic spirit of Protestantism in England particularly tended to foster rather than strangle the new movements),[3] a positive feeling of uneasiness existed amongst the clergy and others concerning this new force.

Such a feeling was justified in their eyes for, as the scientist later became bolder, and the opposition to him weaker, so his undermining of basic theological tenets became more and more dangerous. The scientist after all believed (and believes) in a Law or Laws of Nature, and a principle of causation. On the other hand the Church had (and has) to accommodate miracles. By definition a miracle occurs outside the Law of Nature, and without any connection with the area of causation. Since such events are inadmissible in any scientific system which sets itself up as fully explanatory of phenomena, the scientists found themselves in the position of having implicitly to deny the existence of miracles.[4] Bacon himself favoured investigating them thoroughly and in a scientific manner in order that they might 'be reduced to and comprehended in, some form or certain law'[5] in the hope

---

[1] Cf. Kocher, *op. cit.*, pp. 3–4.

[2] See also John Downame, *The Second Part of Christian Warfare* (1611), Chaps. 10 & 11, pp. 91–103.

[3] Many of the onslaughts against science came of course from the Puritan camp in the persons of Samuel Wright, Henry Smith, Robert Rollock and others. See Kocher, *op. cit.*, pp. 85 ff.

[4] See Kocher, *op. cit.*, p. 117 and note.

[5] *Novum Organum* II, xxviii.

that the common cause of each might be discovered, and their miraculous quality exploded.

But if there had been a revolution, there were many kinds of counter-revolutionary. *Friar Bacon and Friar Bungay* (1594) identifies science with black magic, and *A Looking Glasse for London and England* (1594) denies the scientific idea of natural law and favours miraculous happenings outside the sphere of causation. In Lyly's *Euphues and his Ephoebus* (1579) Euphues renounces the 'hidden mysteries of Philosophy' for the study of Divinity, and Act I, scene iii of *Campaspe* (1584) sees the philosophy of Aristotle as naturalistic, and hence atheistic, compared to the supernaturalism of Plato. A similar revulsion from science permeates Nashe's *Christe's Teares over Jerusalem* (1593), and the advice in Greene's *Vision*,

> . . . so abjure all other studies seeing *Omnia sub coelo vanitas*, and onely give thy selfe to Theologie.

catches much of the spirit of the controversy.

Although the exact nature and extent of Elizabethan science is still a matter for a good deal of research, certain generalizations can be made from the information available. By and large it may be said that the Elizabethan scientist had a distinctive characteristic; he felt he needed to 'explain', to 'account for' events in the natural world and to place them on the level of the predictable. The scientist's position in the culture, and the state of that culture made his main target superstition. In order to attack it, he would 'explain' the movements of the heavenly bodies, comets, falling-stars and the like, by 'accounting for' their 'causes' and thus denying them the 'miraculous' and even portentous significance which they had formerly had.[1] As Donne puts it, Science brought the Heavens down 'about our feet', and

> Loth to goe up the hill, or labour thus
> To goe to heaven, we make heaven come to us.[2]

In this sense, Edmund's derision in *King Lear* of the theory that the stars influenced men's lives, characterizes him in part as a type of the new iconoclasm, and many of Shakespeare's 'villains' in the tragedies strike this sort of attitude; they scoff at the

---

[1] See Kocher, *op. cit.*, pp. 78 ff. for a full account of this process.
[2] *First Anniversarie* ll. 281–2.

miraculous, the unpredictable; they are in essence, 'explainers'.

Soon, fundamental groundworks of belief began to find themselves in danger of being 'explained'. Witches and the like (Satan himself, for a time) went the way of miracles; they could be accounted for. As Robert Recorde claimed,

> . . . Many thynges seem impossible to be done which by arte may very well be wroughte.[1]

A certain indifference, even, to things other than the material colours the work of people like Hood, Charles Turnbull, Robert Hues, Edmund Wright and John Balgrave. Religion was as often as not ignored (after as much of its dogma had been 'explained' as the writers dared) and the way for a 'scientific' view of the function of the reason became open. Reason was of paramount importance to the scientist, for the senses were the means by which he worked, through experiment, and the reason the means by which he ordered and brought significance to the data thus obtained. Hence the growth of science came to be irrevocably tied to a growing certainty in the values of the discursive reason, and a consequent lowering of the status of the non-rational concepts of a theologically-ordered universe. This situation lies behind the urgency of attacks on that faculty such as those of Rollock:

> Renounce that reason of thine, and take it captive, and make it a slave otherwise thou shalt never see GOD to thy consolation for thy naturall reason is an enemie to God and His wisdom . . .[2]

The 'explainer' and the 'reasoner' were one and the same person.

To speak as if one group of ideas can form a positive 'opposition' to or 'reaction' against another contemporary group is perhaps to be misleading. We have noticed the kind of change which the renaissance brought to the status of the former 'lower' reason of Man, and the way in which the effects of that change had caused certain of its activities to be questioned. Without invoking the idea of a 'reaction' against the elevation of the reason's position, it is nevertheless possible to detect in the late sixteenth and early seventeenth centuries the assertion of a contrary point of view. Its focal point lay in the notion of an 'intuitive' mode of thought

[1] *The Pathway to Knowledge* (1551), Preface.
[2] *Cit.* Kocher, *op. cit.*, p. 179.

c

with a higher standing in the mind than that of the reason and, in the circumstances, somewhat opposed to it. The effective roots of this concept are to be found in Neo-platonism.

In the parable of the cave in the *Republic*, Plato distinguishes that area in which the 'intellect' should properly work from that in which the senses operate. He makes a further distinction between two kinds of intellect.[1] The 'higher' intellect is concerned with pure ideas, and its method of gaining knowledge that which we might now call 'intuitive'. The 'lower' intellect is concerned with ideas of a more mathematical sort, and its characteristics are those of the discursive reason.

Aquinas's account of the two aspects of *ratio* is similar to this in so far as it resembles Aristotle's views on the matter which owe, as has been said, a good deal to Plato. In fact, the names which Plato uses for these faculties are reversed by both Aristotle and Aquinas, but it is clear enough that Plato's account of the human mind contains the same notion of a division between faculties (together with a similar insistence on their interdependence). If Aquinas's compellation of them contains little which comes directly from Plato, his description of the limitations which impinge on the reason certainly owes something to the later Neo-platonists who claimed to 'interpret' Plato's thinking.

For example, Aquinas makes the point that the fact that the reason works through and is limited by the senses necessarily confines that faculty to a world of appearances and so of unreality.[2] A fundamental tenet of the Neo-platonic philosophy, as first systematized and promulgated by Plotinus, was that the senses are continually deceived. Consequently, the reason which works through the senses must similarly be deceived. And since the senses cannot gain a knowledge of reality but only an appearance of it, so the reason cannot have access to ultimate truth, but only to a contingent or 'virtual' truth which is less than that. In effect, as Plotinus affirms, only when we exercise the intuitive faculty of spiritual perception (*noesis*), a power 'which all possess but few use', are we able to come into contact at all with the truly real.[3]

[1] Cf. my remarks above p. 8 and n.
[2] *S.T.* I. Q.LXXIX., A. 9 ff. and see above.
[3] Plotinus, V^th *Ennead*. See Emile Bréhier, *The Philosophy of Plotinus*, trans. J. Thomas (Chicago, 1958) pp. 83 ff.

Appearance and Reality

The persistence of Neo-platonism as a considerable influence on Western thought (though its form often undergoes modification in many respects after Plotinus) has frequently been demonstrated. It is discernible both before and after the Elizabethan period, and manifests itself particularly strongly at that time because of the far-reaching authority of the Florentine Academies.[1]

The fact that this philosophy maintained itself as a separate 'stream' of thought both during the Scholastic period and much later in its re-emergence during the renaissance means that the Elizabethan and Jacobean periods were influenced in a sense by both Scholasticism and Neo-platonism at the same time, inheriting the one and re-discovering the other. As a result it also meant that a further element could be added to the division of the mind as a ramification of it, for the Neo-platonic dichotomy between appearance and reality was capable of subsumption within the Scholastic distinction between reason and intuition. The extent to which this was possible depended on the extent to which Aquinas could be misunderstood, for it involved removing his notion of the interdependency of these faculties and replacing it by the idea of an opposition between them.

Thinkers of the period were for many reasons able to do this, so that it became possible to say of the reason that its use resulted only in a knowledge of mere appearances, and of the intuition that it was the only faculty which could ever achieve a knowledge of reality. That this is not wholly compatible with Aquinas's concept of the *ratio* need not be said; in fact the seeds of it are more probably to be found in Plato. In any event, it seems to have been the peculiar renaissance fusion of Neo-platonic ideas with those of the medieval thinkers which made possible a cognate relationship between these elements which was not previously capable of being realized. In short, whilst Aquinas's thinking may have contained implications to this effect, it was the renaissance which, in this as in so many matters, provided

[1] See particularly Frances A. Yates, 'Shakespeare and the Platonic Tradition', *University of Edinburgh Journal*, Vol. 12, No. 1, 1942. Also R. Klibansky, *The Continuity of the Platonic Tradition in the Middle Ages* (London, 1939), W. R. Inge, *The Platonic Tradition in English Religious Thought* (London, 1926). Robert Sencourt, *Outflying Philosophy* (London, 1925), and Ernst Cassirer, *The Platonic Renaissance in England*, trans. Pettegrove (London, 1953), *passim*.

from within itself a catalyst composed of many otherwise disparate forces which made actual what was formerly potential.[1]

The philosopher to whom the renaissance turned as an authoritative source of Neo-platonism was not Plotinus so much as his interpreter Marsilio Ficino. Ficino's translation of the *Enneads* was published in 1492[2] and his philosophy as a whole had a considerable influence on the English writers of this and later periods.[3] A major tenet of his thinking is that the reason is diseased and thus incapable of attaining true (Platonic) reality.[4] A division exists within the mind which Ficino describes in terms of the 'rational' and that which lies behind it, the 'supernatural':

> ... there is a double process of our mind, one rational and the other supernatural.[5]

and he speaks of the *ratio*, the reason, as a power of discursive analysis, moving 'in temporal succession' from one object to another, in the manner of Aquinas's *ratio inferior*. However, the intuitive aspect of the mind, the *mens* or 'mind of the soul', is a higher faculty which has all the angelic qualities of Aquinas's *ratio superior*:

> That mind which is the head and driver of the Soul, imitating by its nature the angels, attains not by succession, but in a moment, whatever it desires.[6]

He claims to speak for all Platonists when he says that intelligence is 'unity' '. . . because it takes place through simple intuition', whereas 'science' (the opposite of 'intelligence') involves 'duality' 'because it proves the conclusion from the

---

[1] Cf. P. O. Kristeller, *Renaissance Thought*, revised edn. (New York, 1961), pp. 48 ff.

[2] An edition of Ficino's translation of and commentaries on Plato was published in London in 1590 and many editions appeared on the continent at the turn of the century. See my article, 'Ficino and Shakespeare', *Notes and Queries*, May 1958, pp. 185 ff.

[3] See Sears Jayne, 'Ficino and English Platonism', *Comparative Literature*, Vol. IV, 1952, pp. 214 ff. Also John Vyvyan, *Shakespeare and Platonic Beauty* (London, 1961), pp. 33 ff.

[4] See P. O. Kristeller, *The Philosophy of Marsilio Ficino* (New York, 1943), pp. 2 ff.

[5] *Cit.* Kristeller, *ibid.*, p. 275.

[6] *Ibid.*, pp. 379–80.

principle . . .' that is, because it involves a process of discursive reasoning.[1]

The life of reason is limited to this earth, and confined by it. The spiritually awakened man who finds himself dissatisfied with the mundane life must turn away from the senses and from the 'rational' mode of thinking, towards an internal and intuitive mode of contemplation. The earthly life, based on reason and sense, is an 'outward' life. The life of the spirit, perceived through the intuition, is 'inward' in character.[2] Cognately, the 'lower' functions of the mind and of the body, reason and the senses, can perceive appearances only. True reality must be achieved in a 'higher' way, by contemplation and intuition.[3] The mundane way of reason and the senses is less than this; it is a life of 'the world', and it has no value at all.[4] In this way, the moment that a man becomes aware of his own 'inward' capabilities and begins to cast off his 'outward' values, he finds that 'reality' as he has hitherto seen it is no longer satisfactory or profitable.[5]

Ficino also insists on a further and collateral division of the mental faculties in his distinction between knowledge and love. Knowledge he sees as earthly, a product of the reason and of the senses; it involves a process of discursive analysis, and is opposed to the non-discursive, non-analytic unity of love.[6] In this way a new metaphor is spun out of the idea of a division of the mind, and it must have struck a chord appropriate to the time for 'Platonic love' in the Ficinian manner became a major force in English writing of the later renaissance, where it is often seen in conflict with its 'worldly' opponents, knowledge and reason.

Ficino had, in fact, made the division of the mind more tractable for literary purposes by the added dimension which he gave it, and this resulted, to make a general statement, in the establishment of that notion as a distinguishing mark of the renaissance in Italy and, subsequently, England. Certainly later writers were not slow to recognize the application of such an idea to their own times. By presenting Man's mind as a Janus-figure, with one face

[1] *Ibid.*, p. 380.
[2] *Ibid.*, pp. 211–16 ff.
[3] *Ibid.*, pp. 218 ff.
[4] *Ibid.*, pp. 238 ff.
[5] *Ibid.*, p. 211.
[6] *Ibid.*, pp. 264–9.

of reason looking downwards to the earth, and another of intuition looking upwards to the heavens, Ficino had placed Man at the centre of the division between temporal and eternal, a configuration of his position which the English renaissance was to take up and emphasize. To many it became a hieroglyph of the condition and therefore the predicament of Man. To some, what was a predicament was also a tragedy.

The transmission of the ideas of Ficinian Neo-platonism from fifteenth century Florence to sixteenth and seventeenth century England is therefore a cultural event of significance for the present argument. There is ample evidence that it took place over a long period, for not only did Ficino's province extend in terms of ideas to Bruno and Campanella in Italy, to Lefèvre d'Etaples and his group, the humanists and poets of Lyons, and the circle of Marguerite de Navarre in France, but in England to Erasmus, Colet and More.[1] It is also possible to detect an apparently Neo-platonic view of the mind's faculties in popular writing in English of the fifteenth century in a form so native that it seems never to have left the British Isles. For example, the Morality play *Wisdom* (c. 1460) contains a fairly full dramatic account of a 'reason' divided into two parts, the 'ouer' and the 'neyther'. As we would expect, the 'lower' reason is said to be concerned merely with earthly things in a discursive manner:

> Be þe neyther parte of reson, he knowyt dyscretly
> All erthely thyngis, how þey xall be vsyde...
> (ll. 145–6)

The 'higher' reason is intuitive in its mode and leads ultimately to knowledge of God; it is itself a Godlike attribute in Man:

> ... þe ouer parte of yowur reasun,
> Be wyche ye haue lyknes of Gode mest,
> Ande of þat mercyfull very congnycion.
> (ll. 1133–35)

The play makes the point that, ideally, the 'lower' reason should be ruled by the 'higher' reason:

[1] Cf. Kristeller, *op. cit.*, Introduction. Also John Vyvyan, *op. cit..* pp. 35 ff.

No thynge xulde offende Gode in no kynde;
Ande yff þer dose þat, þe nether parte of resone
In no wys þer-to lende;
Then þe ouer parte xall haue fre domynacion.
(ll. 297–300)

It is partly in arguing against this very point that Lucifer, tempting 'Will' to sin against God, claims that his (false) arguments are acceptable to the 'lower' reason, and are only denied by the 'higher' reason because it is mad:

Dyspute not to moche in þis with reson;
Yet þe nethyr parte to þis taketh sum instruccion,
And so xulde þe ouerparte, but he were woode.
(ll. 482–4)

An attempt to establish the 'lower' reason as the arbiter of truth and reality (with a consequent dismissal of the intuitive faculty as 'woode', 'irrational') is here crudely labelled devilish because the substitution of appearance for reality is a traditional activity of the devil.[1] The persistence of such an idea – however more subtle its formal statement in drama will become – is readily discernible in later renaissance writing.[2] Iago's temptation of Othello has much in common with Lucifer's arguments here and 'Wysdom's' plea

Yit Mynde, I sey to yow, be-thynke
In what perell ye be now! take hede!
(ll. 903–4)

might serve as an epigraph to both situations, both plays.
S. L. Bethell and Theodore Spencer have remarked[3] that

---

[1] Satan, of course, traditionally holds the role of arch-deceiver in the sense that he tries to deceive man into accepting his evil in place of God's good, which he naturally despises. Total deceit is therefore his *rationale*; he makes evil appear to be preferable to good. As a result he is often described as the archetypal disguiser of reality. He is the 'prince of darkness' and, as the Gospels put it, '. . . there is no truth in him. When he speaketh a lie, he speaketh of his own: for he is a liar, and the father of it.' (*John*, viii, 44).

[2] Significantly, Milton's Satan uses the 'lower' discursive reason (especially to seduce Eve) and the other fallen angels are depicted in Hell, 'reasoning' in this manner, quite pointlessly, about their fate. As a result they are 'in wand'ring mazes lost.' (V. 488–490 and II, 557–561).

[3] S. L. Bethell, *op. cit.*, p. 64. Theodore Spencer, *Shakespeare and the Nature of Man* (Cambridge, 1943), pp. 12 ff.

Shakespeare's contemporaries were well aware of the concept of intuition, through contact with the Neo-platonic philosophy, and there is evidence, as we have seen, for regarding that notion as part of a submerged native tradition which contact with Neo-platonism served to revivify.[1] Spencer points out that in the triumvirate of the mind's faculties, reason, intuition (sometimes called 'understanding') and will, it is the reason's relatively humble job to work 'downwards' on the sense-data which confront it, whereas the intuition or 'understanding' moves in the opposite direction, towards God. Cardinal Bembo's remarks in Castiglione's *Courtier*[2] concerning the 'noblest part' of the soul, that is '. . . understanding, by the which Man may be partner with Angels'[3] reveal the extent to which the notion had retained some of its medieval characteristics.

In the Elizabethan period, the concept of intuition had an immediate and particular significance and was naturally made use of by many writers who wanted to express doubts about the values of the reason. How far this dichotomy between the faculties of the mind may be said to mirror one of a deeper and more crucial nature within the culture itself is open to question.[4] A particular conflict may be related to others in many ways either as cause or effect, and the most fundamental philosophical and social upheavals can be given apparently unconnected literary manifestations. Yet it is possible to detect a deeply seated unease in much contemporary writing about the mind's faculties which the nature of the topic does not apparently warrant.

The charge of Fideism or Scepticism was often levelled at

---

[1] See Frances A. Yates, *art. cit.*, also 'Giordano Bruno's conflict with Oxford', *Journal of the Warburg Institute*, II (1939), pp. 228–31, and 'The Religious Policy of Giordano Bruno', *Journal of the Warburg and Courtauld Institute*, Vol. III (1940), p. 181. See also A. E. Taylor, *Platonism and its Influence* (London, 1925), pp. 41 ff.

[2] 1528 (trans. Hoby 1561).

[3] *Cit.*, Spencer, *op. cit.*, p. 14. Cf. Vyvyan, *op. cit.*, p. 56.

[4] C. P. Snow's *The Two Cultures and the Scientific Revolution* (Cambridge, 1959), although uncertain in its history (see p. 27), is an interesting and perceptive account of the way in which one particular dichotomy has come down to us. Frank Kermode, *op. cit.*, traces a similar process in literary and aesthetic terms (see especially pp. 107 ff.) although he would deny the importance of the renaissance as a focal point.

those who dared to withstand the advance of the reason, and to suggest that it was not the instrument of precision that its champions claimed.[1] The charges were, of course, not wholly justified since such people were often merely advocating the re-instatement and re-alignment of the 'lower' reason into its former, never lowly, position. In this they followed Hooker, whose *via media* had led him to say that, although reason was not worthless, and was Man's necessary light in this world, it should never be allowed to rise above its proper position. Man has, Hooker affirms, an 'understanding', an 'intuitive' faculty, and its necessary counterpart is reason. 'Goodness is seen with the eye of the understanding and the light of that eye is Reason.'[2] He is a 'rationalist' in the way that Aquinas is, because he believes that the proper use of the reason will lead to virtue. He also points out, however, that this 'right' role of the reason can be perverted, either by too great a credence in the values of the senses, or by attaching too great an importance to those scientific discoveries which are made through them.[3] Scientists, he says, who depend on the reason alone, may well

> ... seem the makers of those Laws which indeed are his [God's] and they but only the finders of them out.[4]

and he feels constrained to remind us that

> ... in moral actions, divine law helpeth exceedingly the law of reason to guide man's life; but in supernatural it alone guideth.[5]

Writers such as Sir John Davies and Fulke Greville could scarcely be called Fideists, but they forcefully express a similar view. They are uneasy about any reliance on the reason and the senses, and Davies's distinction between the Divine and the Physician catches that spirit; the Divine is of course necessarily good, the Physician (a natural scientist) is suspect.[6] He makes a similar point in *Nosce Teipsum* in which he says that the senses can never know reality, for that can only be perceived intuitively by

[1] See Hoopes, *op. cit.*, pp. 96–122.
[2] Hooker, *Laws of Ecclesiastical Polity*, I, VII, 2.
[3] *Ibid.*, I, VII, 6.
[4] *Ibid.*, I, VII, 3.
[5] *Ibid.*, I, XVI, 5.
[6] Sir John Davies, *Complete Poems*, ed. Grosart (London, 1876), Vol. II, pp. 66–8.

the Soul, through the 'heavenly powers' which it possesses. The reason can only know an appearance of reality; it must inevitably be deceived because its angelic and intuitive 'light' is obscured by the earth:

> So doth this Earth eclipse our Reason's light
> Which else (in instants) would like Angels see.[1]

The poem *Orchestra* also sees the reason as bound to the earth by logic, and thus limited in its scope.[2]

Similarly, both Greville and Montaigne deny the reason the status which was being claimed for it. Greville's *A Treatise of Humane Learninge* begins by saying that the senses cannot be trusted:

> Sense, Man's first instructor, while it showes
> To free him from deceipt, deceives him most.

and goes on to say that not only is the reason corrupt and worthless, but that it corrupts the spirit as well:

> So Reason stooping to attend the Sense
> Darkens the spirit's clear intelligence.[3]

Indeed the whole of the *Treatise* (conventionally supposed to be in answer to Bacon's *Advancement*) expresses a deep mistrust of this sort, and its argument is expressly directed against those whom Greville dismisses as 'science-mongers'.

Montaigne goes further, occasionally denying the value of any knowledge gained by earthly means, and advocating an inspired 'ignorance' which intuitively grasps at knowledge as the proper alternative.[4] In *An Apologie of Raymond Sebond*, for example, he castigates Man's pride in valuing the reason, and memorably repeats the warning of St. Paul:

---

[1] Davies, *Nosce Teipsum*, edn. *cit.*, Vol. I, p. 77.

[2] *Orchestra*, ed. E. M. W. Tillyard (London, 1945), p. 38, st. 94 ff.

[3] *Poems and Dramas of Fulke Greville*, ed. G. Bullough (London, 1938), Vol. I, pp. 55 ff.

[4] See Ernest Marchand, 'Montaigne and the Cult of Ignorance', *Romanic Review*, XXXVI (1945).

... Ignorance is by our Religion recommended unto us, as an instrument fitting beleefe and obedience ... Take heed lest any man deceive you by Philosophie and vain seducements, according to the rudiments of the world.[1]

The philosophers and scientists who exalt the reason are denounced[2] because of their use of these 'rudiments of the world' and the worth of sense-impressions suffers equal denigration:

... the senses do often maister our discourse, and force it to receive impressions which he knoweth and judgeth to be false ...[3]

And yet, he points out, scientific enquiry bases itself on the evidence of the senses: 'Science begins by them and in them is resolved.' But the senses can never give a true account of reality, for 'Nothing comes unto us but falsified and altered by our senses' and thus the reason is the more deceived:

... Reason, which therein seeketh a reall subsistence, findes her selfe deceived as unable to apprehend any thing subsistent and permanent.[4]

A similar attitude towards the reason, which sees it as a barrier to an intuited and therefore divinely 'ignorant' faith is found throughout the sermons of the first quarter of the seventeenth century. Donne's sermon preached at Whitehall on November 2nd 1617 takes this view, as does his sermon at St. Paul's on Christmas Day 1621, in which he says categorically

Reason is that first, and primogeniall light, and goes no farther in a naturall man; but in a man regenerate by faith, that light does all that reason did, and more.

and his couplet

> Let not my minde be blinded by more light
> Nor Faith, by Reason added, lose her sight.

has that kind of thinking behind it which found the human

---

[1] *Essayes* tr. Florio (Everyman edn. London, 1910), Vol. II, pp. 184–6 ff.
[2] *Ibid.*, pp. 250 ff. and pp. 306–7.
[3] *Ibid.*, p. 312.
[4] *Ibid.*, p. 324.

reason suspect, and was attracted by the contrary doctrine of *sola fides*.[1]

It is not surprising to find different words often used to describe the intuitive faculty in a period not notable for its precision in matters of nomenclature. Thus Hooker will speak at one point of '. . . the intuitive vision of God',[2] and at another of '. . . (that) which angels and glorified saints do intuitively behold . . .,'[3] whereas the Authorized Version of the Bible will use 'understanding' for the intuitive contact with the holy (*Proverbs*, ix, 10), and for the same concept of this angelic faculty in Man, Shakespeare in *Hamlet* will use the word 'apprehension':

> What [a] piece of work is a man, how noble in reason, how infinite in faculties, in form and moving, how express and admirable in action, how like an angel in apprehension, how like a God! (II, ii, 300 ff.)

(the punctuation is that of the second Quarto which, as can be seen, makes better sense in the light of what has been said above than that of the first Folio).[4] Frequently, too, because these concepts are often expressed in Neo-platonic contexts, the reason will be described as able only to perceive mere earthly appearances, whereas the heavenly or ideal reality can be perceived by the soul through the intuition.[5] For example, Spenser's *Faery Queene* shows Red Cross taught on the Mount of Contemplation

---

[1] There is, of course, a large element of Lutheran and Calvinistic thinking about the depravity of man in these ideas, as in those of Greville and Montaigne. Luther's view of the reason was that it was 'blind and dark' and the 'whore of the devil. It can only blaspheme and dishonour everything God has said or done.' *Cit.*, Hoopes, *op. cit.*, p. 103. According to Calvin, 'Reason . . . exhibits nothing but deformity and ruin.' (*Ibid.*, p. 112). The Anglican position was normally in no way as extreme as this. Reason for that Church retained its primacy amongst man's faculties, with the proviso that it should be 'rightly' used. As Hoopes says, '. . . . there is a crucial difference between the "dry light" of unaided reason, the non-moral activity of logical disquisition, and the dictates of "right reason" . . . [i.e. reason] that has been morally purified.' (*Ibid.*, pp. 166–7).

[2] *Laws of Ecclesiastical Polity*, I, xi, 6.

[3] *Ibid.*, V, xlii, 7.

[4] See my note, 'Hamlet's Apprehension', *Modern Language Review*, Vol. LV, No. 2, April 1960, pp. 238 ff.

[5] Cf. J. S. Harrison, *Platonism in English Poetry* (Columbia, 1903), p. 29.

(in the Ficinian manner) to perfect his intuitive 'vision'. Until that time he has been a 'man of earth', and his soul must be purified from the grossness of sense (I, x, 52 ff.). Milton's Comus is an arch-spirit of the senses, and a type of Ficino's 'outward' man. Accordingly, he inhabits a world in which reality is obscured, and his aim is to

> ... cheat the eye with blear illusion
> And give it false presentments ...
>
> (ll. 155–6)

He achieves this, as we would expect, by means of the reason, with

> ... well-plac't words of glozing courtesie,
> Baited with reasons not unplausible ...
>
> (ll. 161–2)

Indeed the Lady accuses him of 'Obtruding false rules pranckt in reason's garb' (l. 759) and the power of her chastity seems to come from a contact with the angels, which enables her to triumph over all bodily and sensual bonds (ll. 453–63); such 'converse with heavenly habitants' is traditionally intuitive in mode. Intuition in effect here becomes the embodiment of a kind of Platonic morality, a saving grace. Comus, truly 'outward', has a temporal happiness of the sense, but the Lady has strength because of her 'inward' vision of moral beauty, achieved through her 'apprehension'.

Similar references to the intuitive faculty are found in Spenser's *Hymne to Heavenly Beautie* (ll. 298 ff.) and in William Drummond's *Song II* 'It autumn was and in our hemisphere', and in many of the devotional poets of the period. An intuitive rising above earthly things to the Beatific Vision occurs in Phineas Fletcher's *The Purple Island* (VI, ll. 75 ff.), and Giles Fletcher mentions the intuitive 'understanding' in his *Christes Triumph after Death* (Stanza 34). Platonic love-poetry as a *genre* contains, of course, many statements of the 'magical' power of love in the Ficinian manner, which lifts the lover above the senses and the reason in an ecstasy of intuition. Herbert of Cherbury describes the process explicitly:

31

> ... our love
> Springing at first but in an earthly mould
> Transplanted to our souls, now doth remove
> Earthly affects ...[1]

Such Platonic love is entirely non-rational in character; the mind is informed with intuitive pleasures rather than the senses gratified with those of an earthly nature.

In *The Governour* Elyot speaks of 'understanding' in the sense of intuition, and admits the difficulty of finding the right word to fit the concept:

> This most pure parte of the soule, and (as Aristotle sayeth) divyne, impassible and incorruptible is named in latine Intellectus, whereunto I can fynde no propre englysshe but understandynge ...[2]

and Montaigne gives an account of it which has the medieval flavour of Aquinas's description of the *ratio superior*:

> As the soules of the Gods, sanse tongues, sanse eyes, and sanse ears, have each one in themselves a feeling of that which the other feel ... so mens soules, when they are free and severed from the body ... divine, prognosticate and see things which being conjoyned to their bodies they could not see.[3]

Speaking of knowledge in Heaven in a sermon preached on Easter Monday 1622, Donne's conceit draws a similarly medieval distinction between the discursive rational knowledge which characterizes Man's earthly lot, and the immediate intuitive knowledge which the Angels possess:

> There ... we shall know how the Angels know, by knowing as they know. We shall not pass from Author to Author, as in a Grammar School, nor from Art to Art as in an University; but, as that General which knighted his whole Army, God shall Create us all Doctors in a minute.

Later in the century references to the concept can be detected in Benlowes's *Theophila* (1652);

---

[1] *Poems*, ed. J. Churton Collins (London, 1881), p. 24.
[2] *The Governour*, ed. H. H. S. Croft (London, 1883), Vol. I, p. 5; see also Vol. II, pp. 371 ff.
[3] Montaigne, *op. cit.*, p. 236; see also pp. 277 ff.

> Might souls converse with souls, by Angel-way
> Enfranchis'd from their pris'ning clay
> What strains by intuition would they then convey.[1]
>
> (I, Stanza 1, ll. 1–3)

and an almost Thomistic account occurs in Milton's *Paradise Lost*; the Angel instructs Adam that

> ... So from the root
> Springs lighter the green stalk, from thence the leaves,
> More aery, last the bright consummate flower
> Spirits odorous breathes: flowers and their fruit
> Man's nourishment, by gradual scale sublimed,
> To vital spirits aspire, to animal,
> To intellectual; give both life and sense,
> Fancy and understanding; whence the Soul
> Reason receives, and Reason is her being,
> Discursive or Intuitive: Discourse
> Is oftest yours, the latter most is ours,
> Differing but in degree, of kind the same.[2]
>
> (V, 479 ff.)

Aquinas's idea that reason and intuition are related ('of kind the same') as aspects of the *ratio* is evident here, although Milton's version of it must have been somewhat old-fashioned by this time.

It has been said that the concept of an opposition between modes of perception can provide a symmetrical and so satisfying configuration of contrary human experiences. One instance of this process in Shakespeare's time may be noticed in the aura surrounding the contrary Elizabethan notions of 'action' and 'contemplation'. Howard Schultz has pointed out that the opposition between these two ways of life (in practice they had to do with the role of man in society) was of some consequence for that culture, even though previous ages had exhibited

---

[1] *Minor Poets of the Caroline Period*, ed. Saintsbury (Oxford, 1905), Vol. I, p. 335.

[2] Coleridge has some interesting comments on this speech in his remarks on Imagination (*Biographia Literaria*, Chapter XIII). The distinction he draws between Fancy and Imagination is very like the medieval distinction between the two aspects of *ratio* (see *Biographia Literaria*, Chapter IV); equally, his application of this concept to Shakespeare, though it hardly touches the surface of the issue, is worthy of note. See my edition of *Coleridge's Writings on Shakespeare* (New York, 1959), pp. 56–7 and 60 ff.

versions of it.[1] The controversies between supporters of each side were heated, sometimes bitter, and plainly lay on the surface of everyday life as an indication of a deeper and farther-reaching opposition beneath it.

The idea of 'action' had as its basis the contention that all knowledge and its acquisition should have the end of practicality. The 'active' man 'actively' involved himself with the world and concerned himself in applying his knowledge to it for the good of the society; 'active' knowledge thus took on the colour of 'applied' science. Bacon, predictably, would concede very little value to any knowledge that was not useful and suggested that 'action' in this sense was a sign of humility in itself since

> ... men must know that in this theatre of Man's life it is reserved only for God and Angels to be lookers on.

He adds that '. . . for contemplation which should be finished in itself, without casting beams upon society, assuredly divinity knoweth it not.'[2]

The 'contemplative' man was the opposite of the 'active' man. He was 'inward', in Ficino's sense, non-worldly in all things; the knowledge which he pursued was essentially non-practical, and could not be put to worldly use, for its end lay in a different direction. As a *modus vivendi* the 'active' life was fairly new to the Englishman, and it had both the appeal of modernity and the approval of the zealous Protestants.[3] It involved him in 'useful' works whose value could be measured, and the idea of 'usefulness' was in consequence 'tacked on' to scientific activities within its ken, together with the idea that 'progress' could be made by such means. Science aided the 'advancement' of man in an 'active' way. Daniel Tuvil puts this point when he says that 'In action doth a man better himself and benefit others.' (*Essayes*, 1609).

A further dimension of the idea can be glimpsed here and it is implicit in the expression of similar sentiments which permeate the writing on this subject (there are hints of it throughout

---

[1] Howard Schultz, *Milton and Forbidden Knowledge* (New York, 1955), pp. 27 ff.

[2] *Advancement of Learning*, II, xx, 8.

[3] See R. Newton Flew, *The Idea of Perfection in Christian Theology* (Oxford, 1934), pp. 251–7.

Bacon's *Advancement*). It implies that action may be metaphorically connected with a kind of 'manliness' which accrues to
a person whose role in society is 'actively' fulfilled. Contemporary extensions of the notion suggest that the active man is the
man who thinks 'rationally' and is a 'man' because of it. He is
thus the opposite of his counterpart, the contemplative man who
thinks 'intuitively' and is, by that token, less than 'manly'.[1]

Such a metaphor, the result of a simple extrapolation of a
basic dichotomy concerning modes of perception which imposes
itself on the mysteries of an apparently cognate dichotomy
concerning modes of sexual activity, suggests a pattern of social
and economic development within the society which other
accounts of it tend to substantiate.[2] In that pattern the role of the
new rational 'man' of action was to be very important; the
modern world by this was to be very much a 'man's' world in
which reason would have a very high status. In consequence,
intuition would be relegated to an opposite position, that of a
merely feminine characteristic. In our own society it fulfils
exactly that function; it has become a faculty which women are
said to have in place of the more valuable (and useful) rational
powers of the man.

Shakespeare's awareness of these ramifications of a situation
central to his time is demonstrable in many of the plays which
will be discussed. Accordingly it may be suggested that they
constitute another facet of the division between the mind's
faculties, and provide cogent instances of the depth to which this
penetrated the whole society. It is interesting to reflect that
Hamlet himself is a confessed contemplative forced unwillingly
to cope with a 'man's' world of action for which circumstances
make him temperamentally unsuited.

The predicament which confronted that society has been said to
be potentially tragic and such a contention should be explained.
Tragedy is not easily defined and the simple notion that it

---

[1] Evidence in support of this will be given in the discussions of the plays
which follow, but the metaphor has a wide provenance in other writings of
the period before and after Shakespeare. The 'opposition' implicit in it
informs Milton's *L'Allegro* and *Il Penseroso*.

[2] Cf. R. H. Tawney, *Religion and the Rise of Capitalism* (London, 1926),
pp. 179 ff.

D

involves a 'fall' from a high position to a lower one will not suffice for most of the English tragic plays of this period. A different conception of 'falling' may be more revealing however, especially if it can be allowed that the idea of a greater and farther-reaching 'Fall' lies behind such a notion for a society whose values and metaphors spring from those of Christianity. The concept of falling from a 'good' position to a 'bad' one may then be said to have as a corollary that of falling from a state of unity to one of dis-unity, since unity in Christian terms presupposes unity with God and the state is one of grace, whereas dis-unity involves the idea of separation from God in a state of disgrace. The notion of separation presupposes that of division, diffraction, breaking-up. In Christian terms (as in those of other religions) a situation in which division pertains suffers by comparison with one in which there is perfect unity, as that of disgrace suffers by comparison with its counterpart. The latter, by definition, precedes the former, and the change, the 'fall' from one state to its opposite, is a tragic one.

One of the most frequent adumbrations of the idea of Man's mind in the Elizabethan period grows in part out of a fundamental implication of the Neo-platonic philosophy: that whatever has the lowest degree of reality on the level of existence must also have the lowest degree of value on the level of morality. Whatever is most real has most good; unreality is therefore totally evil. Since the material world, in that philosophy's terms, must be less real than the spiritual world, then it can be categorized as relatively evil compared to the latter's good. And since the material world is perceived by means of the 'lower' faculty of reason (and it has no higher purpose than this) then that faculty too could be thought of as relatively evil compared to the good of the higher faculty of intuition whose province is the world of the spirit. As soon as such a notion becomes both possible in and acceptable to a society's view of its own method of cognition then the seeds of a certain kind of tragedy have been sown. It has been argued that this came about in the case of the society from within which Shakespeare was writing, and his plays could be said to express that kind of tragedy; it is the tragedy which comes of a breaking-up, and of a division in a culture; much of its action is played out on the level of the human mind.

Shakespeare's age had experienced a radical change in its conception of the structure of that instrument. The old view, well expressed by Aquinas, had conceived of the mind as a unity whose faculties were interdependent and moved in complementary directions to perform the single function which was *ratio*. The renaissance view, however, was of a divided mind whose faculties were opposed to each other because they moved in directions which were mutually contradictory. Neo-platonism, together with certain tensions which were the result of a distinctive change in the culture's own direction, had had the effect of adding moral elements to these faculties which 'labelled' one aspect of the mind's activity good, and the other evil. Division had replaced unity, and a man could be faced with a moral choice to make between two now *opposed* ways of thinking, to both of which he was committed by his very nature. What formerly had needed simple acceptance of oneself as a 'fallen' being who was nonetheless *capax dei* had become a situation which demanded a complicated choosing between alternatives. Two things existed where before there had been only one, and this asked of Man that he should sacrifice one half of himself for the good of the other since he could not retain both. The choice was unavoidable, for even to avoid it was to choose. Tragedy lay, not in whatever alternative was chosen, so much as in the fact that a choice was required. The position of being a 'chooser' was itself tragic because it forced on the individual the tragic disunity of his own culture. With their intense interest in both worlds, material and spiritual, the situation posed an enormous question for the writers who took part in it. Not surprisingly the idea of a 'tragic choosing' becomes a discernible theme in the drama of the period, less as a result than as an expression of this. The choice, significantly, and in spite of the many forms into which it was cast, always seems to have retained one permanent feature: it was one between opposed versions of what called itself 'reality', and the drama, which concerned itself precisely with the difference between kinds of 'reality' as a means of communication between stage and audience, was of course a perfect vehicle for its expression. As a modern writer has put it:

The question for the tragic poet is precisely this: Who is battling whom, and what is really colliding with what?[1]

In another way, the question is the enormous one: 'what is real?', or, more problematically, 'what is not?'; it is one to which Shakespeare's tragic protagonists have to find the answer.

[1] Karl Jaspers, *Tragedy is Not Enough*, trans. K. W. Deutsch (London, 1952), *cit.* Laurence Michel and Richard B. Sewall (eds.) *Tragedy: Modern Essays in Criticism* (New Jersey, 1963), p. 18. See also pp. 19–24.

'HAMLET'

> As I am never better than when I am mad; then methinks I am a
> brave fellow; then I do wonders; but reason abuseth me, and
> there's the torment, there's the hell.
>
> *The Spanish Tragedy* (IV, vi, 165 ff.)

'HAMLET' could be said to share a distinctive quality with its
protagonist: that of hesitancy. Whilst the prince vacillates between alternatives, the play's movement exhibits an irresolution
which embodies Hamlet's own. Accordingly, there has often
been a temptation for critics to confuse Hamlet with *Hamlet* and
to imply in consequence that the former's inadequacy mirrors a
larger one in the play itself. But the implication is invalid;
Hamlet's incompetence (if it is such) must be competently set
forth before it can be affecting. The play achieves as much,
partly by means of imposing on him a choice in which tremendous issues are at stake: matters, literally, of life and death.
Confronted with alternatives, Hamlet takes on the condition of
stasis, and because of his immobility, the play proceeds the more
easily to an anatomization of his role in the society in which he
has been placed. The examination reveals not only Hamlet's
reaction to that society, but the society's to him. As a result
certain qualities of both emerge from a scrutiny more intense
than would otherwise be possible; and in the process the nature
of Hamlet's larger situation becomes a major concern. This has
its structural effects, for Hamlet's role is the momentous and
tragic one of 'chooser' in that society; thus the play's mood of
hesitancy competently and fittingly suggests the indecision
which properly accompanies a choice of such magnitude.

Its 'shape' is in the main diffused through attendant complexities of characterization and motivation and does not receive

a firm statement; it is 'overheard', not heard, when we read the play. So, the alternatives which confront Hamlet manifest themselves in different ways to suit the exigencies of the story. One of these is by means of symbolic localization; two places are set in opposition to each other from the very beginning: the University of Wittenberg from which Hamlet has recently come, and the Court of Denmark at which he has just arrived. The tension between these two provides an impetus for much of the action which follows, for from the first the 'old' values of the University on the Elbe are opposed to the 'new' values of Elsinore. They are mutually contradictory.

If Hamlet's choice is between the ways of life which these values involve, a cognate manifestation of it lies in that which he is also asked to make between a way of life based on contemplation and another which has action as its principle. He can either 'act' and so kill the King, or he can 'contemplate' the deed and allow that to distract him from carrying it out: a formulation of the dilemma which becomes a major element in his own assessment of the situation. Certainly, the play characterizes him as a contemplative person from the first; he is almost the type of the melancholy brooding scholar. The tragedy begins with this figure thrust suddenly and unwillingly into a world of action, for Elsinore is very much a 'man's' world in which that is at a premium. Within its confines heavy drinking and preparations for war signal so much; Laertes is more at home there than Hamlet and he gains easy access at the head of a mob when he wishes, whilst Hamlet stands uncertainly outside. At the start prospects are open for him which are closed to the Prince; permission is granted to go to France, but not to return to Wittenberg.

Hamlet could not be more out of his element. In short, he is a man used to one way of life suddenly faced with another and required to deal with it. In this, he may be said to be a man of his time, for his difficulty suggests an Elizabethan one. Part of what has been called the 'cultural revolution' of that age entailed the replacing of an old medieval culture by a new one which was quite different to it.[1] And if such a process constitutes a permanent human experience, then Hamlet's own becomes universal for that reason. Like all human beings he encounters

[1] Cf. S. L. Bethell, *op. cit.*, pp. 5 ff.

that sense of disruption which the change from past to future brings, and which makes of the present a trap of insecurities. Just as Wittenberg provides a most appropriate localization of a disintegrating past,[1] so Claudius's court exhibits in abundance the 'modern' features which will typify the future. Not surprisingly, Hamlet feels imprisoned in his surroundings.

One of the chief characteristics of Elsinore is its employment of the reason as a weapon, in a consistent effort to subordinate every human activity to it; inevitably, the play argues, this necessitates the substitution of the apparent for the real. At the beginning, Hamlet is urged to join in the process and to accept the attitudes to life which it requires of him. His refusal to do so, and his consequent dilemma, becomes the burden of a plot which, however much it may depend on a tradition of older 'revenge' stories which recount similar events, has nevertheless certain elements within it which cause it to be well suited to a greater purpose. Shakespeare's choice of so hackneyed a vehicle as this 'revenge tragedy' is explicable on the grounds of *Hamlet*'s larger intention. In the course of its telling he relies extensively on the irony which would come of the audience's foreknowledge of the tale. As with *Oedipus Rex*, the horror and its import are the greater because we know what will happen.

If much of the play is 'given' by its title and the expectations which that would have aroused in its own day, a good deal of its force for a modern audience comes from the way in which those are exceeded whilst fulfilled. 'Given' a ghost which may or may not be real, we find the opposite non-ghostly world of Claudius the more sinister because appearances predominate therein. We experience the discomfiture which comes of discovering that reality is not in its expected place, and the play's first line suggests as much in its expression of fundamental bewilderment. Bernardo's nervous challenge, 'Who's there?' (I, i, 1) is disturbing both in itself and because it is wrongly directed. He, after all, is the relieving sentry, a man going on duty. Who on earth, we wonder, would he expect to be 'there' other than the man he should relieve? Unless, that is, there had been 'someone' there, in the sentry's place, on some previous occasion; the 'given'

---

[1] Wittenberg is of course the University of two great 'disintegrators', Faustus and Luther.

ghost stirs at the back of our minds. Francisco corrects the error: 'Nay, answer me. Stand and unfold yourself.' (I, i, 2) and thus elicits the ironic password, 'Long live the King!' (I, i, 3). The King will not live long, we know. This is 'given' along with our knowledge that the previous King did not live long either (it is his ghost which has just been hinted at) and that there has been, and will be, a murder to reckon with in the matter. A note of confusion has been struck; a confusion between the real and the apparent.

The entry of Horatio adds another dimension to the scene. His words 'place' him immediately as a contemplative, an unwilling interloper, like Hamlet himself, into a realm of action. Fittingly, his outlook reveals itself as one in which reason and its 'explanations' of phenomena are subordinate to another point of view. His account of how the 'sheeted dead' rose from their graves before Caesar's death, and how

> . . . the moist star
> Upon whose influence Neptune's empire stands
> Was sick almost to doomsday with eclipse;
>
> (I, i, 118–20)

supplements the atmosphere which has been generated, and has an immediate poetic relevance to the events in which he now takes part. They have to do with ghosts, superstitions and religious mysteries; matters which keep the reason at bay:

> Some say that ever 'gainst that season comes
> Wherein our Saviour's birth is celebrated,
> This bird of dawning singeth all night long;
> And then, they say, no spirit dare stir abroad,
> The nights are wholesome, then no planets strike,
> No fairy takes, nor witch hath power to charm,
> So hallowed and so gracious is that time.
>
> (I, i, 158–64)

Whatever else may be said of these words, they clearly strike an 'old-fashioned' note; their point of view is not a 'modern' one. Their preoccupations are incapable of a certain kind of analysis; they have to do with belief, not fact, and even part-belief (Horatio does 'in part believe' them) is sufficient assent. They speak of a world, perhaps, in which only a higher kind of reasoning has any validity.

That world is quickly replaced by its opposite. The Court of Claudius enters with a flourish. The King, the Queen, the councillors fill the stage and the contrast is deliberate and startling as the 'known' supersedes the unknown, a living monarch supplants the ghost of a dead one. Claudius's opening speech forcefully reminds us of the kind of reasoning whose absence has been felt. And if what we first saw was 'old', then what we see now is decidedly 'new'. The inexplicable is suddenly replaced by that which necessitates 'explanations'. And indeed explanations stiffen Claudius's words; their movement, by contrast with the easy fluidity of Horatio's previous lines about the dawn, have the complex quality of the highly discursive. Careful antitheses in the verse give the sense of a balanced 'argument', a rational progression from premiss to conclusion. The sun has risen on a different world, for the Court is a place of 'wisdom' and 'discretion', where emotions, such as grief, must be subordinated to the social (and nuptial) requirements of government, of order, of utility:

> Though yet of Hamlet our dear brother's death
> The memory be green; and that it us befitted
> To bear our hearts in grief, and our whole kingdom
> To be contracted in one brow of woe;
> Yet so far hath discretion fought with nature
> That we with wisest sorrow think on him,
> Together with remembrance of ourselves.
>
> (I, ii, 1–7)

It proffers an attractive, balanced, rational apportioning of due pleasure and due pain, in which 'discretion' tempers nature, wisdom sorrow, the new King's accession the old King's death. An apparently logical and cyclical order prevails. A king has died, another has taken his place; 'Long live the King!' implies an appropriate degree of inevitability, and the manner of Elsinore, like that of its password, suggests calm self-possession in its acceptance of what seems rationally unavoidable, and so welcome:

> Therefore our sometime sister, now our queen,
> Th'imperial jointress to this warlike state,
> Have we, as 'twere with a defeated joy,
> With an auspicious and a dropping eye,

> With mirth in funeral, and with dirge in marriage,
> In equal scale weighing delight and dole,
> Taken to wife . . .
>
> (I, ii, 8–14)

The words postulate a symmetrical world of an 'equal scale', in which marriage discreetly balances funeral, life death; they speak of a proportioned, complete, and reasonable whole, prepared, 'warlike', to defend itself against all opposition. As Claudius reminds Laertes, the Court is a place where

> You cannot speak of reason to the Dane
> And lose your voice.
>
> (I, ii, 44–5)

It is not profitable to suggest, as some critics have done, that we have no cause to suspect Claudius at this point in the play. The truth lies simply in that his guilt constitutes one of the 'givens' of the *Hamlet* story and of the revenge tradition which is its basis. The tale requires a villain, and the audience knows that Claudius is that villain. Whether Hamlet knows as much does not matter at this stage; more important is the way in which Claudius's words reveal the nature of his villainy. We know him to be a murderer before the play begins, and, by Elizabethan standards, an incestuous one, a cause of the gravest political, moral, and sexual disorder. He is also a practised intriguer, who, in this speech, seems capable of 'explaining away' what he has done. To do so, he uses the method of the discursive reason, the advancement, step by step, from acceptable premiss to logical conclusion; from 'though' and 'yet' to 'therefore'. Not only does he obscure the reality of the situation by this means, but he also creates a political, moral and sexual order of his own in its place, which parodies that which it conceals. Thus the Court becomes his artefact (when it should be God's) and we find him ruling over a synthetic society which he asks us to think of as orderly and good, comprehensible and acceptable. As its King, head of the State, and husband of the Queen, he becomes by such reasoning, and at the climax of its 'ordering' process, the father of her offspring. Hamlet experiences, as a result, the enormity of being called '. . . my cousin Hamlet, and my son—' (I, ii, 64).

At this point Hamlet reveals the strength of his opposition to

Claudius, the Court, and what these stand for. His recognition
that Claudius has masked their true relationship first prompts
him to respond with some belligerence, to assert his real status as
'A little more than kin and less than kind' (I, ii, 65) and thereby
to establish his proper kinship with the Court. He is not
Claudius's son, any more than Claudius is rightfully the Court's
King, or rightfully married to his mother; any more, indeed,
than his father is rightfully dead. His attack focuses on the
banality of such blandishments as Gertrude's

> Thou know'st 'tis common – all that lives must die,
> Passing through nature to eternity.
>
> (I, ii, 72–3)

– a truth whose triteness gives the measure of its debt to the kind
of thinking which informs Claudius's 'explanations'. In fact such
'truths' only 'seem' to have a basis in reality. A husband's death
involves deeper issues than those suggested by her aphorism, and
to call such a death 'common' indicates the shallowness of the
reasoning which expresses it. Death is 'common', certainly; all
men are mortal. But for a mother to ask of her bereaved son why,
since this is the case, he should be so grieved at a 'particular'
occurrence, namely his father's death, surely shows an in-
sensitivity, an abstraction from reality so great as to be monstrous. And in response to this monstrous rationalization Hamlet
attacks that very 'seeming' which it evinces:

> Seems, madam! Nay, it is; I know not seems.
> 'Tis not alone my inky cloak, good mother,
> Nor customary suits of solemn black,
> Nor windy suspiration of forc'd breath,
> No, nor the fruitful river in the eye,
> Nor the dejected haviour of the visage,
> Together with all forms, moods, shapes of grief,
> That can denote me truly. These, indeed, seem;
> For they are actions that a man might play . . .
>
> (I, ii, 76–84)

The last remark is directed at Claudius, of course, and it hits the
target; he is an 'actor', pretending emotions which he does not
feel. It also marks the beginnings of a metaphor which will occur
again in the play, and which has to do with the ramifications of

'play-acting', the kind of dealing in 'appearances' of which Shakespeare as a playwright was obviously intensely aware, as much as were his audience. 'For they are actions that a man might play' points at Claudius's present activities, prefigures Hamlet's feigned madness, and reminds us of *The Mousetrap* to come; all 'givens' in the story of *Hamlet*.[1] The irony is intense, the accusation apt, and the alternatives between which Hamlet will be so tragically torn are thrown into greater relief.

Thus the 'placing' process which has established these of the Court's characteristics also 'places' Hamlet in a position completely opposed to them, one from which a different kind of reasoning on his part will lead to a different kind of reality. Madness, his device for dealing with the Court, and for moving within it, becomes in addition a kind of metaphorical statement of this position, for madness is non-rational. More, in the tradition in which Elizabethan stage-fools are often 'mad', madness can be a legitimate means of reaching a higher level of truth than that of the reason, if there is method in it.

The play places great emphasis on Claudius from the very first as a 'reasoner' in a certain mode. Later, when confronted with Hamlet's dangerous outburst, and the possible collapse of the social structure which he has devised, he hastily attempts to 'reason' with the Prince by fitting the King's death into a rational scheme of consequence, of event following event on a principle of causation:

> But you must know your father lost a father,
> That father lost lost his, and the survivor bound,
> In filial obligation, for some term
> To do obsequious sorrow. . . .
>
> (I, ii, 89–92)

The argument has an air of exactitude and precision. It moves by 'composing and dividing'; it 'explains', and it explains away. In these terms, death becomes commonplace because universal. Accordingly the obligations which it requires to be fulfilled are entirely social; a father's death necessitates only 'filial obligation'. Death in this view forms part of the world of 'fact', the world of the senses:

---

[1] It is also involved in Claudius's 'apparent' praying, which prevents Hamlet from killing him later on, and serves to bring the tragedy to its ironic conclusion.

> For what we know must be, and is as common
> As any the most vulgar thing to sense,
> Why should we in our peevish opposition
> Take it to heart?
>
> (I, ii, 98–101)

Hamlet's wider and more generalized grief thereby becomes unnecessary and so irrational. It is called, significantly, 'unmanly grief' (I, ii, 94) and thus deemed unsuitable to the 'man's' world of Elsinore. It shows 'a will most incorrect to heaven' and 'an understanding simple and unschool'd' (I, ii, 95–7). It constitutes a 'fault against the dead', and a 'fault to nature' (I, ii, 102). Finally, it is 'To reason most absurd . . .' (I, ii, 103). Claudius explains this last point by an account of the way in which such a reason works; it is one

> . . . whose common theme
> Is death of fathers, and who still hath cried,
> From the first corse till he that died today,
> 'This must be so'.
>
> (I, ii, 103–6)

It confines itself to the observation of physical phenomena and its 'common theme' is the construction of propositions on this basis; the climax of its activity is reached with the assertion of necessity: 'This must be so.' It is a reason whose mode is discursive, moving from an irrevocable premiss to an unavoidable conclusion. It is a reason of an essentially 'downward-looking' character, a 'scientific' reason; it is the *ratio inferior*.

As the play progresses, we are left in no doubt of the matter, for we find time and again that it lies in the nature of the 'lower' reason to be confined to such limited truths as have been noticed, and to be unable to go beyond them. The Court as a whole expresses in its actions, its preoccupations, its view of life and death and the methods by which these views are prosecuted, the full limitations of that faculty. For example, it can deal, as has been said, only with the events of this world. The Ghost never appears to Claudius, and when it does so before Gertrude she cannot see it. She sees 'Nothing at all; yet all that is I see.' (III, iv, 133). She sees the material world, 'all that is', nothing beyond that. Claudius, however genuine his desire for repentance, cannot make his thoughts rise above the same level, even when he tries to do so: 'My words fly up, my thoughts remain below.' (III, iii, 97). The tragedy will be played out on the level of such 'thoughts'.

Polonius is an apt representative of the Court, for he takes its *rationale* to absurd lengths. Where Claudius is logical, discursive, Polonius is fantastically so, to the point of becoming ludicrous. But he is not wholly that. The 'few precepts' which he forces on Laertes are, however banal, good advice on one level. They render fully the new 'civility' of the renaissance in the matters of money and manners:[1]

> Give every man thy ear, but few thy voice;
> Take each man's censure, but reserve thy judgment.
> Costly thy habit as thy purse can buy ...
>
> (I, iii, 68–70)

Their tone is 'reasonable' as their preoccupations are worldly. However, this same reasonableness, this same 'worldly' concern becomes a much more sinister and destructive force when its attention is turned beyond its own frame of reference. The love between Hamlet and Ophelia exists in precisely that area; it has nothing to do with money or manners, it is non-worldly, non-physical. In fact, its characteristics are spiritual, even heavenly, for Hamlet

> ... hath given countenance to his speech, my lord,
> With almost all the holy vows of heaven.
>
> (I, iii, 113–14)

Polonius nevertheless seeks to 'explain' this love by the same means that Claudius had used to explain death; they are rational means. Hence, for Polonius, love has no mystery. It is simply a matter of physics and chemistry, with a merely material end in view:

> ... springes to catch woodcocks! I do know,
> When the blood burns, how prodigal the soul
> Lends the tongue vows. ...
>
> (I, iii, 115–17)

The incongruity of the terms he uses is fundamental, and his imagery owes as much to thermodynamics as to anything else:

[1] They have been attributed to Guazzo's *Civile Conversation*; cf. *The Civile Conversation of M. Steeven Guazzo*, ed. Sir Edward Sullivan (London, 1925), Vol. I, pp. li–lvi.

> ... These blazes, daughter,
> Giving more light than heat – extinct in both,
> Even in their promise, as it is a-making –
> You must not take for fire . . . .
>
> (I, iii, 117–20)

This constitutes an 'explanation' of love as rational as anything Claudius could utter, and its 'scientific' quality adds to the effect. Its purpose is to destroy.

Such a method of destruction has great success up to a point, although as one of the Court's chief instruments in the matter Polonius perhaps makes its machinations more deeply sinister by being himself comic, for in his comedy the Court reveals itself more clearly. Set later to 'explain' Hamlet's odd behaviour, he concludes that it is irrational, a kind of 'madness' brought on by love. His expression of this view, his tortuous use of words, parodies and so draws attention to the method by which the words work, the rational one of *discursus*, the logical progression from point to point:

> My liege, and madam, to expostulate
> What majesty should be, what duty is,
> Why day is day, night night, and time is time,
> Were nothing, but to waste night, day, and time.
>
> (II, ii, 86–9)

Such 'expostulation' catches and mocks at much of Claudius's own method in its manner and indeed its matter too; the words, like his, are of time, 'order', government. Throughout the play Polonius seems to offer a debased version of the King's point of view. He is an old and feeble Claudius and it is fitting that Hamlet later kills him in mistake for his master.

Hamlet has confronted the Court with the weapon of non-reason, and that weapon is parried by means of its opposite, the intensely rational. Polonius may attempt to 'expostulate' on Hamlet's madness but his analysis gets no further than the words themselves; his reasoning is self-restricted, it cannot deal with anything outside its province. Its movement is not from point to point in reality (though, characteristically, it 'appears' to be so), so much as circular, confined to this world, to the here and the now; the true nature of Hamlet's madness quite escapes it:

Mad let us grant him, then; and now remains
That we find out the cause of this effect;
Or rather say the cause of this defect,
For this effect defective comes by cause.
Thus it remains, and the remainder thus.
Perpend . . .

(II, ii, 100–5)

The result, though clearly comic, is to reveal how far an excessively rational purpose is not only capable of destruction, but, at its apogee in Polonius, of self-destruction; it destroys the language which carries it, making it impotent as a means of communication. The same point is pressed home later in the play, when we see a further and rather less comic deterioration in the linguistic structures which characterize the Court. If Polonius's speech parodies that of Claudius in one sense, Osric's does so in another. If the barren antitheses of the upstart King's opening lines are mocked by Polonius's strangulated see-sawing between 'cause' and 'effect', then Claudius's proportioned and ordered cosmos, with its balance of 'equal scale' and its artificial symmetry, is parodied by another upstart's 'courtly' euphuisms and exaggerated concern with social ceremonies. Hamlet's effective mimicry of Osric indicates how distant such language and its users are from reality:

> Sir, his definement suffers no perdition in you; though, I know, to divide him inventorially would dozy th'arithmetic of memory . . .
>
> (V, ii, 112 ff.)

If Hamlet's 'madness', like his love for Ophelia which Polonius takes as symptomatic of that, cannot be accounted for by means of the *ratio inferior*, then it writhes, as we see, ineffectually about. The real irony of Polonius's conclusion that as a result of his love the Prince is 'from his reason fall'n' (II, ii, 164) lies in the fact that Hamlet would probably agree with him, and be glad of it; for by this time reason is Hamlet's greatest enemy.

The play, then, presents the Court pre-eminently as an agent of a certain kind of destruction, one prepared to establish itself by means of intellectual as well as physical violence. In the event, Hamlet is inspired to attack this evil by an account of it which is both appropriate and accurate. The Ghost insists on Claudius's

bestiality as well as on the fact that he can work 'witchcraft' with
his reason, his 'wit':

> Ay, that incestuous, that adulterate beast,
> With witchcraft of his wits, with traitorous gifts –
> O wicked wit and gifts that have the power
> So to seduce!...

> (I, v, 42–5)

The two are not unconnected. Reason has been seen to be
capable of destroying language, and it is by extension possible
to suggest, as the Ghost does, that it also destroys its user's very
humanity. Claudius the 'reasoner' is also Claudius the animal,
and this is a notion which has already occurred to Hamlet in
another connection before he meets the Ghost.

From the beginning of the play, Hamlet's opposition to the
Court has a very broad front. Given to introspection, and
detesting the material world about him, his words have the tone
of the sceptic; they catch the world-weariness of Montaigne and
Ficino:

> How weary, stale, flat, and unprofitable,
> Seem to me all the uses of this world!

> (I, ii, 133–4)

His distaste centres, initially, on his mother, and on her marriage.
The aspect of that which disgusts him most is not so much its
haste, nor its incestuous nature (though these receive memorable
comment), but its deplorable bestiality, its animal involvement
with the 'solid' (or 'sullied') flesh. More particularly, Hamlet
seems to want to link her behaviour with the very faculty
normally thought to raise human beings above the level of the
animals, the reason:

> O God! a beast that wants discourse of reason
> Would have mourned longer –

> (I, ii, 150–1)

Animals do not have the discursive *ratio*, the 'discourse of
reason'. But this woman, who does possess it, has behaved worse
than any animal, and Hamlet's remark suggests in a paradox
that her 'discourse of reason' has in some way caused this to be so.
To be 'rational' to that degree is to be *less* than human.

The same scene (I, ii) also hints at an opposite notion, for in it the view is affirmed that beyond the fleshly and animal 'uses of this world' there exists a higher realm to which the body cannot reach. The incorporeal figure of the Ghost has already brought this to mind, and its spectral presence can be felt here as in every scene. Not only is the Ghost a manifestation of a spiritual world which demands attention for itself in the face of the 'rational' and physical activities of the Court, but its imminence throughout insistently asserts the 'reality' of Gertrude's original, lawful marriage; the 'ghostly' King Hamlet was her 'real' husband, the fleshly Claudius only appears to be such. Hamlet's sardonic juxtaposition of the two, his father's funeral with his mother's wedding which 'followed hard upon', therefore serves a complex purpose. It indicates the extent to which the destruction of reality has resulted in the construction of an appearance in its place, and his account reveals by contrast the full shabbiness of Claudius's version of the same event which, in an attempt to cloak an unseemly haste with the tritest of conceits, speaks of 'mirth' in connection with the funeral, and 'dirge' with the marriage. Finally, talk of this event with Horatio and the others who have seen the Ghost brings Hamlet a vision of his father by means of a mode of perception poetically relevant to the Ghost's spiritual nature; he sees him in his 'mind's eye' (I, ii, 185), and the reference to a supra-sensual mode of cognition is quickly followed by the suggestion that it involves an activity of the soul, not the body:

> I doubt some foul play. Would the night were come!
> Till then sit still, my soul. . . .
>
> (I, ii, 255–6)

It will be confirmed later that Hamlet's soul can acquire a kind of knowledge which lies beyond the confines of mere reason: it is 'prophetic' (I, v, 40) and informed by a spirit which is not rational. Even at this very early point Hamlet adopts the role of antagonist to the reason, as a corollary of his antagonism towards its counterpart, the physical world of the flesh which has just left the stage in the persons of Claudius and Gertrude. Significantly, he acquires precise information laid against that world from a source totally opposed to it. Indeed, his perception of his father in his 'mind's eye' is exactly opposite to that kind of perception of which Gertrude speaks when she earlier counsels him,

> Do not for ever with thy vailed lids
> Seek for thy noble father in the dust.
>
> (I, ii, 70–1)

She speaks of the mode of cognition appropriate to Elsinore, where men see by physical means, and look 'downwards'. Hamlet's 'seeing' is of another sort, the obverse of that; it employs the mind, not the eyes, and it looks 'upwards'.

In fact Hamlet's first encounter with the Ghost stresses the point for it requires of him a renunciation of the rational as the necessary preliminary to a mystical communion with a spiritual power. The Ghost has already been associated with an 'old' and mysterious way of thinking opposed to the Court's way, so that, in his vehement acceptance of the Ghost's part, Hamlet must renounce the kind of reason upheld by Claudius as well as the way of life in which that results. By the Court's standards thereafter he can only be, as Polonius says, 'nothing else but mad.' (II, ii, 94).

Just before the encounter, Hamlet himself seems to re-affirm this when he speaks disparagingly of the animal behaviour of the King to the accompaniment of noises off-stage which supplement his account (I, iv, 8 ff.). He goes on to enlarge a psychological theory that the human 'pales and forts of reason', man's defence against the mystery which surrounds him, may be breached and overrun in 'particular men' by something in their nature. He speaks of Claudius, but, ironically, his words apply to himself with greater significance for, almost immediately, his own reason is confronted with a force which seems to overthrow it in another way. Claudius's *ratio* has been 'unbalanced' to the extent that the *ratio inferior* dominates it; he is merely 'rational' in that sense and, by Hamlet's paradox of his mother, merely animal as a result. 'Manliness' for Claudius lies in his present behaviour; by the same paradox, such 'manliness' is bestial. On the other hand Hamlet's own *ratio* now experiences contact with a different, 'higher' force. Appropriately, he turns to meet it with a prayer on his lips: 'Angels and ministers of grace defend us!' (I, iv, 39).

At first a certain ambiguity naturally surrounds the Ghost. It could be either 'a spirit of health' or 'a goblin damn'd', and by mortal standards an association with it could lead to madness. Horatio, their representative, pleads this case. The Ghost might well

> ... deprive your sovereignty of reason
> And draw you into madness.
>
> (I, iv, 73–4)

This represents a 'normal' view, and it is Horatio's function throughout the play to put it. But Hamlet's situation is abnormal. Only by means of accepting a level of truth and perception beyond that of the reason can he overcome the reason's limitations. The madness which he embraces may be as far, perhaps, from the reason as insanity, but it lies in a different direction. It will not involve irrationality so much as super-rationality, of a sort which Polonius's notion of 'true madness' has failed 'to define'. A choice between two opposed ways of life therefore confronts him. A struggle ensues, literally, for as the Ghost beckons, Hamlet's friends in this world hold him back. In breaking free, in choosing, Hamlet takes a momentous decision. He rejects one way of life and embraces another. He rejects an 'apparent' father, Claudius, in favour of a 'real' father, the Ghost; he chooses against reason in favour of something beyond it. In following the Ghost off the stage, Hamlet follows the source of the truth of his own 'mind's eye', for he follows his own source, his father. And the knowledge which he acquires from that source, in the sense that it apprises him of the role he must now assume, is self-knowledge; his choice fulfils the precept *nosce teipsum*.

Unfortunately such knowledge also destroys him for it reveals that the role, the traditional one of Revenger, fits ill with the man. A contemplative, he is required to act, and this demands that he should sacrifice one part of himself for the good of the other, for the man and the role are mutually contradictory.

The Ghost's revelations indicate the exactness of Hamlet's 'prophetic' soul-knowledge. And, asked to join battle with the 'witchcraft' of Claudius's 'wit', he resolves, by contrast, to fly

> ... with wings as swift
> As meditation or the thoughts of love ...
>
> (I, v, 29–30)

to the revenge demanded. Plainly, his method of dealing with
reason will be that of its opposite. It will be attacked with
'meditation', just as murder and lust will be opposed by 'thoughts
of love'.

After his communion with the Ghost, Hamlet does indeed
appear mad to his friends. Yet already the 'method' is discernible. His 'wild and whirling words' have little of one kind of
reason in them perhaps, but they elicit the truth in another way.
Apparent tautologies,

> There's never a villain dwelling in all Denmark
> But he's an arrant knave. . . .
>
> > (I, v, 123)

contain the necessary degree of veracity which all tautologies
must, as well as truths of a larger sort, and Horatio's objection,

> There needs no ghost, my lord, come from the grave
> To tell us this.
>
> > (I, v, 125–6)

reveals how little he understands Hamlet's position. Elsinore is
vulnerable only to something beyond itself; only the Ghost can
and does reveal the reality which underlies the appearance of the
'smiling villain', and Hamlet argues strongly for the necessity of a
super-rational access to truth in such circumstances when he
makes his formidable statement of an 'intuitive' faith in the
Ghost's words:

> There are more things in heaven and earth, Horatio,
> Than are dreamt of in your philosophy. . . .
>
> > (I, v, 166–7)

In this way, Hamlet's 'madness' is nearer to the kind of barbed
non-reason of the traditional Elizabethan 'wise fool' than to
insanity.[1] By means of it he gains admission to the Court, and a
tacit, if momentary, acceptance of his role of 'fool' within it. As a
'fool' he makes play with words and speaks in riddles. Yet what
he says persistently harries the reason, chastises its 'apparent'
values, and points to the truths which it cannot attain. Ironically,
it is the 'rational' Polonius who notices this peculiarity:

---

[1] *Vid.* Enid Welsford, *The Fool* (London, 1935), pp. 76 ff.

How pregnant sometimes his replies are! a happiness that often madness hits on, which reason and sanity could not so prosperously be delivered of.

(II, ii, 208 ff.)

As a 'fool', Hamlet can attack the Court in a summary manner, and without fear. Even Rosencrantz and Guildenstern's attempts to trap him are brushed aside and neatly parried by his disarming refusal to submit himself to their kind of reasoning: 'Shall we to th' court? for, by my fay, I cannot reason'. (II, ii, 264).

His madness, therefore, has a distinctive quality, and his condition at this point in the play suggests, not surprisingly, that of the man, described by Ficino, who is beginning to adopt a process of intuitive reflection as his mode of thought. The moment a mind thus engaged begins to cast off outside impressions and awakens to its own life, it feels, says Ficino, a profound uneasiness and grief:

> . . . the whole time the sublime Soul lives in this base body, our mind, as though it were ill, is thrown into a continual disquiet – here and there, up and down – and is always asleep and delirious; and the individual movements, actions, passions of men are nothing but vertigos of the sick, dreams of the sleeping, deliriums of the insane, so that Euripides rightly called this life the dream of a shadow.[1]

Ficino also remarks that in the initial stages of the movement away from this world, and towards an 'intuitive' way of life, of piercing the dream to touch reality, a man will experience a vague sorrow, a distaste for worldly things, a disgust with material values, for,

> . . . in this exile no earthly pleasures can comfort the human mind, since it is eager for better things.[2]

Hamlet has already chaffed Rosencrantz and Guildenstern about the distinction between dreams, shadows and reality (II, ii, 258 ff.). Now he gives full expression to a similar revulsion from the world:

---

[1] *Cit.* Kristeller, *op. cit.*, p. 209.
[2] *Ibid.*, p. 211.

I have of late – but wherefore I know not – lost all my mirth, for-
gone all custom of exercises; and indeed it goes so heavily with my
disposition that this goodly frame, the earth, seems to me a sterile
promontory . . .   (II, ii, 296–301)

He anatomizes man, presented as the humanist thought of him,
as the wonder of the Universe:

What [a] piece of work is a man, how noble in reason, how
infinite in faculties, in form and moving, how express and
admirable in action, how like an angel in apprehension, how
like a God![1]

Yet this spectacle does not delight Hamlet, it disgusts him now
that his intuitive mode of 'seeing' has shown him its reality. Such
insight has torn aside the veil of appearances which cover
Claudius's world. Aptly, Rosencrantz and Guildenstern intro-
duce into it the first mention of another world of appearances,
that of the stage:

To think, my lord, if you delight not in man, what lenten enter-
tainment the players shall receive from you.

(II, ii, 313–14)

Yet Hamlet's reaction is the opposite of that. Disgusted by an
appearance which masquerades as reality for gain, he is delighted
by the prospect which a troup of professional 'maskers' affords.
For they, the actors who 'render' life on the stage and present an
admitted 'appearance' of it, offer him, as they offered Shakespeare himself, a world that can be ordered and manipulated to
serve truth and justice. Drama, to the dramatist (and Hamlet
becomes one; he constructs the most potent part of *The Mousetrap*) makes of appearance an instrument by whose means
reality can be revealed. So he accepts this play-world gladly,
with its microcosmic social structure of 'apparent' Kings,
Queens and courtiers, for it is a weapon he can use to reach
reality in the face of deceit. 'The play' will certainly be the
'thing' by whose means the conscience of the King will be caught.

The madness of Ophelia, like that of Hamlet, presents itself
as a kind of intuitive reaching after truth. Her words have little
rational import; she

[1] I have, as noted in the previous chapter, adopted the punctuation of the
Second Quarto.

> ... speaks things in doubt,
> That carry but half sense. Her speech is nothing,
> Yet the unshaped use of it doth move
> The hearers to collection; they yawn at it
> And botch the words up fit to their own thoughts;
>
> (IV, v, 6–10)

She engages in no 'discourse of reason' yet her words have meaning and significance in another way. She

> would make one think there might be thought,
> Though nothing sure, yet much unhappily.
>
> (IV, v, 12–13)

Accordingly, when Claudius takes on the role of 'reasoner' in the face of a rebellious mob, Ophelia can expose his pretensions simply by singing and speaking the non-discursive and non-rational 'language' of flowers. A mode of thought above the level of the reason, and above the 'hugger-mugger' of Claudius's plots and schemes has the capacity to disturb the Court in a fundamental way. Ophelia's 'intuitive' grasp of the situation (she could not possibly know anything about it on a rational level) constitutes a real danger to Claudius. And yet his lack of perception about Ophelia is remarkable; to him, she has sunk below, not risen above, the level of human discourse:

> ... poor Ophelia
> Divided from herself and her fair judgment,
> Without the which we are pictures, or mere beasts;
>
> (IV, v, 81–3)

Ironically, this gives more a measure of his own animality than of hers. Laertes comes closer to the mark when he recognizes that 'This nothing's more than matter' (IV, v, 171) and that her words are a 'document in madness – thoughts and remembrance fitted' (IV, v, 175–6), though to regard the truly meaningful as 'madness' is by now a predictable reaction on the part of anyone having to do with the Court and its machinations (Ophelia herself, when 'sane', has already dismissed Hamlet as 'mad', at a time when she was acting as the Court's agent).

Later, at the height of Claudius's plotting with Laertes, when he is at his most cunning, his most 'reasonable' (IV, vii, 150 ff.) Ophelia again takes on her role of disruption, only this time by news of her death. That event suggests in itself something non-rational, impossible and beautiful;

> ... Her clothes spread wide
> And, mermaid-like, awhile they bore her up;
> Which time she chanted snatches of old tunes,
> As one incapable of her own distress ...
> (IV, vii, 176–9)

At this Laertes may weep, but Claudius's reaction is characteristic:

> ... Let's follow, Gertrude.
> How much I had to do to calm his rage!
> Now fear I this will give it start again ...
> (IV, vii, 192–4)

'Madness' in this play, then, may be said to be the dramatic expression of a form of mental activity higher and farther-reaching than that of the reason. As such, it becomes the weapon which Hamlet finds most effective against Claudius, and indeed the structure of the play yields itself quite easily to such a view. On a more complex level, a cognate opposition has been said to exist within this structure, as part of it, which manifests itself by means of another set of images. It is that between appearance and reality.

The images used by the Court to express its own opinion of its activities are often (especially in the play's 'depersonalized' moments, when the action is suspended and commented on by the participants, whatever their persuasion on the level of the plot) those of an 'appearance' which covers up an unwholesome reality. The third and fourth acts of the play abound in poetic structures of this kind, and it could be argued (though warily) that where the first two acts develop the opposition of Hamlet and the Court in terms of an intuitive 'madness' opposed to reason, the third and fourth acts ramify this structure in the cognate terms of a reality opposed to an appearance.

Polonius, in an oddly mixed metaphor, first makes us aware of this aspect of the Court's activity (ironically, he is at this moment instructing Ophelia how to deceive Hamlet by appearing to be what she is not):

> ... We are oft to blame in this:
> 'Tis too much prov'd, that with devotion's visage
> And pious action we do sugar o'er
> The devil himself.
>
> (III, i, 46–9)

At which 'the devil himself' of the play, Claudius, feels constrained to murmur

> O, 'tis too true!
> . . . .
> The harlot's cheek, beautied with plast'ring art,
> Is not more ugly to the thing that helps it
> Than is my deed to my most painted word. . . .
>
> (III, i, 49–53)

Both men (the Court's chief representatives) are talking about an appearance with which they themselves are disguising reality. Polonius's image is of taste: an apparent 'sweetness' disguises the devil's real 'bitterness'. Claudius, fittingly for him in a way which beggars description, uses a more traditional metaphor of cosmetics. Perhaps it is fitting because it is traditional (the drama of the time abounds in like metaphors, almost to the point of exhibiting an obsession with the implications of 'making-up'), for he is describing his own activities, and they are 'traditionally' evil, 'traditionally' devilish.

Hamlet's soliloquy, 'To be, or not to be', which follows immediately, has as its immediate concern the problem of suicide. But its formulation of that (which we might have expected to be expressed specifically in the imagery of the intuition-reason dichotomy) takes on the colour of its surroundings, and develops the note struck by Claudius and Polonius. Its theme is potentially the traditional conflict of action and contemplation, in that 'conscience' is said to make cowards of us all, thus destroying the will to action (which the present situation demands), for

> ... enterprises of great pitch and moment,
> With this regard, their currents turn awry
> And lose the name of action. . . .
>
> (III, i, 86–8)

What frustrates action here, however, is not its opposite 'contemplation', for that belongs to the 'intuitive' mode of thinking, like the 'meditation' that has been mentioned earlier, whose 'swift wings' were to 'sweep' Hamlet to his revenge. Rather, it is said to be 'thought', since

> ... the native hue of resolution
> Is sicklied o'er with the pale cast of thought ...
> (III, i, 84–5)

The image is of cosmetics. 'Thought', reasoning of the Court's type, becomes by this related to the 'plast'ring art'; it is an agent of sterility; it negates and cannot create, for it denies action, and, like a cosmetic, covers up truth. 'Thought' of this kind makes sick what is healthy, gives the apparent preference over the real; as Hamlet comments a few lines later in another 'cosmetic' image:

> ... the power of beauty will sooner transform honesty from what it is to a bawd than the force of honesty can translate beauty into his likeness. (III, i, 111 ff.)

The paradox, perhaps a development of the earlier one whereby his mother was the less human as she was the more rational, the less a beautiful woman the more she hid her beauty in animality, lies close to the heart of the play and it catches the temper of the times. As Hamlet laconically comments, 'This was sometime a paradox, but now the time gives it proof. . . .' (III, i, 113 ff.). Ophelia, whom he treats, rightly now, as a mere agent of the Court, ceases in consequence to be the woman he loved, and becomes another creature (whom he has not loved) painted, by means of cosmetics, over her former innocence:

> I have heard of your paintings too, well enough; God hath given you one face, and you make yourselves another.
> (III, i, 142 ff.)

The kind of reasoning in which the Court has involved her has, like a cosmetic, hidden the truth which she once represented. She belongs to Elsinore now, and reflects its image rather than God's. And indeed, Ophelia's 'other' face, the present 'appearance' which dominates her until her 'reality' emerges in madness, now 'sees' Hamlet in the Court's way as merely insane. She, whose non-rational affection for him was once linked with 'almost all the holy vows of heaven', has become something else, 'painted' and 'made up' by the Court for its own purposes. She therefore regards his mind as 'o'erthrown', regrets the deterioration of his social status (he was once 'Th' expectancy and rose of the fair state'), and with deepest irony, because she uses such terms without hesitation, laments his loss of a reason which she conceives of as 'noble':

> Now see that noble and most sovereign reason,
> Like sweet bells jangled, out of time and harsh . . .
> (III, i, 157–8)

Until her release, she remains a prisoner of the reason she admires. However, as the scene ends, Claudius finds himself forced to admit that Hamlet's 'madness' is not mere irrationality. It has pierced the cosmetic veil, and touched the flesh beneath; it reaches above and beyond the level of the reason to that of the 'soul':

> . . . what he spake, though it lack'd form a little,
> Was not like madness. There's something in his soul
> O'er which his melancholy sits on brood . . .
> (III, i, 163–5)

The play exploits the paradoxes of appearance and reality in many other ways. The most intriguing of these may be said to be that which probably intrigued Shakespeare most of all because it involves a probing of the nature of theatrical communication. 'Acting', the concept of 'assuming a role', of 'pretending' to be something one is not, forms a common basis for metaphor in the drama of the period. In a theatre whose mode of communication with its audience was non-naturalistic, the possibilities of a 'witty' use of theatrical convention to make a point about plays, within a play itself, need not be gone into here. It is sufficient to note that the drama was conceived (by audience and dramatists) to be a perfectly proper means of moral instruction, and of getting to and talking about the truth. Hamlet's claim that

> . . . I have heard
> That guilty creatures, sitting at a play,
> Have by the very cunning of the scene
> Been struck so to the soul that presently
> They have proclaim'd their malefactions;
> (II, ii, 584–8)

is as commonplace as it sounds, and his device of *The Mousetrap* gives us in miniature what perhaps we may assume to be Shakespeare's larger design in *Hamlet*. The play is directed at 'guilty' members of its Elizabethan audience as much as *The Mousetrap* is directed at Claudius.

As a device for revealing reality and exposing appearance, a play, itself an 'appearance' of reality, has an ironic and paradoxical rightness; it fights fire with fire, it sets (as *The Mousetrap* does) an 'apparent' murderer to catch a real one, a player of one sort to condemn a 'player' of another. Claudius, whose 'seeming' grief Hamlet had earlier recognized as one of the 'actions that a man might play' will thus be given an appropriate *quid pro quo*. That Hamlet is concerned with the 'play within the play' for these reasons there can be no doubt, for the sum of his advice to the Players is that the play should be given 'straight', untrammelled by stage 'business', in order that its effect shall be immediate and positive. This will be achieved by means of showing the audience its own face; by showing '. . . the very age and body of the time his form and pressure' (III, ii, 25 ff.). 'Appearance' will be ripped aside by use of appearance; the true face of reality will be revealed by the false faces of the actors (or, to adapt a previous metaphor, cosmetics will be wiped off by means of stage make-up, itself the 'cosmetic' process writ large).

Indeed, we have seen, prior to the performance of *The Mousetrap*, how far Hamlet himself can be affected by play-acting. His speech 'Oh what a rogue and peasant slave am I' (II, ii, 543 ff.), gives a full account of his 'real' self, as it has been rudely exposed to him by the Player's 'Hecuba' speeches. Such 'reality' has been revealed in consequence of the Player's simulation of weeping, his 'apparent' embodiment of the passion which Hamlet lacks. Dramatic representation has elicited the truth, since the actor has achieved in his 'acted' revenge for Hecuba exactly what is proper to Hamlet's own situation; it has therefore seemed monstrous that

>   . . . this player here,
> But in a fiction, in a dream of passion,
> Could force his soul so to his own conceit
>
> . . . .
> . . . . And all for nothing!

For Hecuba!
What's Hecuba to him or he to Hecuba,
That he should weep for her? What would he do,
Had he the motive and the cue for passion
That I have?

(II, ii, 544–55)

The Mousetrap, then, becomes in this way a major mani-festation of the play's conflict on the level of appearance and reality. Its very formality gives it the air of a 'set piece', a *tour de force*. The stage takes on another dimension and becomes both stage and auditorium; at this moment there are two plays and two audiences in the theatre, and Hamlet's role of 'chorus' applies to both plays and to both audiences. He 'interprets' both *The Mousetrap* and *Hamlet* which contains it, and the barbed shafts which hit Claudius hit us with no less accuracy.

Situated at two removes from our 'reality', *The Mousetrap* quite properly seems very stilted and artificial to us, the audience of *Hamlet*. But for the audience on the stage it reveals the truth, just as *Hamlet* does for us. Hence its awkward lines reveal nevertheless (for they are perhaps the lines written by Hamlet himself) the essence of Claudius's situation. The 'appearance' which he had constructed in his account of his accession to the throne at the beginning of the play, that 'ordered' and grandly secure world he then spoke of in which 'discretion' had fought with 'nature' and over which there presided an 'equal scale weighing delight and dole' so that you could not 'speak of reason to the Dane / And lose your voice' is now replaced by the shabby and trite little reality of a world in which

> The instances that second marriage move
> Are base respects of thrift, but none of love.
> A second time I kill my husband dead,
> When second husband kisses me in bed.
> (III, ii, 177–80)

The triteness and the shabbiness are real, frighteningly so, as Claudius's reaction shows. Reality emerges for Hamlet, too,

> What to ourselves in passion we propose,
> The passion ending, doth the purpose lose. . . .
> (III, ii, 189–90)

– but not in the same way. We know the true nature of his dilemma for he has told us of it. This is a mere versification of the way in which his 'passion' has become neutralized by 'thoughts', which, the Player King assumes, can never have claim to reality or truth. However much we may rationalize, the 'ends' of events are not in our hands:

> Our wills and fates do so contrary run
> That our devices still are overthrown;
> Our thoughts are ours, their ends none of our own.
> (III, ii, 206–8)

However, the play's work is quickly done. Claudius's world of appearances has indeed reached 'ends' not of his own, and the truth is brutally, even crudely, exposed so that by the time Hamlet gives his hysterical summation of the plot,

> 'A poisons him i' th' garden for his estate.
> His name's Gonzago. . . . You shall see anon how the murderer
> gets the love of Gonzago's wife.   (III, ii, 256 ff.)

reality, through the medium of drama, has dispelled appearance.

Having revealed the truth, Hamlet has only to deal with it, and he hastens to do so. So exhilarated is he at having hoist the Court with its own petard that he can confuse Polonius in a similar way, confidently ringing the changes of an 'appearance' of camel, weasel, whale, on the reality of a cloud (III, ii, 365 ff.) before charging to his mother's closet. Yet the battle is not over, the skein of appearance not yet fully broken, the transition from play to action not fully effected. He is still deceivable, and is deceived by the 'appearance' of Claudius's praying (III, iii, 37 ff.); moreover, in his interview with his mother, where he tries to show her the difference between the appearance of virtue and its reality by means of a picture, a 'counterfeit presentment', he fails completely. He tries to use the method of the play, the confrontation of guilt by guilt:

> You go not till I set you up a glass
> Where you may see the inmost part of you.
> (III, iv, 19–20)

But Gertrude has become part of Claudius's world; she has taken appearance for reality, Claudius the pseudo-King for King

Hamlet, the real King. She has left the 'fair mountain' to 'batten on this moor', and has preferred the body, the flesh, to that which lies above it; her act has the taint of the kind of blasphemy which 'sweet religion makes / A rhapsody of words' (III, iv, 47–8). And of all her faculties, Hamlet lays most blame for this on her reason, for it has acted as 'pander' to her will (III, iv, 88).

By this time, Polonius is dead, killed, ironically, because he was an 'appearance' of Claudius. Yet his death shows that Hamlet's sword is still unable to cope with the web of appearances in which it is caught. To underline the point, the Ghost appears to Hamlet at the height of his tirade against his mother. As this 'family group', husband, wife and son, ironically and briefly forms on the stage, the play's 'shape' crystallizes momentarily about them. Hamlet's language reverts suddenly from the appropriately bestial epithets he has been using to Gertrude, to an equally appropriate prayer (which recalls his original prayer on first encountering the Ghost):

> Save me, and hover o'er me with your wings,
> You heavenly guards!
>
> (III, iv, 103–4)

But even as he forms words of Angels and Heaven, Gertrude unwittingly reveals herself by her comment:

> Alas, he's mad!
> (III, iv, 105)

The nub of the play lies in this tableau: Hamlet, in touch with a higher form of intuitive reality, Gertrude, unseeing (the Ghost is invisible to her), judging him by the 'rational' reality of Elsinore. The world of the spirit cannot communicate with that of the flesh; Hamlet, its chosen go-between, is tragically unfitted for the task.

Hamlet's fitting of himself for the role imposed on him by the Ghost occupies the rest of the play. It involves bridging the gap between the Ghost and Gertrude, between husband and wife, father and mother. In the terms of this discussion, that necessitates a reconciliation between the opposing forces of appearance and reality, and reason and intuition. Hamlet's resolve, his determination, and his ultimate (if qualified) ability to achieve this all come about, in a sense, off-stage. Yet the difference between the man we see at this point and the man who brings the play to its conclusion after the abortive voyage to England is not as great as some critics have suggested. The seeds of the 'new' Hamlet are quite obvious on this side of the voyage; the 'sea change' exhibits no change, but a development. In fact on his way to the boat, Hamlet formulates an argument to himself which contains the key to all his subsequent behaviour, and which gives the essence of the opposing forces which have been discussed. He is watching the troops of Fortinbras pass over the stage, those same troops which will restore political order to Denmark when Hamlet's task is finished; they are the forces of reality:

> Exposing what is mortal and unsure
> To all that fortune, death, and danger dare.
> (IV, iv, 51–2)

Looking at them, Hamlet feels constrained to reiterate a view of mankind which he has held throughout the play. Man is more than fleshly, more than a beast:

> ... What is a man,
> If his chief good and market of his time
> Be but to sleep and feed? A beast, no more!
> (IV, iv, 33–5)

He has told us before that a beast lacks that 'discourse of reason' which a man has. He has spoken of man's 'noble' reason and his angelic 'apprehension' (II, ii, 301 ff.). Now he argues more explicitly. Man's reason has two aspects, one discursive (the *ratio inferior*) one 'godlike' (the *ratio superior*), and God has commanded us to use the latter as well as the former:

> Sure he that made us with such large discourse,
> Looking before and after, gave us not
> That capability and godlike reason
> To fust in us unus'd. ...
> (IV, iv, 36–9)

If we use less we are less than human, and Hamlet condemns himself as much as Claudius by this. He has allowed his own 'bestial oblivion', his immersion in the flesh, and his own 'craven scruple' of discursive reasoning – or, as he puts it, of '... thinking too precisely on th'event' (IV, iv, 41) to overcome that intuitive faculty in himself which would have swept him to truly 'manly' action, as a 'complete' human being. He has allowed it to 'fust . . unus'd'. The veil of appearance must be pierced, the reason must be overcome. He therefore resolves from now on to act only intuitively, to neglect the 'great argument' of reason, and to rush heroically to do what has to be done whenever the opportunity presents itself. His words suggest an intuitive groping after reality itself:

> . . . O, from this time forth,
> My thoughts be bloody, or be nothing worth!
> (IV, iv, 65–6)

Hamlet comes full circle in more than one way. The 'tale' is completed, the problems solved, wrongs righted, and order restored. But what fascinates about the play is the way in which the original conflict is resolved, simply if enigmatically, by an extension of those terms which began it in the first Act. Gertrude's original assertion of death, that it was 'common', was a rational enormity in its context. Nevertheless, the end of the play seems to suggest in that same idea of death's 'commonness' a solution to Hamlet's problems.

In effect it becomes elevated to the level of a kind of quietism about life itself, an intuitive assertion that Hamlet's dilemma is capable of resolution by death. To this the play adds a cognate notion of a providential design to life, the natural end to which is a death ordained by a higher power, providentially, at whatever point it chooses. Hamlet certainly accepts death after his voyage, welcomes it even, because it overrides all presumption, all appearance, even reason itself. Everyone comes to this end, the highest as well as the lowest:

> Imperious Caesar, dead and turn'd to clay.
> Might stop a hole to keep the wind away.
> (V, i, 207–8)

Death, indeed, provides its own solution, this side of the grave, to the problems of life; its final reality mocks at all appearances. Hence the 'cosmetic' imagery with which these are associated in this play takes on a quieter tone in Hamlet's conversation with those hearty realists, the gravediggers. The savagery formerly directed against Ophelia's 'painting' has a larger dimension:

. . . get you to my lady's chamber, and tell her, let her paint an inch thick, to this favour she must come . . .

(V, i, 187–9)

The facts defeat rational argument; Yorick's skull gives comfort because it is undeniably and finally real. As a result of this kind of thinking Hamlet acquires a terrible calm; he leans on death, as something providentially ordained, planned from above: 'there is a special providence in the fall of a sparrow.' (V, ii, 212). Such a conclusion suggests that man's problems are merely temporary, for they await this final solution. In such a belief, 'indiscretion', immediate non-rational action, is felt to be better than the 'deep plots' of our reasoning, because whatever we reason, that faculty must fall short of the absolute truth. The world after all is God's, not man's creation, and

> Our indiscretion sometime serves us well,
> When our deep plots do pall; and that should learn us
> There's a divinity that shapes our ends,
> Rough-hew them how we will.
>
> (V, ii, 8–11)

Claudius's plot, rationally worked out,

> . . . an exact command
> Larded with many several sorts of reasons.
> (V, ii, 19–20)

is a true product of his 'discretion', but it will be met, and has on the voyage been met, with Hamlet's kind of intuitive 'indiscretion'. And, thus armed, the Court loses for Hamlet its monstrous aspect and becomes the mere buzzing 'waterfly' of Osric, whose 'reasoning' he meets with mockery since it is worth no more. He lives, like the rest of the Court that this 'drossy age dotes on' only on the 'outside' of life; he has

> only got the tune of the time and outward habit of encounter –
> a kind of yesty collection, which carries them through and
> through the most fann'd and winnowed opinions.
>
> (V, ii, 183 ff.)

Claudius's 'rational' world has come only to this.

Hamlet himself, on the other hand, has a deeper insight. He 'sees' more clearly for he possesses an intuitive knowledge of a larger meaning to life which, if inexpressible, must be affirmed in a readiness to meet it:

> If it be now, 'tis not to come; if it be not to come, it will be now; if it be not now, yet it will come – the readiness is all. Since no man owes of aught he leaves, what is't to leave betimes? Let be.
>
> (V, ii, 213 ff.)

That 'Let be' expresses a powerful intuitive faith which the end of the play shows in action in the final duel to the death between Hamlet and the newly-won Court's representative, Laertes.

Symbolically, the duel constitutes a *reprise* of the various modes which Hamlet's opposition to Claudius has taken. Laertes, nothing if not the man of action, here fights the man of contemplation. The King's reason has planned the fight, but Hamlet's intuition has rendered the result pointless before it has begun. If Laertes must win because his sword is poisoned, Hamlet cannot lose because the fight on another level is already over. All that remains is for Death to solve this, as all struggles. And as if to underline the universal quality of the event, Claudius himself raises the conflict almost to cosmic level, far beyond the confined space of Elsinore:

> ... let the kettle to the trumpet speak,
> The trumpet to the cannoneer without,
> The cannons to the heavens, the heaven to earth ...
>
> (V, ii, 267–9)

The duel, like the play, expands beyond the limits of the theatre in this climax. The action's irresolution vanishes with its violence.

Significantly, Claudius, Gertrude, and Laertes all die as a result of miscalculated reasoning; Claudius's rational plan shows itself to be inadequate for dealing with Hamlet's 'indiscreet' attacks, and subject, like all 'deep plots', to error, in a deadly way. Death, as Hamlet intuitively knew, solves the problem for all of them. His task, of killing the King, is done, as is Claudius's purpose of killing Hamlet; nevertheless, the latter act is only accidentally achieved by means which mock at its rational planning. As if to emphasize the 'intuitive' spirit in which Hamlet meets his death, Horatio commands that 'flights of angels' sing him to his rest, and thus joins him, at the end, with that spiritual world which played so important a part in his struggle against the physical. Ironically, Hamlet finally gets the best of both 'worlds', and bridges the gap between contemplation and action, the world of the mind and the 'manly' world of the body, when Fortinbras accords him a soldier's funeral. In death, as he seemed to know he would, he becomes the sort of 'man' he could never be in life, for in death he combines the spiritual and the physical.

Before he dies Hamlet vehemently demands of Horatio that his whole story should be told accurately and in full. On the surface it is enigmatic, as the play is, a confused and hesitant tale of strange horrors resulting in an inexplicable carnage. But, as Hamlet insists, a true account of it will reveal something far deeper than the apparent pattern of events, and of greater moment than the few bodies which now litter the stage. He therefore charges his friend to

> ... report me and my cause aright
> To the unsatisfied.
>
> (V, ii, 331–2)

Such a report will, he hopes, reveal the true nature of the conflict.

3

THE PROBLEM PLAYS

When my love swears that she is made of truth,
I do believe her, though I know she lies.
(*Sonnet* 138)

THE CONFLICT with which *Hamlet* is concerned does not perhaps receive a satisfactory resolution in that play, and most
critics would number themselves among 'the unsatisfied' to
whom Horatio's explanatory account ought to be addressed.
The bodies on the stage seem nevertheless to 'say' something to
us, however mutely; they state a problem if they do not solve it,
and the play's ending contains a hint, perhaps, of the much more
satisfactory conclusion of *King Lear* in which Cordelia's body
serves a similar purpose.

The questions posed by *Hamlet* are momentous ones. How
should a man distinguish between alternative versions of reality?
How should a man deal with a world based on one set of values,
one version of what is 'real', from the standpoint of another set
of values, another 'reality'? What is truth and how should it be
perceived, 'intuitively' or 'rationally'?

In the plays which follow *Hamlet* the same issues undergo
statement and re-statement in different forms until in the later
tragedies a clearer view of them emerges; the process reaches its
climax in the tragic clarity of *King Lear*. At this stage, however,
it seems that the major difficulty surrounding such questions lies
in the effective framing of them. Indeed, their answers seem not
to depend on choosing the 'right' alternative over the 'wrong'
one, so much as on the recognition that such alternatives exist,
that there are questions to be answered. The dramatist's
problem lies in the inculcation of such recognition.

It seems appropriate, therefore, that those plays which were

72

written after *Hamlet* and before *Othello* should be called the 'problem plays', although for many reasons the term is not a happy one. It suggests something in them, the treatment of 'problems' of a certain kind and in a certain way, which the plays themselves belie; ever since the term was invented by F. S. Boas, critics have been unhappy with it.[1] One reason for this has been the kind of problem with which these plays deal. Boas thought of them as social 'problems' treated in the manner of Ibsen, and although it has become fashionable to scorn this view, it may nonetheless be tenable and indeed perceptive in its way. To deny it is to deny that moral or metaphysical problems have a good deal of relevance to society, which should be much less tenable. Human beings exist invariably in 'societal' groupings, so that their problems must in some way manifest (or be manifestations of) human society. These plays are about 'social' matters because all human dilemmas have this dimension. But, and this constitutes a greater objection to Boas's view, they involve much more; all three, *Troilus and Cressida*, *All's Well That Ends Well* and *Measure for Measure*, construct entirely artificial 'societies' which become 'backgrounds' for the treatment of human problems only incidentally connected with them; the problems have priority over their 'social' setting. As a result, they overflow the confines of Troy, Rousillon, Paris, Florence, Marseilles or Vienna, and take on the 'universal' status of Hamlet's problem, itself no more confined to Elsinore than Othello's is to Venice and Cyprus, or Macbeth's to Scotland. Only in *King Lear* will the 'setting' of the play in England be of a greater order of importance and it would diminish that play to think of it as concerned simply with 'social problems'.

A further objection to Boas's view must be that these plays are in no sense 'self-contained' or conclusive as a group about the kind of problem with which they deal. They might perhaps more profitably be regarded as tentative movements towards the framing of the larger questions of *Othello* and *Macbeth* rather than as satisfactory statements of those in themselves. In this sense they constitute experiments in finding more adequate means of 'talking about' the issues which *Hamlet* considered. They look forward to the positivity of the later tragedies, and their style

[1] See Peter Ure, *Shakespeare: The Problem Plays* (London, 1961), pp. 7 ff. and Ernest Schanzer, *Shakespeare's Problem Plays* (London, 1963), *passim*.

gropes in that direction. In them Shakespeare learns to speak with his tragic voice. What that voice speaks of may be said to constitute one of the most fundamental of human 'problems', the conflict between two opposed views of the world, the rational and the non-rational, the conflict between appearance and reality.

G. Wilson Knight's essay on *Troilus and Cressida*[1] brilliantly argues exactly this. The play, he says, rests on a 'central idea' embodied by the two embattled armies, which express, each in its own way, a set of mutually opposed values. The values of the Greeks are essentially those of the reason (Knight's term is 'intellect'). Two voices characterize this army, those of Ulysses and Thersites, and in both can be heard the coldly cynical analysis of events which recalls the voice of Claudius in *Hamlet* and which will be recalled in those of Iago, Lady Macbeth, Goneril, Regan and Edmund. By contrast, the values of the Trojans are of an opposite kind. In Troy the voices speak of love, honour, romance, and their most obvious representative is Troilus. The play chronicles the defeat of Trojan values by those of the Greeks, in a way which prefigures the ultimate end of the Trojan War itself. And the 'pivot incident' which brings this about is therefore the handing over of Cressida to the Greeks. The 'symbolic suggestion' of such an event naturally becomes very powerful when the play is viewed in this light, for the inability of Trojan values to sustain themselves in the face of Greek opposition undergoes a withering scrutiny as a result, and these same values seem to be implicitly condemned for being vulnerable to the onslaught of their opposite.[2] Intuition of the kind which Troilus employs reveals its own inadequacy in a world which conspires against it, and he is mercilessly punished in a manner which looks forward to a later treatment of a similar idea in *Othello*.

The 'rational' voice reaches one of its heights in Ulysses's famous speech on 'order' (I, iii, 78 ff.). The tone of these words has so often been miscalculated that it is necessary to set them in context. The speech occurs as the Greeks argue amongst themselves about the progress of the battle, and Ulysses seems to

[1] G. Wilson Knight, *op. cit.*, p. 47.

[2] Cf. L. C. Knights's comment on G. Wilson Knight in *Some Shakespearean Themes* (London, 1959), p. 77.

intend it as an antidote to the somewhat absurd magniloquence of Agamemnon and his colleagues. Yet it is itself coloured with something of the same overstatement, and makes rather too much of a very simple point. In this it parodies, somewhat cynically, the ridiculous grandeur to which Agamemnon and his generals lay claim. It serves thus as an example of the 'policy' for which Ulysses was noted, the 'cunning' for which Homer admired him; the speech in fact exemplifies the kind of rational scheming which we have seen Claudius employ. After all, Ulysses' main point is capable of direct statement at first:

> The specialty of rule hath been neglected;
> (I, iii, 78)

and this simple (and, perhaps, as Shakespeare intended it to seem, questionable) premiss provides the peg on which the rest of the speech hangs. In it, Ulysses puts forward an idea of a rationally constructed social order, which postulates itself as one 'divinely' ordained and thus the necessary opposition to a non-rational, non-'ordered' individualism on the basis of which the Trojans operate. Cleverly, he tailors his expression to suit the mood of his colleagues; his words begin with a reasonable premiss, but, moments later, they become absurdly exaggerated:

> The heavens themselves, the planets, and this centre
> Observe degree, priority, and place,
> Insisture, course, proportion, season, form,
> Office, and custom, in all line of order;
> And therefore is the glorious planet Sol
> In noble eminence enthron'd and spher'd
> Amidst the other . . .
> (I, iii, 85–91)

The insistence on medieval principles such as 'priority' and 'place' is clearly over-emphasized, and we are surely not meant to take this in any other way, though Ulysses knows what he is doing, for his colleagues take it seriously enough (and so successful is his plan that it has convinced critics of Shakespeare to do so too). In other words, in this speech, Ulysses uses 'old' notions to effect a 'modern' purpose. The play provides no further evidence that he believes in what he says here; indeed subsequent events point the other way, for Ulysses seems quite prepared to upset the 'order' which he now recommends and to let Ajax fight

Hector instead of requiring Achilles to do so, which would fulfil the 'specialty of rule' he so eloquently urges. He uses these notions, then, as a political instrument in a highly rational game of politics. In fact, the subsequent conduct of the war on the Greek side shows that such 'degree' and 'order' as he advocates have little to do with it. The speech creates an 'appearance' of reality: it describes what perhaps ought to be the case, whereas actual events belie it. Ulysses' 'reasoning' in the matter therefore fits well with his behaviour in the rest of the play.

On the Trojan side, Troilus expresses an opposite view of the battle. Of course, we will hear rational arguments powerfully put in the Trojan camp but only in order that they may be knocked down by the force of Troilus' non-rational point of view; 'reasoning' in Troy serves as a foil to Troilus' 'intuition', and, significantly, his arguments carry the day. So, in the debate whether the Trojans should keep Helen or send her back, he argues a case completely opposed to the more rational one of Hector who is concerned to assess the price which Helen has cost in Trojan lives. Troilus, on the other hand, makes the point, later made by Cordelia at her most non-rational, that values like 'worth', 'honour' and 'love' cannot be 'priced' and made the subject of such calculation:

> Fie, fie, my brother!
> Weigh you the worth and honour of a king,
> So great as our dread father's, in a scale
> Of common ounces? Will you with counters sum
> The past-proportion of his infinite,
> And buckle in a waist most fathomless
> With spans and inches so diminutive
> As fears and reasons? Fie, for godly shame.
>
> (II, ii, 25–32)

Helenus' reply to this chides Troilus for his lack of reason:

> No marvel though you bite so sharp at reasons,
> You are so empty of them. Should not our father
> Bear the great sway of his affairs with reasons,
> Because your speech hath none that tells him so?
>
> (II, ii, 33–6)

Troilus, however, argues even more forcefully against the subjection of such values to rational analysis. He mocks Helenus,

'You fur your gloves with reason', and goes on to claim that reasoning of this type destroys 'manhood and honour', thus making a point that we have heard before, and will again, about the kind of 'manliness' that reason supposedly inculcates:

> ... Nay, if we talk of reason,
> Let's shut our gates and sleep. Manhood and honour
> Should have hare hearts, would they but fat their thoughts
> With this cramm'd reason. Reason and respect
> Make livers pale and lustihood deject.
>
> (II, ii, 46–50)

Troy accepts this anti-rational argument, and acts henceforth on this basis. Helen is retained, the war goes on. The discussion has centred on a problem which *Hamlet* dealt with, and with which *Othello* and *Lear* will be particularly concerned. Can 'love', or any spiritual quality, be 'measured'? Can its 'worth' or 'value' be rationally 'assessed'? Is Helen, as Hector now wearily puts it, 'worth what she doth cost / The keeping'? Troilus' arguments depend on the idea that love may not be 'reasoned' about and his rejection of the opposite notion might be a reply to Polonius' 'rational' assessment of the love of Hamlet and Ophelia. In this sense, Troilus argues Hamlet's case, in words that Othello might well have used, and with arguments that Cordelia will imply by her silence in another situation. As the proponent of such a view, he thereby takes on the role of an intuitive thinker, one to whom the arguments of reason in such matters are improper.

Nevertheless the play now proceeds to subject his views to a withering examination which reveals their ultimate impotence in a world hostile to them. As in the case of Othello, such high-sounding professions as Troilus makes are shown to be tragically vulnerable to a rational force committed to their destruction; that proves the measure of their inadequacy. Sadly, as Wilson Knight points out, Time, which belongs to the world of the flesh, and which can negate the values of the spirit if they are made subject to it, lies on the side of the Greeks. As Ulysses cynically comments:

> Time hath, my lord, a wallet at his back,
> Wherein he puts alms for oblivion,
> A great-siz'd monster of ingratitudes.

> Those scraps are good deeds past, which are devour'd
> As fast as they are made, forgot as soon
> As done. . . .
>
> (III, iii, 145–50)

And indeed, the 'good deeds' of Troilus and Cressida and, the play hints, of Paris and Helen, for the two couples are constantly related (III, i, 32 ff.) and of Troy itself, will be 'forgot as soon as done'. We know, and that irony casts its shadow over the whole play, what will happen to Troy in the end. The voice of Thersites expresses its fulness; he reduces the whole affair, not only of Troilus and Cressida, but of Troy and Greece, to the level of its worldly components, with a belittling and 'rational' analysis of the total situation:

> All the argument is a whore and a cuckold – a good quarrel to draw emulous factions and bleed to death upon.
>
> (II, iii, 68 ff.)

He refers to all the play's events, and his words apply equally to them all; on this level, the story is not one of heroic battles and great loves, but of 'war and lechery' as he says.

The end of the play shows the triumph of reason. Hector, who ought to have died heroically, is basely murdered. The 'old' honourable way of life of Troy is overwhelmed by a 'new' Greek 'honour'. The word itself has a 'modern' ring in Ulysses' speech which sees it as something of only relative value which can be rationally calculated; it involves merely the 'opinion' of others. He advises Achilles in this way: honour has no worth other than that which it possesses at the present point in time; time acts as the rational assessor of all these 'spiritual' matters:

> For beauty, wit,
> High birth, vigour of bone, desert in service,
> Love, friendship, charity, are subjects all
> To envious and calumniating Time.
> One touch of nature makes the whole world kin . . .
>
> (III, iii, 171–5)

In a sense, Time is the villain of this piece, and it performs the role which, say, Iago primarily has in *Othello*, of reducing spiritual values to a merely worldly status. It constitutes, by this, a 'rational' force, and Ulysses, as a Greek, regards it in this light.

The effect of Time, of 'reason' of this kind on Troilus' non-rational love for Cressida is therefore to destroy it, because of its vulnerability to such an attack. An almost predictable situation ensues. We have heard Troilus advance a non-rational argument in the debate over Helen, and we have heard Hector comment that his 'blood' is

> So madly hot that no discourse of reason,
> Nor fear of bad success in a bad cause,
> Can qualify the same.
>> (II, ii, 116–18)

In his relationship with Cressida, then, we should be quite prepared for his non-rational 'bad success' in what from the first seems to be a very 'bad cause' indeed. For, if Troilus' love for her takes no account of worldly values,

> I am giddy; expectation whirls me round.
> Th'imaginary relish is so sweet.
>> (III, ii, 17–18)

Cressida's love proves of a different order; worldly, fleshly, it has a rational aspect to it:

> *Troilus*   Fears make devils of cherubins; they never see truly.
> *Cressida* Blind fear, that seeing reason leads, finds safer footing
>   than blind reason stumbling without fear.
>> (III, ii, 66–9)

She finds 'seeing reason' of a 'downward looking' kind better than that non-rational 'blind reason' with which Troilus looks upwards. He may be

> ... as true as truth's simplicity
> And simpler than the infancy of truth;
>> (III, ii, 165–6)

but, even on first view, she reveals herself to be coquettish (I, ii, 187 ff.), interested in other men (I, ii, 240 ff.), not overly concerned with 'truth's simplicity', and even capable of duplicity in the matter (she finds her own statement made in badinage with Pandarus, 'To say the truth, true and not true' (I, ii, 93), perfectly acceptable).

Her falsity is not altogether surprising since, in addition, Shakespeare has made it quite clear through Pandarus that he regards her, and all the characters, as eponymous; 'all false women' are 'Cressids' (III, ii, 199) and her behaviour supports the view; she shows, as she unwittingly admits of herself, 'more craft than love' (III, ii, 149), whereas Troilus' 'vice' lies in the reverse of this, his 'simplicity':

> ... Alas, it is my vice, my fault!
> Whiles others fish with craft for great opinion
> I with great truth catch mere simplicity.
>
> (IV, iv, 101-3)

Such intuitive 'simplicity' and 'truth' in fact makes him unable to deal with Cressida's defection, for, confronted with her duplicity, he sees, not one 'great truth', but two literally opposed 'truths'.

These are presented to him in effect by the two aspects of his *ratio*. His *ratio inferior* sees one Cressida, his *ratio superior* another; his reason tells him one thing about her, his intuition another. Thus, in the scene (V, ii) in which he physically perceives Cressida's unfaithfulness, he expresses bewilderment that what he has seen with his eyes and understood, therefore, rationally, can be belied by what he believes in his 'heart', intuitively:

> But if I tell how these two did coact,
> Shall I not lie in publishing a truth?
> Sith yet there is a credence in my heart,
> An esperance so obstinately strong,
> That doth invert th'attest of eyes and ears.
>
> (V, ii, 116-20)

The situation must raise the question of the difference between appearance and reality. Which Cressida is the real one? Is the Cressida he has rationally observed just now really her? 'This she? No; this is Diomed's Cressida.' (V, ii, 135). He swears by the activities of the soul, which are intuitive not rational, that it was not. The concept of unity, the idea of 'truth's simplicity' will not permit it:

> If beauty have a soul, this is not she;
> If souls guide vows, if vows be sanctimonies,
> If sanctimony be the gods' delight,
> If there be rule in unity itself,
> This was not she.
>
> (V, ii, 136-40)

Nevertheless, reason cannot be so easily dismissed, and its discursive quality causes him to recognize that it tells its own kind of truth.[1] The rationally-perceived Cressida is also real:

>   ... O madness of discourse,
> That cause sets up with and against itself!
> Bifold authority! where reason can revolt
> Without perdition, and loss assume all reason
> Without revolt:
>
>   (V, ii, 140–4)

At this point, faced with the 'bifold authority' of two opposed modes of perception, Troilus expresses the essence of his tragic situation. He, like Hamlet before him, and like Othello after him, has been confronted with a choice, one between reason and intuition, appearance and reality, 'Cressida' and Cressida. He utters as a result the amazing conclusion that gives us the problem directly: 'this is, and is not, Cressid' (V, ii, 144), and we recall in this the irony of Cressida's former 'to say the truth, true and not true' (I, ii, 93). The tragedy lies in the fact that there are two Cressidas, that he is caught between them, and that he has become a chooser; his mind becomes a battleground like Troy itself: 'Within my soul there doth conduce a fight...' (V, ii, 145). The 'fight' quickly becomes subsumed into the larger struggle between Greece and Troy which Troilus now re-joins with tragic vigour (V, ii, 165 ff.). But the irony of Troy's fate lies over all, underlined by Thersites' cynically repeated version of it, 'Lechery, lechery! Still wars and lechery!' (V, ii, 194 ff.) and the problem remains unresolved to the end of the play which quickly follows. Significantly, Troy's end is the theme of the 'mad' prophecies of Cassandra, whose lack of reason is greater than that of her brothers. She sees, consequently, much more clearly. Troilus, foolishly, ignores what she says, preferring his version of 'honour' to her kind of truth (II, ii, 118 ff.). By clinging to his 'soul's' intuitive perception of Cressida, despite all evidence to the contrary, Troilus becomes, in terms of the greater battle, foolishly heroic. He will go under with Troy; the Greeks will triumph, as reason has done, over a world vulnerable to their

[1] Whilst Troilus can here affirm an intuitive faith that 'vows be sanctimonies' in support of his love, Iago later turns this table, and can 'reason away' Othello's love for Desdemona as 'sanctimony and a frail vow betwixt an erring barbarian and a super-subtle Venetian' (*Othello*, I, iii, 351).

attack. Troilus' 'simplicity' causes his downfall, for because of it he becomes unfitted to deal with the situation in which fate has placed him. He is destroyed because he is caught, unprepared, between two poles, two Cressidas, two opposed ways of looking at the world. His tragedy lies, not in the fact that one Cressida is 'better' than another, but that, in the modern world, there are two of them. The Greek world which has created the situation is thereby implicitly condemned. It has divided the mind, caused fragmentation of experience, created a 'bifold authority' in place of a 'rule in unity'.

Whilst Shakespeare may be said to prefer Trojan ideals to the cynical denial of these which characterizes the Greeks, he seems to recognize that if they are to survive they need to be much more firmly grounded than those represented by Troilus' 'intuitive' conception of Cressida. Both she and Helen (whose retention keeps the war going and so ensures the ultimate defeat of Troy) are worthless objects of such ideals, for they cause them to crumble and to be doubted. Just as Othello's love for Desdemona will show itself to be totally unprepared for and vulnerable to Iago's attack, so Troilus' love for Cressida, and the Trojans' 'love' for their ideals, collapse for lack of the right kind of support. Intuition, as *Othello* makes plain, is an aspect of *ratio*, and should properly have a *basis* in reason. Without that it becomes merely romantic. At the end of this play Troilus becomes a 'baseless' romantic who foolishly believes that Troy will revenge itself on the Greeks and himself on Diomed. We know in advance the verdict of history, that this cannot be so.

Troilus and Cressida is not as pessimistic a play as at first sight it might seem. A great deal of its apparent cynicism probably results from its intellectual 'brightness'. Written perhaps for an Inns of Court audience,[1] it has a sophisticated quality which may give the impression of flippancy in its treatment of fundamentally serious issues, but in many respects this impression is erroneous. Essentially, the play's thematic structure conditions its tone, for it gives us on one level a sophisticated view of a young man's lack of sophistication, and a sense of apparent cynicism possibly springs out of this.

In *All's Well That Ends Well*, the reverse is true. Bertram, the

[1] Cf. Peter Alexander, *Shakespeare's Life and Art* (London, 1939), pp. 193 ff.

protagonist, may himself be something of a sophisticate, but the view we are given of him is entirely unsophisticated, with the result that the play has an opposite tone, one which has more to do with the unsophisticated manner of the 'folk-tale' than with the intellectual analysis of metaphysical problems. W. W. Lawrence points out[1] that the plot combines two traditional elements, the 'healing of the King', and the 'fulfillment of apparently impossible tasks'. Even stated in abstraction, a certain pattern can be discerned, for in both cases what appears to be, on a 'rational' level, unchangeable or irrevocable changes in a way which is not, in the situation's terms, 'rational' at all. The King's physicians pronounce him incurable, yet he is cured by 'magical' means on a level higher than that of mere medicine; the tasks seem 'rationally' impossible to fulfil, yet they are fulfilled in another way. The total situation in which the impossible comes 'magically' about traditionally forms part of the 'folk-tale' of this kind, and it may be that the plot was selected from (probably) Painter's version of one of the stories from the *Decameron*, in his *Palace of Pleasure*,[2] for exactly this reason.

The 'sub-plot' of Parolles is apparently Shakespeare's own invention. Whereas in the 'main' plots the stories themselves contain a tacit opposition between reason and something higher, or more effective, the Parolles plot evinces a cognate opposition between the apparent and the real. Parolles is a creature of words as his name implies, and this receives comment three or four times in the play. A 'manifold linguist' (IV, iii, 220), not only does he use words to obscure reality, but he is also duped by them himself. He is led to believe that he has been captured by the enemy, by means of a *pastiche* of language whose use mocks his own (IV, i). In his relationships with Bertram and Helena in the main plot, he has therefore a role which suggests an early version of Iago's in respect of Othello and Desdemona. He trafficks in appearances, and persuades Bertram to believe in matters which are not really as he describes them. The fact that Shakespeare has added this story to the 'traditional' one which the main plot tells, indicates, perhaps, a larger design. Certainly,

[1] W. W. Lawrence, *Shakespeare's Problem Comedies* (New York, 1931), pp. 67 ff. See also G. K. Hunter, *Introduction* to the *Arden* edition of the play (London, 1959), pp. xxv ff.
[2] See Hunter, *op. cit.*, p. xxvi.

in so far as the two plots of *King Lear* serve a similar purpose it may be suggested that this play constitutes an early attempt at a complex thematic construction which the later play more perfectly achieves.

In many ways, then, the play looks forward to the great tragedies, and, poor play though it is, it must be interesting for that reason. Like Hamlet, and certainly Troilus, a choice between two ways of life based on opposed principles confronts Bertram. He has to choose between the values represented by Helena on the one hand and by Parolles on the other. At first he chooses in favour of the latter and the play chronicles his eventual rejection of that for the 'virtue' which Helena embodies. His initial rejection of her is meanwhile condemned as a rejection of real virtue for its appearance.

A 'heavenly' aura surrounds Helena from the first. She seems aware that whatever power she possesses comes not from herself but from a higher source:

> It is not so with Him that all things knows,
> As 'tis with us that square our guess by shows;
> But most it is presumption in us when
> The help of heaven we count the act of men,
> Dear sir, to my endeavours give consent;
> Of heaven, not me, make an experiment.
> (II, i, 148–53)

The King, to whom she addresses these words, accepts her view, and sees a 'blessed spirit' in her:

> Methinks in thee some blessed spirit doth speak
> His powerful sound within an organ weak;
> And what impossibility would slay
> In common sense, sense saves another way.
> (II, i, 174–7)

Her 'curing' of the King will be effected in 'another way' than that of the physician's science. She works by means higher than those of 'common sense', and, as a result, she is able, despite their rational 'impossibility', to restore, to redeem. As she says, having effected the cure, 'Heaven hath through me restor'd the King to health' (II, iii, 62).

The atmosphere of death and loss which is strong at the beginning of the play changes gradually to one of birth and marriage at the end; that which is 'lost' is regained. At the beginning, the moral laxity which the King's illness perhaps symbolizes permeates the Court, and seems specifically associated with an attitude to life which reveals itself as materialistic, rational, 'explaining' in mode. Miracles, Lafeu tells us, are past, because the new men, 'philosophical persons', have explained them away:

> They say miracles are past; and we have our philosophical persons to make modern and familiar, things supernatural and causeless. Hence is it that we make trifles of terrors, ensconcing ourselves into seeming knowledge when we should submit ourselves to an unknown fear. (II, iii, 1 ff.)

And yet, in the face of this 'seeming knowledge' which Lafeu sees as characteristic of the 'modern' age, the King is cured by 'supernatural' means.

G. K. Hunter notes that the young people of the Court are 'modern' in this way.[1] The older people (the King, the Countess) have an 'older' faith; although physically ill, like the King, they are spiritually healthy. On the level of the body they are sick, on that of the spirit they are not (though, it is implied, the young people are). Helena's magical cure carries associations with that 'older' world; it works by 'magic'. The 'new' world's representative, appropriately, is a dealer in mere words.

From the very first, Parolles is characterized as a rationalist. Talking with Helena about virginity, his views exhibit 'reasoning' in an extreme form; he speaks of the 'politic' uses of virginity and the 'rational' purposes which its loss serves:

> It is not politic in the commonwealth of nature to preserve virginity. Loss of virginity is rational increase.
> (I, i, 119 ff.)

Not surprisingly, when the King forces Bertram to marry Helena, Parolles urges him away from her, claiming typically as a 'reasoner' that true 'manliness' lies elsewhere, in the wars:

> To th'wars, my boy, to th'wars!
> He wears his honour in a box unseen
> That hugs his kicky-wicky here at home,
> Spending his manly marrow in her arms,

[1] *Op. cit.*, p. xxxvii ff.

> Which should sustain the bound and high curvet
> Of Mars's fiery steed.
>
> (II, iii, 271–6)

And later:

> A young man married is a man that's marr'd.
> Therefore away, and leave her bravely . . .
>
> (II, iii, 291–2)

Since, as the play ultimately shows, real 'manliness' lies for Bertram more properly in his marriage to Helena, Parolles' advice takes on the now familiar pattern of presenting an appearance in place of a reality. His words themselves provide the means by which this is achieved, and in this respect the play looks forward to *Macbeth*, where language undergoes a closer examination in connection with its ability to construct 'appearances'.

Parolles' role therefore embodies one of the main themes in the play. The long speech of the King to Bertram on 'honour' indicates something of its status, for in it he makes the point quite clearly that mere words like 'honour' can hide reality. Bertram has refused to accept Helena as his wife because of her poor breeding; she has no title, no family 'name'. The King argues that 'names', mere words, are worthless, are appearances; 'honour' is a name, 'virtue' is a reality:

> If she be
> All that is virtuous – save what thou dislik'st,
> A poor physician's daughter – thou dislik'st
> Of virtue for the name; but do not so.
> From lowest place when virtuous things proceed,
> The place is dignified by th' doer's deed;
> Where great additions swell's, and virtue none,
> It is a dropsied honour. Good alone
> Is good without a name. Vileness is so:
> The property by what it is should go,
> Not by the title. She is young, wise, fair;
> In these to nature she's immediate heir;
> And these breed honour. That is honour's scorn
> Which challenges itself as honour's born
> And is not like the sire. Honours thrive
> When rather from our acts we them derive

86

Than our fore-goers. The mere word's a slave
Debauch'd on every tomb, on every grave
A lying trophy . . .

(II, iii, 119–37)[1]

The spring of the play's action lies here. Bertram has to choose between Parolles (who deals in words, mere 'names' like 'honour') and Helena (who offers him real 'virtue'). His own promises at the moment are 'mere words', appearances, and he has to learn to deal with and to recognize the reality that they do not encompass. His 'deeds' should match his words. G. K. Hunter puts it: 'The superiority of virtue to honour as of realities to names is a point the play makes without qualification.'[1]

At the end of the play, Bertram's false 'honour' dissolves, and the reality of virtue is thrust upon him by the resourceful Helena. Notably, she has to involve herself in 'appearances' (the 'bed-trick') to effect this, in order to force Bertram to acquiesce in the reality of their baby; true 'manliness' lies there, in the creation of a child. Parolles, exposed for what he is, as 'Simply the thing I am' (IV, iii, 310) is cast aside. Bertram finally accepts what Helena's 'name' itself represents: love. He resolves thereafter to 'love her dearly, ever, ever dearly' (V, iii, 310). The 'impossible task' is overcome in this 'non-rational' way; intuition and reality in the name of 'virtue' have triumphed over reason and appearance in the name of 'honour', and the play 'ends well', thus triumphing over its own 'name', as a result.[2]

In so far as Bertram is a sophisticated young man quaintly made aware of the value of virtuous innocence in Helena, the play contains, as has been said, a 'folk-tale' element which is completely traditional. However, that Shakespeare chose the idea of 'mere words' to indicate Bertram's blind sophistication, and that of 'magical' curing to indicate Helena's innocence, suggests a larger dimension. It can be argued that both these characteristics might respectively be considered to represent the activities of reason and intuition. In this quite minor work,

---

[1] *Op. cit.*, p. xl.
[2] In a play in which 'names' are such an issue, the play's own 'name' is referred to as the proverbial saying which it is, more than once in the action (IV, iv, 35; V, i, 25). Perhaps Shakespeare is becoming more and more aware of the power which such drawing attention to the play as a play could have; *Macbeth*, as will be shown later, makes a great deal of this device.

Shakespeare clearly rehearsed a number of devices and concepts which later burgeoned in the tragic plays to form part of their grandeur. Helena's virtue with its 'heavenly' connotations, and its non-rational mode, becomes that of Desdemona, and Cordelia. Bertram's 'honour' already has a slight ring of Othello's 'occupation', though their roles are quite different. His refusal to recognize the reality of Helena's virtue suggests Lear's similar intransigence when confronted by Cordelia's honesty, as it does Gloucester's 'blindness' to the equal qualities of his son Edgar. Parolles' use of words to deceive perhaps makes him a forerunner of Iago, and even of the Witches in *Macbeth*. The entire play, although not a great and perhaps even a less than satisfactory dramatic construct, has a pattern of conflict within it which the tragedies will more fully explore. For the moment, the conflict is simply, perhaps tritely, and certainly 'proverbially' (as the play's title indicates), resolved. The 'problem' once stated (and the King's speech on 'honour' both states and 'solves' it) is never seen without the shadow of its solution hanging over it. The play remains one of Shakespeare's most artificial works in this sense, and a good deal of our feeling of dissatisfaction comes from that. However, in the last of these 'problem' plays, a similar problem undergoes a much fuller treatment, and the solution which emerges is neither simple nor trite, but deeply suggestive in many ways of the tragedies which will follow.

Measure for Measure is concerned to a great extent with the opposition of and the difference between Justice and Mercy.[1] Justice, that development of the ancient *lex talionis* which computes a punishment in accordance with the crime committed, is inflicted on Claudio at the beginning of the play.[2] The play implicitly argues thereafter against the exact computation involved, for to compute measure for measure, an eye for an eye, a tooth for a tooth, even 'an Angelo for Claudio, death for death' reveals itself as a formula inadequate to deal with the nature and complexities of the sins which abound in Vienna. Nevertheless,

[1] Harold Wilson's article 'Action and Symbol in *Measure for Measure* and *The Tempest*', *Shakespeare Quarterly*, Vol. 4, 1953, gives a good account of this.
[2] On the Elizabethan and Jacobean concept of the *lex talionis*, see F. T. Bowers, *Elizabethan Revenge Tragedy* (Princeton, 1940), pp. 15 ff.

such computing lays claim to the very thing which it lacks: it professes complete adequacy. Mercy, on the other hand, is said to be a divine quality which can only be obtained through God's grace. It is that god-like activity by whose means Man's limited vision of the true and the right must be modified. Justice should be tempered with mercy, and the play embodies this principle in its final scenes, when the Duke sits in 'judgement' on Angelo and the events which he has brought about; he dispenses mercy as well as justice.

Roy Battenhouse sees the play as an 'atonement drama' in which the Christian doctrine of Atonement for sin, the central 'mystery' of the Gospel, is acted out.[1] This view suggests, again, the notion of Justice as merely an earthly human activity, which requires divine Mercy as its complement. Angelo, who practises mere Justice, becomes (in accordance with the tradition of the 'atonement' play) devilish, until he and indeed the whole of Vienna is redeemed by the God-like Duke.[2]

Justice, then, is created and imposed by Man. Mercy exists as a divine quality complementary to it. Justice without mercy is blind and evil, as Man is without God, and as the body is without the soul. In a real sense, Justice may be thought of as a product of Man's reason, and so earthly and fleshly in its mode (its 'computing' nature supports this view; the *lex talionis* constitutes a practical application of a rational principle). Mercy on the other hand, and by the same token, is not at all rational, for it overrides the computation of punishment for crime, and rejects the rational 'equalities' of measure for measure. Mercy is apprehended on a higher level than that of the reason. It cannot be codified like Justice, nor is it subject to earthly and fleshly considerations. It comes, as Portia in *The Merchant of Venice* tells us, from the highest spiritual source:

> It droppeth as the gentle rain from heaven . . .
> (*Merchant of Venice*, IV, i, 180)

And it is

[1] Roy W. Battenhouse, '*Measure for Measure* and the Christian doctrine of the Atonement', *P.M.L.A.*, Vol. 61, 1946, pp. 1029 ff.

[2] G. Wilson Knight, *op. cit.*, pp. 73–96, has a similar view of the Duke's function.

> ... an attribute to God himself;
> And earthly power doth then show likest God's
> When mercy seasons justice.
>
> (Ibid. IV, i, 190–2)

Angelo, the chief dispenser of Justice in this play, is nothing if not rational and fleshly in his pursuit of it. He

> ... doth rebate and blunt his natural edge
> With profits of the mind, study and fast.

And, as Lucio goes on to tell us, he

> ... follows close the rigour of the statute
> To make him an example.
>
> (I, iv, 60–8)

Both the Duke and Claudio refer to him as 'precise' (I, iii, 50 and III, i, 95) in his thinking and his actions, and when he gives his 'arguments' in favour of executing Claudio,

> It is the law, not I condemn your brother.
> Were he my kinsman, brother, or my son,
> It should be thus with him.
>
> (II, ii, 80–2)

they are conclusive, unassailable, and they strike a 'rational' chord in us. Angelo's voice here comes close enough to our own to be uncomfortable. He argues, we must unwillingly admit, as most of us would in this case. His tone is 'modern' in a disturbing way. But, like the other 'reasoners' of these plays, he deals in appearances, not reality. He is one of the 'seemers' whom the Duke wishes to expose (I, iii, 54) and as such, he is frequently referred to as a devil. His 'pernicious purpose', Isabella tells us, is 'Seeming, seeming' (II, iv, 150). His version of 'mercy', she says, is 'devilish' (III, i, 66) (it appears to be merciful, in reality it is not), and she denounces him as

> ... yet a devil;
> His filth within being cast, he would appear
> A pond as deep as hell.
>
> (III, i, 93–5)

When, later, the Duke pretends to believe in Angelo, and asks Isabella to give an account to him of how she has been wronged, she objects that 'You bid me seek redemption of the devil!' (V, i, 29). Angelo (whose name suggests the opposite of his true character, he is 'outward-sainted' [III, i, 90] a devil not an angel) 'seems', like the devil, to be what he is not, and he uses 'precise' reasoning to this end. As Isabella puts it, he hides his devilishness under the very rational precision which embodies it, and by whose means he computes justice:

> O, 'tis the cunning livery of hell
> The damned'st body to invest and cover
> In precise guards!
>
> (III, i, 96–8)

We are not surprised, then, when Angelo shows himself capable of extending his rational 'computation' into an area not proper to it, that of love. A true 'reasoner', like Polonius, and later Iago and Goneril and Regan, he sets a price on love, and calculates its 'worth'. Hence, his 'computative' justice takes the turn of computing a price, Isabella's virtue, for the release of her condemned brother. As he speaks, we almost hear the voice of Claudius:[1]

> I, now the voice of the recorded law,
> Pronounce a sentence on your brother's life;
> Might there not be a charity in sin
> To save this brother's life?
>
> (II, iv, 61–4)

Isabella's reply, however, strikes a note surprisingly similar to this. Indeed, mistaking Angelo's purpose, she more than agrees with him:

> ... Please you to do 't,
> I'll take it as a peril to my soul
> It is no sin at all, but charity.
>
> (II, iv, 64–6)

Although, as Angelo says, 'Your sense pursues not mine' (II, iv, 74) and she has not grasped the full import of his proposal, she is plainly prepared to consider the matter as 'rationally' in her own way as he. And although she later totally rejects his suggestion, she does so by arguments as 'reasoned' as those of the pro-

[1] Notably, like Claudius, Angelo is also unable to pray for absolution from his sin (II, iv, 1 ff.).

position itself. For a different purpose, and from a different point of departure, Isabella nevertheless 'computes' values in exactly Angelo's manner. A wholly rational mode of thinking prompts such of her replies as those which assess the 'price' of moral actions:

> *Angelo* Then must your brother die.
> *Isabella* And 'twere the *cheaper* way:
> Better it were a brother died at once
> Than that a sister, by redeeming him,
> Should die for ever.
>
> (II, iv, 104–8)

Such reasoning must lead to exactly the same end as that of Angelo: her brother's death. In both cases it is informed by a particularly rigorous moral code, and G. Wilson Knight's judgement that Isabella 'stands for sainted purity'[1] should be regarded in this light. In fact her 'purity' is that of the most extreme kind of puritanism, which Shakespeare surely finds offensive, both here and elsewhere.

The play focuses a good deal of its attention on Isabella's puritanical lack of mercy, and points out that she has almost as much to learn from the Duke as Angelo has in the matter. Before we see her we learn that she thinks, as Angelo does, in a similarly 'precise' way. Claudio says of her that

> . . . she hath prosperous art
> When she will play with reason and discourse,
> And well she can persuade.
>
> (I, ii, 177–9)

In fact we first encounter her when she is about to enter a nunnery, and she tells us then that she was hoping for 'a more strict restraint/Upon the sisterhood' (I, iv, 4–5) than that which she finds. Lucio's extravagant compliment at this point,

> I hold you as a thing enskied and sainted,
> By your renouncement an immortal spirit,
> And to be talk'd with in sincerity,
> As with a saint.
>
> (I, iv, 34–7)

---

[1] *Op. cit.*, p. 74.

remains, despite his protestations to the contrary, as 'mocking' as Isabella finds it (I, iv, 38). It mocks her partly by means of its extravagance, since Lucio hints, perhaps, at Isabella's object in entering the nunnery. All the 'precise' piety which Angelo exhibits manifests itself in her, so that when she comes before him to plead for her brother's life, against what she surprisingly admits to be a 'just but severe law' (II, ii, 41), we can feel the need for the Provost's prayer that Heaven will give her the 'moving graces' (II, ii, 36) which she lacks, and we may agree with Lucio's repeated injunction, 'You are too cold' (II, ii, 45 and 56).[1]

Angelo himself suggests that her rejection of his proposal is 'cold' and 'precise' in this way:

> Were not you, then, as cruel as the sentence
> That you have slander'd so?
> (II, iv, 109–10)

– and we are forced, willy-nilly, to agree with him. The rest of their argument in this scene has the same tone. Reason pits itself against reason, and Isabella's admission that

> I something do excuse the thing I hate
> For his advantage that I dearly love.
> (II, iv, 119–20)

---

[1] Much is made by sympathetic critics of Isabella's subsequent plea for mercy in this scene:

> Why, all the souls that were were forfeit once;
> And He that might the vantage best have took
> Found out the remedy. How would you be,
> If He, which is the top of judgment, should
> But judge you as you are? O, think on that;
> And mercy then will breathe within your lips,
> Like man new made.
> (II, ii, 73–9)

It should be pointed out that, in context, this speech is entirely subsequent to what Lucio says: it is delivered in response to his urgings that Isabella's first approach is too 'cold'. In a real sense, it is 'tailored' to the occasion, and a good deal of 'reasoning' therefore lies behind these words. As an instance of Isabella's imperfection, they are perfect; she only says the 'right' things when required to do so by the fact that what she really wants to say is not effective. Her later treatment of Claudio seems hardly merciful, and she condemns herself here as much as Angelo.

does not endear her to us, for it smacks very much of Angelo's own practice (he is prepared himself to commit the sin for which he has sentenced Claudio). After all, Isabella has previously told us that Claudio's offence is

> ...a vice that most I do abhor,
> And most desire should meet the blow of Justice.
>
> (II, ii, 29–30)

and she has come to her brother's defence very unwillingly.

It soon becomes quite clear that neither Isabella nor Angelo can win the argument, for they are swapping equal terms of 'Justice', computing equations about the 'worth' of her virtue. This is a world of rational assessment in which prices are fixed for moral commodities, and the discussion takes on an air of 'bargaining' as if it were taking place in a market:

> *Angelo*   ...Your brother is to die.
> *Isabella* So.
> *Angelo*   And his offence is so, as it appears,
>   Accountant to the law upon that pain.
> *Isabella* True.
>
> (II, iv, 83–6)

The result is the kind of stalemate reached in a world which thinks only in terms of what is 'accountant' and susceptible to rational calculation. Angelo contents himself with simply claiming that he is right:

> Say what you can: my false o'erweighs your true.
>
> (II, iv, 170)

'Falsity' and 'truth' are by now merely relative terms in the argument. Isabella's final statement of the computed 'value' of her virtue,

> Then, Isabel, live chaste, and, brother, die:
> More than our brother is our chastity.
>
> (II, iv, 184–5)

is so tritely expressed, so puritanical in its sentiments and so dubious in its morality, that her visit to her brother, to 'fit his mind to death' seems to be undertaken in a spirit not too far removed from that which has passed the sentence itself.

Happily, her visit is preceded by that of the Duke, who offers Claudio an attitude to death which, whilst equally rigorous, is much more acceptable. His long speech, 'Be absolute for death . . .' (III, i, 5 ff.) expresses an orthodox Christian view of contempt for the world, and its reasoning is of a higher order than that which calculates the value of one thing as opposed to another. Rather, the Duke's reasoning has to do with 'absolute' terms which will ensure that

> . . . either death or life
> Shall thereby be the sweeter.
> (III, i, 5–6)

This kind of 'reasoning' defeats the computative sort in which Angelo and Isabella have been seen to involve themselves, and Claudio is well advised by the Duke to

> . . . Reason thus with life;
> If I do lose thee, I do lose a thing
> That none but fools would keep.
> (III, i, 6–8)

Such 'reasoning' takes proper account of death, and welcomes it, paradoxically, on a level of intuitive acceptance. It exhibits the ideal blending of *ratio superior* and *ratio inferior*, and its acceptance leads Claudio to an understanding of the fundamentally non-rational Christian paradox of life-in-death:

> To sue to live, I find I seek to die;
> And, seeking death, find life. Let it come on.
> (III, i, 42–3)

Nevertheless, when Isabella presents her case to him, it shakes Claudio's resolve. He begs her to let Angelo have his way, in order to save his life, and she falls to cursing him violently (III, i, 137 ff.) and finally dismisses him in terms which show openly that she lacks herself the mercy for which she has pleaded:

> Thy sin's not accidental, but a trade.
> Mercy to thee would prove itself a bawd;
> 'Tis best that thou diest quickly.
> (III, i, 150–2)

She speaks here almost with the voice of Angelo.

The Duke's task now lies in the inculcation of mercy in Isabella as well as the dispensation of it to Angelo. Both have been tested and found in need of instruction in the matter, and this becomes the burden of the play from now on, for Claudio's execution will, we know, never take place. The Duke, God-like, has knowledge of all that has happened and controls all that will happen; his purpose is to bring Isabella from the appearance of Justice to the reality of Mercy.

As in the case of *All's Well That Ends Well*, appearances themselves are used to bring about this change by means of a 'bed-trick'. And just as appearance will be used to fight appearance and to disclose reality, just as reason will be fought by reason (the Duke has earlier decided that

> By cold gradation and well-balanc'd form,
> We shall proceed with Angelo.
>
> (IV, iii, 96–7)

– so a 'computed' form of Justice will be used to bring about Mercy. Angelo's deception has been calculated to make him commit the same crime as that for which he has condemned Claudio. We learn that, on those grounds, he may be considered to be Mariana's 'husband on a pre-contract' so that

> To bring you thus together 'tis no sin,
> Sith that the justice of your title to him
> Doth flourish the deceit. . . .
>
> (IV, i, 70–3)

In other words, since Claudio's relationship with Juliet was exactly the same as that, the present situation is one in which measure will be set against measure, where, in the Duke's words, 'Craft against vice I must apply' (III, ii, 259).

As a result a change comes about in Isabella. She begins, as has been said, as a 'rational' person whose reasoning in its own way exhibits limitations as strict as those of Angelo himself. However, when the Duke appears in his true form on the stage, when reality emerges, Isabella renounces this same reasoning in pleading her case to him. She accuses Angelo in the Duke's presence, which causes her to be called 'mad'. But the Duke accepts such 'irrationality' as having access to the truth:

> Her madness hath the oddest frame of sense,
> Such a dependency of thing on thing,
> As e'er I heard in madness.
>
> (V, i, 61–3)

It is the sort of 'madness' which Hamlet acquired, the sort which is not so much 'mad' as beyond the limits of the reason. And, indeed, Isabella makes a similar point to the Duke, urging him to use his reason properly, to make it a means of getting at the truth, not of hiding it. She advocates thereby 'reasoning' of a different order to that which we have seen her use herself. She pleads for Mercy, the 'irrational' counterpart of Justice:

> Isabella   O gracious Duke,
>   Harp not on that; nor do not banish reason
>   For inequality; but let your reason serve
>   To make the truth appear where it seems hid,
>   And hide the false seems true.
> Duke   Many that are not mad
>   Have, sure, more lack of reason.
>
>   (V, i, 63–8)

Isabella has thus become 'mad' by rational standards, but in the way in which Lear will later be seen to have achieved 'reason in madness'. She asks that 'reason' be not rejected for its 'in-equality', that is because it does not 'compute' the equalities of the *lex talionis* in the 'equal' balancing of an eye for an eye, measure for measure. A reason which does not do this may, perhaps, by the standards of Angelo (and earlier Isabella herself) be not rational at all. But behind Isabella's words there lies a higher kind of reasoning, one which reveals reality. Such intuitive reasoning has the qualities which 'many that are not mad' lack.

We should not be surprised therefore when, later, Isabella pleads 'against all sense' (V, i, 431) for mercy for Angelo. She does not know that Claudio is still alive, and this situation has been created by the Duke in order that her plea would have to be made against all the dictates of the reason, which would normally demand rational Justice in the case.[1] Nevertheless, she pleads for Angelo's life against reason, against Justice, against the Duke's feigned verdict of 'An Angelo for Claudio, death for death.'

---

[1] The original story has been changed by Shakespeare in order to allow this point to be made. In the Cinthio-Whetstone plot, the King does not know that Claudio is still alive. The fact that the Duke does know this makes the situation a deliberate creation of his own, whose purpose is to place Isabella in circumstances in which her plea for mercy will be totally 'non-rational'.

(V, i, 407). The fact that she does so signals that her 'education' has been completed. The reasoning with which she bargained with Angelo for her virtue has been replaced by a higher kind which becomes in these circumstances as divinely irrational as the Mercy for which she pleads. It has the standing, we remember in Portia's words, of 'an attribute to God himself.' Isabella, who began the play on the threshold of a convent, about to retreat from the world, ends it (it is implied) on the threshold of marriage with the Duke, about to embrace the responsibilities to the 'world' of Vienna which that requires. Her 'marriage' to the Church, which, as we saw, was to be a coldly restricted affair, is replaced by marriage to the Duke who, God-like, seems to have a status higher than that of the Church at least in matters of matrimony. Justice, the cold product of the reason, has been replaced (or at least augmented) by Mercy from a higher source.

Viewed in this way, *Measure for Measure* falls into a pattern similar to that of the other 'problem plays'. The three protagonists, Troilus, Bertram, and Isabella, each face a dichotomy between the values and way of life involved in the use of reason and those involved in the use of the intuition. Their fates are different, but their situations are alike. Troilus, clinging immoderately to an intuitive vision of Cressida, goes, foolishly and romantically, to his inevitable doom. Bertram learns that what Helena offers him is valuable and necessary when compared to the barrenness of Parolles' way of life. He chooses her, 'deeds', rather than him, 'words', intuition and reality rather than reason and appearance. Isabella learns, in a harsher way perhaps, that Mercy is divinely 'irrational' but a necessary complement to a too-rational Justice.

Both Bertram and Isabella are 'educated' (as Lear and Gloucester will be) from one way of thinking to another, and their plays end 'well' as a result. Poor Troilus, who, it might be argued, ought never to have suffered since he begins on the 'right' side, has another message for us. It is simply that, as Isabella discovers as well as Bertram, reason and intuition are complementary and ought properly to constitute a unity. Too much of one leads as far from reality as too much of the other. The dichotomy has no 'right' side. Essentially, the fact that a choice exists seems to be the tragic element in these, and certainly in the later plays. The choice of one side or the other does not seem to make much difference; either side is vulnerable without the other's support. Those characters who escape tragedy (they are Bertram and Isabella here) are those who manage to combine both sides of the dichotomy, and who thereby avoid making the choice (although, like Bertram, they perhaps make wrong choices initially). As has been said, the problem seems to be not so much that of choosing as of avoiding the role of chooser.

It would be foolish to claim that the 'problem plays' are wholly satisfactory as dramatic works. They are full of weaknesses of design and they communicate only imperfectly with us. This account of what they 'say' is of course affected by that situation and reflects at least that imperfection. Nevertheless, a pattern can be discerned, if faintly at times. *Hamlet*, with all its imperfections, probably belongs more with these plays than with the great tragedies which follow. If this view is taken, it means that it may legitimately be argued that these four plays, *Hamlet*, *Troilus and Cressida*, *All's Well That Ends Well*, and *Measure for Measure*, are imperfect movements towards the kind of statement which the later plays bring to perfection. As G. Wilson Knight puts it, in them 'we find the profound thought of the supreme tragedies already emergent.'[1] I think that this is so, and that the relatively simple structures of *Othello*, *Macbeth*, and *King Lear* have been bought at that price. It is as if, when *Measure for Measure* was finished, Shakespeare began to see more clearly what he wanted to do. His next work has, as might be expected, a design and a structure which is absolutely simple and clear, a stark quality reminiscent of the Morality play.

[1] *Op. cit.*, p. 84.

H

4

'OTHELLO'

'For the mind of man is far from the nature of a clear and equal glass, wherein the beams of things should reflect according to their true incidence; nay, it is rather like an enchanted glass, full of superstition and imposture, if it be not delivered and reduced.'

(Bacon, *Advancement of Learning* II, xiv, 9)

COLERIDGE REGARDED *Othello* as representing the union of the poetry of *Lear* and the meditation of *Hamlet*; in it, he said, 'every thing assumes its due place and proportion, and the whole mature powers of his [Shakespeare's] mind are displayed in admirable equilibrium.' Certainly there would be a kind of blindness in suggesting that *Macbeth*, in the state in which it has come down to us, is comparable to *Othello*, scene for scene, in the felicity of its dramatic construction; and while both *Lear* and *Hamlet* may claim to be more powerful plays in terms of theatrical impact, the former's implacable grandeur and the latter's questing nervousness are perhaps only so perfectly achieved at the cost of the 'due place and proportion' and the 'admirable equilibrium' of the undoubtedly lesser, but certainly no less impressive *Othello*. Indeed perhaps the very 'neatness' of this play, its essential simplicity of dramatic design, has caused it to fare less well with the critics than the others, at least in the matter of how much attention is paid to it. For all Coleridge's praise of the play, his remarks on it are generally less pithy than his comments on the other tragedies, and he tends to dismiss it by admiration; inevitably, it must be supposed, simplicity will defeat criticism.

Of course, a simple design may or may not contain a simple issue; but if the issue, as it is in *Othello*, is shaped by the play's structure into the form of a struggle to the death between Good and Evil, then such matters are clearly not so much 'simple' as fundamental. It is this kind of structural simplicity, which forces the events of a play into a discernible significance, that Coleridge had in mind when he said that 'Schiller . . . sets you a whole town on fire and throws infants with their mothers into the flames . . . But Shakespeare drops a handkerchief, and the same or greater effects follow.' It is those 'greater effects' which engage our interest.

The events of the plot are taxed from the very beginning with the weight of something ulterior. Cinthio's tale has suffered a sea-change which has transformed it from a mere account of passions ill-founded and led astray to an incisive dramatic probing of the simple values of human existence. And they are quite simple. Iago represents simple Evil (the simplicity is underlined in that the sea-change has left him 'motiveless' or virtually so), Desdemona simple Good (a condition which has so defeated critics that they have charged her with naïveté), and Othello, quite simply, is forced to choose between the two. Such an uncompromising structure must be the basis of any analysis of the play, and it ensures that the play's action concerns itself primarily with Othello's choice.

The fact that such a choice faces him comes about largely as a result of what Iago says and does in the play. The choice itself is manufactured and offered to Othello by Iago; the decision in the matter reached by Othello and the action he takes (including his last) are therefore conditioned and controlled by Iago. Desdemona throughout is a passive entity; she is *there*, but no action comes from her, all action is done to her (with the climax of the tragic action of the murder). Because the play is fundamentally concerned with an attack by Evil on Good, it invites a precise investigation of the nature of Iago's Evil, its background, its basis, how it works and to what end. And we could surely not as a result do less than examine the process by which this, as Coleridge calls him, 'being next to devil, only *not* quite devil,' sparks the tragedy, dupes Othello, causes Desdemona's murder, and provides the means to those 'greater effects' which rear themselves on the story. The process is a rational one.

In these terms it may be contended that *Othello* contains an examination of certain aspects of the 'lower' sort of reasoning, and of the effect such reasoning has on a world which lies beyond its province, and yet cannot defend itself. It is the story of the corruption of one way of life based on one sort of reasoning, by another, based on a 'lower' sort. The gradual poisoning of the intuitive world of Desdemona by the rational world of Iago constitutes the main theme of the play. Othello's tragedy lies in the nature of his choice between these two; it becomes thereby a tragedy whose terms and location are those of the human mind.

Iago's conclusion that

> The Moor is of a free and open nature
> That thinks men honest that but seem to be so.
>
> (I, iii, 393–4)

provides a clue to both Othello and himself. The play tells a story, on one level, in which a simple substitution of appearance for reality takes place. But although this dimension is discernible, it in no way dominates but serves, rather, a subsidiary purpose complementary to that larger design outlined above.

Nevertheless, it is necessary to isolate this level from the play temporarily, in order to see how it exemplifies the conflict of reason and intuition in other terms. For example, the plot requires that the major characters of Iago and Othello should be recognizable in their respective roles of deceiver and deceived at the same time as they take part in a greater struggle which involves the nature of the love between Desdemona and Othello. As a result, Iago's use of reason to destroy that love may be simultaneously seen as the substitution of an 'appearance' of it in place of its reality.

The situation exists potentially in the play from its beginning and on the simplest visual level; people's looks belie their reality. However attractive Othello may be to Desdemona, his physical appearance clearly exhibits the reverse of this. He is black (the devil's colour), ugly (by Elizabethan standards), and bizarre to the eyes of a somewhat enclosed society (Roderigo calls him an 'extravagant and wheeling stranger'). At least, Iago and the others paint this 'appearance' of Othello before we meet him; the 'reality' is quite different. On the other hand, Iago, who is devilish in reality,[1] a villain who should be quite socially unacceptable, moves with ease in polite society, (he is adept at social badinage with Desdemona and her attendants on arrival

---

[1] The point is conclusively made at the end of the play when Othello suggests that Iago has cloven feet (V, ii, 289).

at Cyprus (II, i, 82 ff.) and he has an 'appearance' which is handsome and attractive; Cinthio's *novella* describes him as extremely good-looking. The irony is perfect, and it begins the play's pattern of 'deceitful appearance' on all its levels. The one person whose looks in fact indicate her reality, Desdemona, is made to appear deceitful in just this respect.

In this way Othello's frequent use of the term 'honest' of Iago not only indicates his own lack of perception but also shows the extent of Iago's ability as a 'deceiver'. The play makes the point explicitly and affords Iago ample opportunity to boast of his prowess in that field. He prides himself on being one of those who

> ... throwing but shows of service on their lords,
> Do well thrive by 'em ...
>
> (I, i, 52–3)

and who works by means of 'seeming';

> ... not I for love and duty,
> But seeming so for my peculiar end.
>
> (I, i, 60–61)

Significantly, he swears 'By Janus' (I, ii, 33), the god with two faces, and his version of what has happened between Othello and Desdemona as the play opens is literally 'two-faced'; it 'seems' to be the truth. Indeed, when it is later put forward by the deluded Brabantio, the Duke roundly denounces that point of view as

> ... these thin habits and poor likelihoods
> Of modern seeming ...
>
> (I, iii, 108–9)

Iago, then, constitutes the source of all the 'seeming' in the play, and in that capacity supplements and parallels his activities as a 'reasoner'. From the very first his two roles are cognate. In the Duke's words, they are both 'modern', and so commonplace.

Othello's trust in Iago, and his belief in his 'honesty', must therefore assume proportions far beyond those of a simple 'mistake' about a man's character. His belief opens the way to momentous attacks on his love, and the irony of the many statements such as

> A man he is of honesty and trust:
> To his conveyance I assign my wife.
>
> (I, iii, 284–5)

is enormous, not because Iago is not honest and trustworthy, but because it is Desdemona, Othello's 'pearl', who has been 'assigned' to him. For, if Iago acts as the agent of 'appearance' in this play, Desdemona has within her the very essence of that 'reality' which he proposes to destroy. The play reaches one of its climactic points in this respect as soon as Othello thanks Iago for the 'information' he has laid against Desdemona with the words 'I am bound to thee for ever' (III, iii, 217). Because Othello is by this time inextricably and permanently involved with Iago's world of appearance, they are literally true.

The steps which lead up to this point may be traced as the story unfolds. Iago makes Cassio his first target, because through him Desdemona may be approached. Accordingly, he manufactures a situation in which Cassio's 'reality' is destroyed and he 'appears' to be other than he is. Of course, Iago finds Cassio worthless nonetheless, for he has no faith in any kind of 'real' virtue. To him, Cassio has the quality of a mere pretender, like himself:

> ... A knave very voluble; no further conscionable than in putting on the mere form of civil and humane seeming ...
> (II, i, 232 f.)

and once the trap has been set, he hastens to spring it. As he moves gradually closer to Desdemona, Iago makes it clear that he regards all women in the same light; like Cassio they become versions of his own deceit. His contempt for them indicates the shallowness of the kind of 'manliness' which he thereby claims for himself, for from this point of view they are mere creatures of constant change, who imperfectly hide their reality under an appearance; more, they are animals or deceitful 'pictures' who do this, not human beings:

> Come on, come on; you are pictures out a-doors, bells in your parlours, wildcats in your kitchens ...
> (II, i, 109 ff.)

The end of such thinking later reveals itself as that of convincing Othello that Desdemona shares these characteristics with all women. If they are deceivers, she too may be deceitful, and he will argue the 'rational' necessity of this:

She did deceive her father, marrying you;
And when she seem'd to shake and fear your looks,
She loved them most. . . .

(III, iii, 210–12)

The premisses of such arguments are sound enough: as Othello says, 'And so she did' (III, iii, 212). But Iago uses sound premisses to reach conclusions which are unsound. As a result, an 'appearance' of the truth comes to be substituted for its 'reality'. Having once practised deceit, Desdemona may 'apparently' do so again. However, Iago makes the merely apparent seem 'really' inevitable. Of course her original deceit was only a means to the end of reality, her love for Othello; having achieved that, she would be unlikely to relinquish it. Nevertheless, by this time Othello has been effectively deceived himself. Thereafter, Iago quickly frustrates any attempt on Othello's part to break through the framework of appearances which he has constructed. Thus, when Othello demands 'proof', Iago can easily provide it, as long as he maintains control over what it 'proves'. Having constructed his own 'reality', he describes the real proof which would destroy it in terms so gross that Othello shrinks from any suggestion that it might be brought into evidence:

. . . how satisfied, my lord?
Would you, the supervisor, grossly gape on –
Behold her topp'd?

(III, iii, 398–400)

He makes use here of the same crudity which, earlier, had urged Brabantio to examine the facts; Othello, in a similar situation, feels impelled to shun them. If 'reality' is such, 'appearance' is more inviting.

In the event, Othello allows Iago to 'prove' his case in his own way, and thereby tacitly allows him to manufacture his own world of cause and effect, and to lead Othello into it. Thus Othello sees and hears only as much as Iago wants of the dialogue with Cassio in Act IV. Where before, image, epithet and innuendo created the appearance, now Iago presents it literally on the stage as a little 'play' within the real play. Where a similar device in *Hamlet* led to reality, here the reverse is true, and appearances are accepted as real. Othello feels thereby convinced that the case against Desdemona is 'proved'.

As a result she ceases, in his mind, to be his wife, and becomes the opposite of a wife, a whore; such a change is fitting for it makes her fulfil an appropriate function in the spuriously 'manly' world in which Othello now moves. Their love, something very real at the beginning of the play, changes into an 'appearance' of itself, prostitution; their bedroom becomes a brothel, and Desdemona assumes the role that Iago had intended for her:

> ... that cunning whore of Venice
> That married with Othello ...
> (IV, ii, 90–1)

Finally, as the play ends, Othello vainly tries to grope his way back to his former reality, that of the noble warrior, by reiterating his old triumphs to himself and his accusers:

> And say besides that in Aleppo once,
> Where a malignant and a turban'd Turk
> Beat a Venetian and traduc'd the state,
> I took by th' throat the circumcised dog
> And smote him – thus.
> (V, ii, 355–9)

Significantly the 'dog' he stabs to death is himself; no longer a real man, he has become a beast, and the only reality left for him now is that of death.[1]

The simplicity of the structure of *Othello*, its deliberate categorization of Evil pitted against Good must require us, then, in an analysis of the nature and mode of that evil to bear such considerations in mind. The very character of Iago, his apparently 'motiveless' course of destruction, and more especially, the precise methods by which he achieves it, must surely lead to the conviction that he is involved to the hilt in the 'devilish' manipulation of appearances to deceive. Using as he does the precise methods of analysis and rational 'explanation' of the *ratio inferior*, he is, like Claudius in *Hamlet*, who 'explains' murder, like Edmund in *Lear*, who 'explains' nature, and like Macbeth, who involves himself in a whole world of devilish 'explanation' and prediction, a disguiser of reality, a destroyer of harmony, a

---

[1] Cf. John Holloway's persuasive argument, *The Story of the Night* (London, 1961), p. 56, that Othello here is re-enacting his own crimes; he has himself 'Beat a Venetian (Desdemona) and traduc'd the state'.

bringer of chaos, a force of evil whose entry into the world is through Man's mind. The type of sin in which this evil results may be characterized, in Elizabethan terms, as Adam's sin, the pursuit of the knowledge which destroys; and Othello, who is seduced by Iago 'according to the rudiments of the world,' commits this sin, and perhaps suffers Adam's fate as a result.

Iago's role as 'reasoner' is easily demonstrated. From the first, he attempts a rational 'explanation' of the phenomenon of Desdemona's love for Othello. In his account of the affair to Brabantio, he presents his version of what has happened as an actuality, based on empirically observable fact. The obscenity is actually happening now:

> Even now, now, very now, an old black ram
> Is tupping your white ewe.
> (I, i, 89–90)

He convinces Brabantio by the reasonableness of such arguments. But the plain fact is that Iago's arguments are not *really* true, they do not fully account for what has happened. This has been no rape, no abduction, no clandestine affair wrought by 'foul charms', but an affair of the heart of an order above and beyond the 'explanation' that Iago gives it. Desdemona's world is incapable of 'explanation' by these rational means; indeed, it is left to Othello to tell us quite simply what has happened (I, iii, 78–81), and his 'round unvarnish'd tale' reveals a love based, not on the 'lower' reason, but on something beyond it. There is nothing 'rational' in this sense about Desdemona's love for Othello; in fact it seems irrational and illogical almost, so much is it higher than the 'lower' level on which Iago treats it. She loves Othello, not in a way that can be 'explained' or 'reasoned' about, but because she

> saw Othello's visage in his mind;
> And to his honours and his valiant parts
> Did I my soul and fortunes consecrate.
> (I, iii, 252 ff.)

It is communion of minds and souls rather than of bodies.

It is against this that Iago will pit the destructive force of his reasoning, and the love-match between Othello and Desdemona is examined as a disintegrating structure for the rest of the play. Iago's methods of destruction are exactly those of the 'lower' reason. He will observe, analyse, explain, define, and so interpret to Othello, with such validity, logical necessity, and rational certitude, that the seemingly impregnable fortress will crumble. He begins, immediately after this edifice has been raised on the stage, to rationalize it, to analyse it, to explain it away.

Reason, not love, he insists, governs man in the face of desire: 'If the balance of our lives had not one scale of reason to poise another of sensuality, the blood and baseness of our natures would conduct us to most preposterous conclusions' (I, iii, 326 ff.). Reason is the prime, the only governing factor in our lives: 'we have reason to cool our raging motions, our carnal stings, our unbitted lusts' (I, iii, 330 ff.), and this is a perfectly acceptable argument. But as a result of it Iago is able to 'rationalize' love as nothing but a 'sect or scion' of these 'raging motions', and to offer a 'definition' of it in these terms as merely '... a lust of the blood and a permission of the will' (I, iii, 333 ff.).

As an 'explanation' this is hardly accurate, hardly complete, but, by the lights of the 'lower' reason, it holds water; it exists typically enough in the context of an avowed 'manliness'. Iago's opinion of women has been seen to be small; his present urging of the weak Roderigo to 'be a man' (I, iii, 333) is a predictable aspect of his role as 'reasoner'. As if to insist on the propriety of his 'definition' of love, Iago can even predicate certain events of it, as a matter of rational and physical necessity; 'She must change for youth; when she is sated with his body, she will find the error of her choice.' (I, iii, 345 ff.). Such words impose a worldly element on the situation which it hardly warrants. The climax of such a process of analytical destruction is indicated when what we have seen as a holy, sanctified, and spiritual communion between two people of honour and beauty becomes, in Iago's reasoned 'explanation' of it, 'sanctimony and a frail vow betwixt an erring barbarian and a super-subtle Venetian' (I, iii, 360–61), and Desdemona's own explanation of her love becomes, in terms of the 'lower' reasoning, 'she first loved the Moor, but for bragging and telling her fantastical lies' (II, i, 220–2). Indeed Iago can see nothing above this 'lower' level in Desdemona. Significantly he thinks of her spiritual relationship with Othello only in physical terms, and those of the grossest kind. Roderigo can expostulate, recognizing something holy, something not susceptible to rational analysis in her; he speaks (II, i, 245), of her 'blest condition'. But Iago sees nothing which lifts her above the level of his way of thinking, nothing inexplicable, nothing above the world: 'If she had been blest, she would never have lov'd the Moor. Blest pudding!' (II, i, 247 f.). He links himself accordingly in a 'Divinity of hell' with the blackest forces of evil (II, iii, 339 ff.), and at the same time draws attention to the fact that the method by which he works his evil is the use of reasoning, the wit, that is, by traditionally devilish means: 'Thou know'st we work by wit, and not by witchcraft' (II, iii, 360). It is a distinction of which Claudius would have wholeheartedly approved.

It has been pointed out that Iago's substitution of validity for truth proves fundamental to his method of working evil. As we have seen, he wishes to achieve an effect of verity arrived at through a process of reasoning, and the extent to which Iago's reasoning neatly avoids the whole truth of any situation becomes the measure of its success. At first Othello can dismiss the 'exsufflicate and blown surmises' of Iago's 'inference' by reference to a higher reality where the 'surmises' reveal themselves as merely that. In his super-rational world of love, 'Chaos is come again' only if he ceases to believe. But the play charts unerringly an exact course of gradual cessation of belief. The moment Othello asks for proof of Iago, he has stepped down from the 'higher' world into the world of that 'lower' reasoning which will destroy him; he has stepped from the world of the spirit to that of the flesh. Of course Iago can easily supply him with rational 'proof' of a sort, but only that sort which takes the form of being capable of logical assent, valid, rather than of ultimate consent, true. Right down to the incident of the handkerchief, Iago imposes the necessity of his 'lower' reasoning on matters not properly susceptible to it.

Finally, with his repeated demands for 'the ocular proof' (III, iii, 359 ff.),

> Make me to see't; or, at the least, so prove it
> That the probation bear no hinge nor loop
> To hang a doubt on . . .
>
> (III, iii, 368 ff.)

Othello becomes firmly tied down to the level and necessities of the *ratio inferior*; on this level his world becomes tragically vulnerable. Iago's method reveals itself from now on as openly rational; it works by an inductive process, by means of 'imputation and strong circumstances' (III, iii, 410) which may lead 'to the door of truth', but, as we have seen, only to that sort of truth, or that part of it, which suits his purpose.

Othello's avid seizing of the most minute scraps of evidence that Iago offers him at this stage indicates just how far he has fallen from his former state, and indeed surprises Iago by its extent. Iago can easily see how this new craving 'may help to thicken other proofs / That do demonstrate thinly' (III, iii, 434 f.). Just how thinly his 'proofs' do 'demonstrate' has been seen to be a very important part of the play. The 'lower' reason, as we have noticed, does little more than place an 'explicable' and predictable pattern of its own over certain events (the eavesdropping scene provides the climax of this process). The world that such a reason reveals is not the true world, but a construct of the reasoner; it cannot compare with, or explain the whole cosmos that Othello's and Desdemona's love involves in itself. Nevertheless, in the grip of Iago's reasoning, Othello slips into easy 'rational' categorization. Desdemona becomes for him the familiar 'Venetian wife', the 'super-subtle Venetian' that Iago had said she was. The 'lower' reason, in triumph over the 'higher', casts Othello in a role as avenger now, and makes him part of that lower world which as a lover he had formerly transcended. In that world Desdemona's guilt is rationally obvious, and 'by reason' proved. As Brabantio at first, Othello is at last convinced by Iago's reasoning. As the latter says, laconically, 'He is much chang'd' (IV, i, 265).

The 'change' has taken place in Othello's mind. Even before he appears, we have had an inkling that his judgments do not move on the 'rational' level. It was not reason (Iago tells us) which made him choose Cassio as his lieutenant, and in one sense Iago's campaign against him takes its departure from this point. When we first see Othello, his complete confidence in himself is most striking. In a confusing situation he maintains a remarkable clarity of vision, and has a faith in the eventual emergence of the truth surprising in its power. There is nothing 'rational' in this faith; it simply assumes that

> My parts, my title, and my perfect soul
> Shall manifest me rightly.
> (I, ii, 31–2)

They do. For despite the doubts cast by Brabantio on his 'parts' and his 'title' – Othello, after all, merits only a 'general mock'; the 'sooty bosom / Of such a thing as thou' is plainly considered contemptible, despite his somewhat grandiose claims to 'royal' lineage (I, ii, 21–2) – his 'soul' contains greatness, and he claims, significantly, perfection for it. Such simple perfection (it recalls Troilus' 'truth's simplicity') appears invulnerable at first. It is enough, it seems, that the facts are stated about the affair, for the truth to be revealed:

> She lov'd me for the dangers I had pass'd;
> And I lov'd her that she did pity them.
> (I, iii, 167–8)

From such a viewpoint 'love' can claim to be sufficient in itself to overcome all 'rational' opposition.

Indeed, love of this sort has qualities of a traditionally non-rational and non-physical nature; its location lies not in the body, for 'Love looks not with the eyes, but with the mind' (*MND* I, i, 234) and the minds of lovers, like those of 'madmen', have access to a level of truth beyond that of the reason:

> Lovers and madmen have such seething brains,
> Such shaping fantasies, that apprehend
> More than cool reason ever comprehends.
> (*Ibid.* V, i, 4–6)

The love which exists between Othello and Desdemona has exactly this 'intuitive' quality; it operates far more on the level of the mind than of the body. What Iago has presented as a purely physical affair reveals itself in the early scenes of the play to be the reverse of this. The means by which this love has come into being are expressly said to be imaginative in their mode of communication, disdainful of mere physical fact. Hence, we are told, Desdemona has been won against all 'rational' expectations, by romantic travellers' tales:

Wherein of antres vast and deserts idle,
Rough quarries, rocks, and hills whose heads touch heaven,
It was my hint of speak – such was the process;
And of the Cannibals that each other eat,
The Anthropophagi, and men whose heads
Do grow beneath their shoulders. . . .

(I, iii, 140–5)

There is little of 'reason' in this; in fact the events described go 'against' a rational view of the world and speak of the mysterious, the far-fetched, the 'old'. They spring from the kind of viewpoint against which reason, as a 'modern' force, must always be pitted.

Indeed, mystery envelopes their love and little of a tangible nature characterizes it. Its merely physical aspect, although it exists, is 'played down' to a surprising extent. Othello does not beg for Desdemona to accompany him to Cyprus for any fleshly reason,

. . . I therefore beg it not
To please the palate of my appetite;
Nor to comply with heat . . .

(I, iii, 261–3)

but for reasons above the level of the body: 'But to be free and bounteous to her mind' (I, iii, 265). However oddly this may strike our modern ears, we should recall the conventions of love as an earlier age saw them. Plainly, the play does not move on a 'naturalistic' level here, and Othello's 'love' for Desdemona becomes, by this, a symbolic entity not susceptible to the questions of naturalism. (Indeed, if we ask those questions, we react to their love as Iago does; on this level, his role is that of our world's representative.)

The lovers, on the other hand, inhabit for the moment the world of the 'perfect soul', spiritual in its love, intuitive and non-rational in its mode of thinking. Othello's romantic assertion of his relationship with Desdemona expresses this to the full but, even as he does so, 'My life upon her faith!' (I, iii, 294), a terrible irony can be detected, for his words may be interpreted literally and rationally in a rational and literal-minded world. When faith does vanish from that world his life will be forfeit. So far above the physical level, so non-rational is Othello's love, that Iago's attack on it (armed for the most part in opposite, physical terms) could perhaps be said to succeed for this reason. Sexuality appears to be almost entirely absent from Othello's relationship with Desdemona (however much critics sentimentally aver that it does not; it is significant, surely, that both the lovers deny physical passion at the beginning of the play, and that their bedroom is ultimately described in epithets appropriate first to a brothel, then to a slaughter-house). Accordingly, sexuality becomes a feature of Iago's attack. And if his initial, and successfully repulsed, attempt to destroy their love makes use of sexual images in their most bestial aspect, his subsequent machinations take on the related colouring of something foul being brought to birth. He speaks of horrific gestation :

> There are many events in the womb of time which will be delivered. (I, iii, 366)

– and, more particularly :

> ... Hell and night
> Must bring this monstrous birth to the world's light.
> (I, iii, 397–8)

His own actions are thus given connotations of the 'manly' sexual act which precedes birth, and we have already noticed that he has been poetically cast in the role of a 'seducer' (like the serpent) of Othello's mind. The notion that Iago's reasoning contains the seeds of some monstrous progeny is reiterated later in Othello's image :

> ... By heaven, he echoes me,
> As if there were some monster in his thought
> Too hideous to be shown.
> (III, iii, 110–12)

This implies that the 'monster' which Iago has brought to birth 'echoes' a similar one forming in Othello's own mind. In a parody of 'manly' sexuality, Iago's reasoning has 'inseminated' Othello's mind to produce such offspring.[1]

By contrast with the sexual and 'hellish' images which characterize Iago's schemes, Othello and Desdemona are surrounded by linguistic structures which connote a 'higher'

[1] In this Iago is traditionally serpentine. The serpent, conventionally phallic, nevertheless seduces Eve *via* the ear and the mind, by words and 'reasoning'.

world of blessings, heaven, and prayer.[1] Othello's grandiose 'good-evening', 'The goodness of the night upon you' (I, ii, 35) is a blessing. Cassio encircles Desdemona with words of 'heaven':

> Hail to thee, lady! and the grace of heaven,
> Before, behind thee, and on every hand,
> Enwheel thee round!
>
> (II, i, 85–7)

– and Desdemona herself, in the meeting with Othello at Cyprus, sets their love in a 'holy' atmosphere:

> . . . The heavens forbid
> But that our loves and comforts should increase
> Even as our days do grow!
>
> (II, i, 191–3)

Othello responds fittingly to this prayer: 'Amen to that, sweet powers!' (II, i, 193). He has told us that Desdemona is his 'soul's joy' (II, i, 182), and their love's communion takes place on the level of the soul. If it fails, the loss thereby takes on the universal proportions of 'perdition' (III, iii, 91–3) for it will be a soul that will be lost.

The 'change' which comes about in Othello and which results in such a loss comprises the whole story of the play, and receives carefully documentation in each of its stages. The collapse does not occur immediately but gradually. As Iago's attack gains ground, Othello's non-rational mode of thinking in fact reasserts itself as if in desperation, from time to time. He makes statements in the face of seemingly irrefutable 'proof' which hark back to his original viewpoint:

> If she be false, O, then heaven mocks itself!
> I'll not believe it.
>
> (III, iii, 282–3)

Such an avowal of love owes nothing to the reason, and it upholds principles which might be called Neo-platonic. In their Christianized form, they imply that the spiritual world, the 'idea' of God, makes up the reality of which our material world is

---

[1] Cf. S. L. Bethell, 'The Diabolic Images in *Othello*', *Shakespeare Survey*, Vol. V. 1952. Also F. R. Leavis, 'The Diabolic Intellect and the Noble Hero', in *The Common Pursuit* (London, 1952).

merely an 'appearance', a copy. Othello's sudden and surprising affirmation here (Iago has all but convinced him of Desdemona's infidelity, suddenly she enters) rests on the conceit that Desdemona's perfection in all things, and in particular her truth, reflects directly the ideal truth in God's mind, being almost an exact copy of it. It represents an act of intuitive thinking on Othello's part, which enables him to reach in his mind, beyond the level of the world, and to communicate directly with the Ideal world (with, in Christian terms, 'heaven'). His remark justifies itself, for, if this perfect earthly copy of God's truth is in fact not true at all, then heaven does indeed 'mock itself' in Desdemona. Such an idea cannot be acceptable, Othello cannot 'believe it'. At a later point, his vision revives briefly yet again. Utterly convinced by the trick in which Cassio appears to speak of an affair with Desdemona, Othello can still say 'O the world hath not a sweeter creature' (IV, i, 179), but Iago quickly challenges this 'heaven-directed' line of thought: 'Nay, that's not your way' (IV, i, 182).

Unfortunately, these are only moments. As the play progresses, and as Othello becomes dominated more and more by Iago's version of the truth, so the intuitive vision which reached to heaven fades. His mind wavers backwards and forwards, his sights become lowered to the level of the world, and he swears by that:

> ... By the world'
> I think my wife be honest, and think she is not;
> I think that thou art just, and think thou art not.
> I'll have some proof.
>
> (III, iii, 387–90)

The tragic dilemma which makes it necessary to choose between two opposed versions of the truth receives as clear a statement here as it did in *Troilus and Cressida*. The great gulf which lies, in the matter of belief, between the *assent* of reason to evidence, and the intuitive *consent* of love to a truth which lies beyond the evidence, underwent dramatic exploration in the earlier play. Troilus'

> ... this is, and is not, Cressid.
> (*Troilus and Cressida*, V, ii, 144)

I

expresses Othello's own position. His tragedy lies in his awareness of a 'bifold authority' as much as did Troilus'. As a result,
his position inevitably deteriorates, once he has admitted Iago
the slightest of footholds in his world. He touches pitch and is
defiled. Indeed, a witty extension of Troilus' paradox that a
person can both be and not be the same thing subsequently
embodies much of the nature of Othello's 'change'. Thus, where
Iago's boast 'I am not what I am' (I, i, 66) characterizes him
early in the play and marks him as a deceiver (and a blas-
phemous one at that, since his words 'devilishly' reverse God's
statement, 'I am that I am', *Exodus* iii, 14), Othello's 'change'
from what he was has so radical a nature that it constitutes a
change in his whole personality. Desdemona's later comment,
'My lord is not my lord' (III, iv, 125) hints, in its meaning and
structure, at a link between Othello's personality and that of
Iago. Metaphorically, the play chronicles the transformation of
one man into another. In terms of his function in the play,
Othello 'becomes' Iago as his role changes to suit Iago's speci-
fications, and his way of thinking becomes Iago's way. Othello
himself finally recognizes his own metamorphosis and wryly
draws attention to it with his 'That's he that was Othello – here
I am' (V, ii, 287).

The business of the handkerchief illustrates the extent of the
change quite clearly. Ultimately it becomes what Iago wants to
make of it, part of a structure of 'rational' proof. The handkerchief itself, however, belongs to another realm of experience. It
has the same aura as that which surrounds Othello's and
Desdemona's relationship at the beginning of the play, and the
words which describe it connote an 'older' world of 'charms'
and of non-rational mystery:

> ... That handkerchief
> Did an Egyptian to my mother give.
> She was a charmer, and could almost read
> The thoughts of people ...
> (III, iv, 55–8)

Like the love it symbolizes, the handkerchief has 'magic in the
web of it'. It has a holy and sanctified quality: 'The worms were
hallowed that did breed the silk' (III, iv, 73) – and it was sewn by
a sibyl 'In her prophetic fury'. Nevertheless, Othello finds himself

subsequently forced to make 'evidence' of the handkerchief, and to subject it to the sort of rational analysis for which, on the basis of his own description above, it is not suited. But, as he has already said, '. . . our new heraldry is hands, not hearts' (III, iv, 44). Truth lies for him only in the realm of the physical, of the body, of Desdemona's hand which he now holds. Her heart lies out of his reach, as the handkerchief (which the 'hand' should contain as the body does the spirit) has been lost. By now, too, the 'holy' nature of their love has been destroyed, and Othello begins to use Iago's 'devilish' terminology; 'Damn her, lewd minx! O, damn her, damn her!' (III, iii, 479) The 'heavenly' Desdemona has been replaced by her 'hellish' opposite; she has become his 'fair devil' (III, iii, 482).

If Othello's love for Desdemona cannot preserve itself, and is incapable of defence against the attacks of reason, Desdemona's love for Othello seems to be of a rather different order. The extent of the tragedy reveals itself in this situation, for Desdemona confronts Othello as a living *exemplum* of the 'right' sort of love, perfectly capable of dealing with attacks upon itself. Intuition, after all, must have its basis in reason however far it may rise above it. Love, one of the manifestations of the *ratio superior* in action, and pre-eminently that in this play, should be grounded in *ratio*. Othello's love, however, shows itself to be too much above the level of mere humanity, and this makes it vulnerable to an attack from exactly that quarter. Abstracted from the world, it falls an easy prey to the forces of the world, and Othello's proud scorn in this respect of anything below the exalted level at which he tells us that he wooed Desdemona, makes him fall in the end to the debased level from which Iago's campaign proceeds. He loves, as he realizes too late, 'not wisely, but too well'.

Desdemona's love then, has the 'wisdom' which Othello's lacks.[1] Like his, its mode is partly intuitive, beyond the realm of flesh; she sees Othello's 'visage in his mind'. Nevertheless, it rests on a sufficient degree of reason. She can combine the two aspects of the *ratio* in a way that he cannot, and she points thereby the moral of the play. She overcomes a fundamental bifurcation of the modes of perception in a manner which neither Othello, nor

[1] It exhibits reason of the 'right' sort, the *recta ratio* (see Robert Hoopes, *op. cit.*, p. 2 ff.).

Troilus, nor Hamlet could emulate, and which Lear achieves only at the cost of his sanity (and of the life of Desdemona's later embodiment, Cordelia).

Thus Desdemona knows the 'place' of her love in the world, and the social obligations which it lays on her. Her speech to Brabantio at the beginning of the play serves as a paradigm for an Elizabethan audience of responsible recognition of the division of her duties between husband and father – Cordelia recognizes the same duties, and points to the dereliction of them in her sisters, at the beginning of *Lear* (I, i, 98 f.). In an age as conscious as the Elizabethan of the structure of society, and the social responsibilities of love and marriage within it, her words would have been approved.

Thus supported, Desdemona's love remains wholly uncontaminated by Iago's plots. Her 'innocence' proves no mere flimsy thing, but has a tough quality which will not yield. To kill it, she must be murdered, and even that cannot be easily done. Until the end the 'holy' atmosphere of her love remains undispelled. If Othello looks 'downward' and swears by 'the world', her thoughts move in a different direction; she swears 'By heaven, you do me wrong' (IV, ii, 82). Her denial of Othello's charges has a religious vehemence: '. . . No, as I am a Christian!' (IV, ii, 83) and her repudiation of them makes constant reference to a power higher than that of the reason: 'No, as I shall be saved!' (IV, ii, 87). The extent to which such 'heavenly' concepts 'surround' Desdemona has been noted before, and it seems reasonable to suggest that these indicate the source of her strength. She asks 'heaven' to 'pardon' whoever has brought Othello to this point (IV, ii, 136), and her 'religious' epithets suffuse the whole of the accusatory scene in her bedroom to such an extent that it becomes, after Othello has gone, virtually a 'holy' place. She swears, kneeling in prayer,[1] 'by this light of heaven' (IV, ii, 151) that the accusations are false; her 'discourse of thought' has not, as Othello suggests, led her to be unfaithful. She would not 'do such a deed for all the world', and she repeats later: 'No, by this heavenly light!' (IV, iii, 63). Indeed, such a 'sanctified' way of life (and her prayer at the end

---

[1] In a way which ironically recalls the kneeling of Othello and Iago (III, iii, 464 ff.) as they swear a 'sacred vow' of vengeance in which blasphemy is implicit.

of IV, iii, 'God me such uses send,/Not to pick bad from bad, but by bad mend!' implies that it is such) is opposed to and has nothing in common with that 'lower' way which lies, as Roderigo puts it '. . . within reason and compass' (IV, ii, 218).

Even at her death, Desdemona's love retains its original characteristics. It is spiritual and intuitive in mode, and well complemented by her 'rational' awareness of the inadequacy of the human reason to deal with things like itself: 'All's one. Good faith, how foolish are our minds!' (IV, iii, 22). Her quietness, as she prepares for what will be her deathbed, recalls that of Hamlet's ultimate acceptance of a providential ordering in the world which lies above the level of the human reason. Her 'willow' song, non-discursive, beyond the reason's scope, recalls Ophelia's 'mad' yet effortless reaching after truth:

> I call'd my love false love; but what said he then?
> Sing willow, willow, willow:
> If I court moe women, you'll couch with moe men . . .
>
> (IV, iii, 53–5)

It has the 'prophetic' mode of intuitive thought for, only moments later, Othello will murder her for the 'rational' reason which that last line mocks at '. . . she must die, else she'll betray more men' (V, ii, 6).

In murdering Desdemona, Othello murders a whole realm of 'holy' non-rational belief, and he does so on the basis of rational 'proof' by whose profane calculation the act seems both necessary and just. The murder itself springs, on the level of the plot, out of the attack on Cassio which has been made because Iago, Roderigo tells us, '. . . hath given me satisfying reasons' (V, i, 9). Othello's account of his own 'reasons' for committing the crime are explicitly given in his speech, 'It is the cause' (V, ii, 1 ff.). Its rational quality immediately and significantly draws attention to itself. Beginning with the idea of a 'cause', a 'causal' relationship between the 'facts' as Othello sees them, his words go on to argue a 'case' against Desdemona in a manner which recalls that of Angelo in the earlier play.[1] However, the argument which emerges burlesques real argument in a grotesque parody of 'reasoning'. The 'facts' on which it depends are not facts, and the

---

[1] Cf. John Money, 'Othello's "It is the cause"', *Shakespeare Survey*, Vol. 6, 1958.

reasoning becomes pointless and circular; the famous 'Put out the light, and then put out the light' (V, ii, 7) gives its flavour. Such reasoning (like that of Polonius) gets no further than the words themselves, and becomes tangled inextricably in a web of false equations. The two 'lights', Desdemona's life and the candle, may have a conventional 'poetic' equivalence (it is typical of Othello's predilection for the grandiose to make it so), but such notional analogies have no proper place in argument of this sort.[1] Even the 'cause' itself receives no satisfactory definition: it cannot be named, its presence can only be reiterated:

> It is the cause, it is the cause, my soul –
> Let me not name it to you, you chaste stars –
> It is the cause ...
>
> (V, ii, 1–3)

'Causal' assertions such as '. . . she must die, else she'll betray more men' (V, ii, 6) clearly have no basis in fact. No men have been betrayed, and the reasoning behind such words is plainly degraded. In effect, although the argument goes through the motions of a 'cause and effect' analysis, it contains nothing but contention, and emotional weighting. Even Iago, one feels, would have scorned this, for it exhibits the method of reasoning abstracted from any real purpose, save that of self-justification. Such a parody (and here Othello's thinking 'parodies' Iago's much as Polonius' parodied that of Claudius) leads to a ridiculous parallelism such as that of the 'light', and to maniacal paradoxes in which the killing purports to be done, not in hate, but in love:

> . . . I will kill thee,
> And love thee after.
> (V, ii, 18–19)

The picture which this gives, of the murderer kissing his victim, provides an emblem, almost, of the final absurdities to which 'reason', remorselessly and improperly applied to an emotional

[1] Cf. Montaigne, 'Thus, seeing all things are subject to passe from one change to another; *reason, which therein seeketh a reall subsistence, findes herself deceived* as unable to apprehend any thing subsistent and permanent.' *Op. cit.*, p. 323.

situation, can reach. By a process of 'rational' argument, Othello has caused himself to cease to be a lover, a husband, and to become a 'judge' pronouncing sentence on a criminal.[1] Love, a spiritual entity beyond the scope of the reason at the beginning of the play, has been 'reasoned' away by a notion of 'justice' involving 'judgement'. 'Justice' and 'judgement' are essentially the ends to which reason reaches, as *Measure for Measure* has demonstrated. They depend on worldly and rational factors such as causality and the computation of punishments. Othello's love, formerly able to override such limitations, has now been finally and completely defeated by them. As 'judge' he dooms Desdemona, and kills his love because he kills that which he loves. At the climax of the speech he becomes 'justice' itself:

> O balmy breath, that doth almost persuade
> Justice to break her sword! ...
>
> (V, ii, 16–17)

– and is as blind to a higher reality as that figure often is. The kind of 'reason' in which Justice deals now grips Othello so firmly that he can go further and give it the sanction of love itself, a process which he chooses to regard as 'heavenly':[2]

> ... This sorrow's heavenly;
> It strikes where it doth love.
> (V, ii, 21–2)

The fundamental incompatibility of the world of love and the world of reason could not be better expressed. And Othello's speech at this point provides a fitting climax to a play which has dealt primarily with the difference which exists between the kind of belief required for the forming of rational judgements, and another and 'higher' kind of belief relevant to the nature of love. Because of its nature, love cannot be susceptible to 'proof', to 'evidence', to the 'testimony' to which Othello has subjected it. The result of such a subjection is the loss of love itself, and such a loss, universalized by Othello when he realizes its

[1] W. M. T. Nowottny's article 'Justice and Love in *Othello*', *University of Toronto Quarterly*, Vol. 21, 1951, demonstrates this brilliantly.

[2] Cf. Montaigne: 'To judge of the apparences that we receive of subjects, we had need have a judicatorie instrument: to verify this instrument, we should have demonstration; and to approve demonstration, an instrument; thus are we ever turning round.' *Op. cit.*, p. 322.

dimensions, lies at the heart of his tragedy. He has become one who

> Like the base Iudean, threw a pearl away
> Richer than all his tribe . . .
>
> (V, ii, 350–1)

Like Judas,[1] he has betrayed that which he should have loved. Reason has demanded in both cases that love 'justify' itself; it has argued that love is capable of being measured and that its value can be 'computed'. Instead of rejecting such demands as improper, Othello has tried, and failed, to fulfil them. Chaos has come into the world again and, as Gratiano remarks, 'All that is spoke is marr'd (V, ii, 360). The 'change' is complete.

Simplicity of construction in a play contains its own kind of satisfaction, and it is this which *Othello* notably gives. However harrowing the experiences of the protagonists, the pattern of the events which the plot chronicles brings a comfort with it which cushions any impact which the play may have on a modern audience. The sense of tragic loss with which it concludes is balanced by a sense of completeness which Othello's suicide perhaps brings to a modern non-Christian culture. By it, the murderer punishes himself and the sight of the villain being dragged off to tortures completes the picture. Time, and a series of cultural revolutions have robbed the play of the full implications of its ending, of the certainty of a tragedy which still remains forcefully to be played out on the other side of the grave. For us, Othello's death balances Desdemona's; the suggestion in the play that her soul has gone to Heaven and his to Hell must for most people be of academic interest alone. Its symmetry pleases, but we are not moved as Shakespeare intended.

There is no remedying this, and, of course, there is no reason why that should be done. The interest of the play lies for us in the quality of Othello's dramatic 'journey' towards his final act rather than in that act's nature and its ultimate results. It has been suggested that this movement is one away from one way of thinking and towards another. The perfection of the structure

---

[1] The crux 'Indean/Iudean' is important here. I choose the Folio reading because the preceding argument seems to support it. But cf. M. R. Ridley in the *Arden* edition of the play (London 1958), pp. 195–6 n.

depends to a great extent on there being a 'constant' in the process, Desdemona, on whom the different ways of thinking focus. Her static role means that she can be seen by us through various eyes in different aspects, and the play gives a devastating account of Othello's gradual change from an intuitive vision of her to one in which reason predominates. From whatever social or psychological point of view may be adopted, this remains dramatically satisfying.

The play also exhibits the same process in other terms; those of Othello's changing notion of reality. At first he sees Desdemona as she is; at last, he sees only her appearance. This latter element seems of less interest in this play than its counterpart, and receives less powerful expression than that of the opposition between reason and intuition. Perhaps Shakespeare felt the need to probe one aspect of the issue more fully and to reach conclusions about it before considering the other. Certainly in his next great tragedy, *Macbeth*, the problem of appearance and reality in all of its dimensions becomes an overriding preoccupation.

5

'MACBETH'

Dreams, dreams, visions, fantasies, chimaeras, imaginations,
tricks, conceits: *The Malcontent* (I, iii, 72)

IT HAS BEEN a critical axiom for a long time, that, of all the
tragedies, *Macbeth* most methodically exploits the device of
'deceitful appearance.' In the majority of plays this inevitably
results in a confusion on the stage between the apparent and the
real together with a consequent mistaking of the one for the
other. An Aristotelian *peripeteia* often results in which the
protagonist's 'reversal' of circumstances mirrors the preference
he has shown for appearances which are the 'reverse' of reality.[1]
In the case of *Macbeth* it may be argued that appearance
gradually takes precedence over reality in the mind of Macbeth
himself as an analogue of the use of reason of the 'lower' sort.
The play seems to say that only by means of intuitive mental
action can reality be reached. Further, in a play which is
surprisingly explicit in its comment and structure, these faculties
and the activities they involve seem quite positively labelled as
'evil' and 'good' respectively on all levels at which the play
operates.

Macbeth is clearly a play of 'opposites' and its most manifest
structural pattern consists of the antithetical juxtaposition of
'opposed' scenes, themes, characters, and even words. Thus
scenes in which witches and their 'magic' appear precede those
in which mortal men exhibit their mere mortality: they bleed,
and die (I, i and I, ii); the theme of 'disorder' invokes its opposite,
that of order; Macbeth, an evil king, undergoes direct comparison with his English counterpart, who cures the 'King's
evil'; words like 'fair' inevitably call up their opposite, 'foul';

---

[1] Cf. L. C. Knights, *Explorations* (London, 1946), pp. 18 ff.

throughout the play 'darkness' opposes itself to 'light', night to day, and the antipodes of human experience are poetically brought together. Hence Kenneth Muir speaks for much modern criticism in saying that 'one of the predominant characteristics of the general style of the play . . . consists of multitudinous antitheses.'[1] As Mgr. Kolbe has put it, we find ourselves confronted with a 'picture of a special battle in a universal war';[2] the war between grace and sin, between good and evil.

It may be contended that this 'special battle' finds itself expressed in this play in the terms of appearance *versus* reality, and that these are not merely terms in which one of its aspects may be viewed, but that they are preponderant; they have the status of a matrix from which most if not all of the other antithetical structures in the play seem to spring. As such they take on the colouring of the 'universal war' between good and evil, and thus constitute the basis from which poetic 'comment' on it (by means of images, characterization, thematic design, as aspects of the antithetical structure) is elicited as the action proceeds.

Thus, one of the most frequent antithetical images in the play, that of ill-fitting garments so often used of Macbeth's assumption of power, effectively suggests that the clothes which a man wears present an appearance of himself, which hides his reality.[3] More, what a man looks like, the play insists, often deliberately masks what he really is like. Similarly, wherever 'discord' or 'disorder' of some sort is opposed to concord and order (and to a large extent this constitutes the play's pre-eminent concern), reality seems to be invested in concord and order, and their opposites only 'appear' to be real. It will be noticed that only those events which have happened, or which are happening on the stage are real; those which will (or may) happen (and Macbeth gambles on these and the witches constantly urge him towards them by their 'prophecies') are unreal, are 'appearances'. Hence the play often

---

[1] *Macbeth*, ed. Kenneth Muir (*Arden* edn., London, 1951), Introduction, p. xxxi.

[2] *Shakespeare's Way* (London, 1930), cit. Muir, *loc. cit.*

[3] Cf. Caroline Spurgeon, *Shakespeare's Imagery and what it tells us* (Cambridge, 1935), pp. 98 ff. Also Cleanth Brooks, 'The Naked Babe and the Cloak of Manliness', *The Well Wrought Urn* (New York, 1947), pp. 22 ff.

opposes 'actual', and so real, events in the past and the present, to 'potential', and so unreal, events in the future. In addition, here as in other plays (*Timon of Athens* in particular), whatever belongs to 'nature' is presented as real, whatever belongs to 'art' (even the art of the theatre) is spoken of as unreal, wherever it gives only an 'appearance' of nature, and thereby denies reality.

The play treats these issues through the medium in which a dramatist must necessarily work, that of language in action on the stage, and in so doing, comments on that medium itself. Indeed, Macbeth's tragedy springs out of his belief in certain words, and the 'playing' on words in which the Witches indulge proves to be the means by which his downfall is brought about. Such a use of language, the juggling with 'meanings', the ambiguous juxtapositioning of contradictory senses and the use of words to obscure what should be their purpose, communication, has been noticed in previous chapters. Claudius's public pronouncements have this quality, and those of Polonius share it in its comic mode. Iago's words are of this kind, and by them he seduces Othello to a point where, as we have seen, his words virtually 'become' Iago's, as does the thinking, and the personality behind them. A common voice runs through these tragedies, and it speaks thus; it is the voice of reason.

In *Macbeth* both the voice and the manner receive a careful examination, and in respect of the play's overriding preoccupation the results of such a scrutiny are quite positive. One use of language results in an appearance of the truth, another gives the reality. In the sense that so much of the play depends on the linguistic device of 'double' meaning and its dramatic use to create obscurity and confusion in the mind of the protagonist, the concept of 'equivocation' has an important status in the action. Indeed, in so far as 'equivocation' depends on the idea of opposed meanings contained within the same linguistic structure, on the idea of a 'double' sense which an utterance can be given, the term contains within itself a configuration of that 'antithetical' movement from one thing to its opposite so characteristic of the play.

The question of such a use of language (for political purposes which affected the country at large) was in fact very much in the minds of intelligent people at the time when *Macbeth* was first performed before its royal audience. Kenneth Muir[1] has noted that in the spring and summer of 1606, equivocation and verbal double-dealing in general had become a much-discussed topic in London following the trial of Father 'Farmer' Garnet for implication in the Gunpowder Plot. John Chamberlaine's letter to Winwood on the 5th of April says that, although Garnet was confronted with the evidence of spies who had overheard his conversations with another priest in the Tower, and having been informed that such evidence was forthcoming and irrefutable, he

> ... persisted still, with Protestation upon his Soul and Salvation that there had passed no such Interlocution: till at last being confronted with Hall, he was driven to confess; And being now asked in this Audience how he could salve this lewd Perjury, he answered, that so long as he thought they had no Proof he was not bound to accuse himself: but when he saw they had Proof, he stood not long in it. And then fell into a large Discourse of defending Equivocations, with many weak and frivolous Distinctions.[2]

He also affirmed that in his opinion, and that of the Schoolmen, equivocation may be confirmed by oath or sacrament, without perjury, 'if just necessity so require'.

Such views would undoubtedly have outraged a society already disposed to think the worst of Roman Catholic priests, and although the accounts of it are probably exaggerated, they express, perhaps because of this, the kind of moral horror which Shakespeare's contemporaries would have prided themselves on feeling in connection with the misuse of statements which purport to be factual. Because its 'evil' characters are involved in equivocation and are deliberately labelled as 'devilish', *Macbeth* strikes a firm contemporary note, and points a particular moral as well as a more generalized one. The burden of the trials of disguised Catholic priests was always to unmask and to expose them for what they were, to pierce the appearance and reveal the reality. As a result, their use of equivocation would have taken on by this time the character of being part of their disguise, a verbal appearance which hid the truth's reality. Simple 'lying' was not in question; equivocation dealt not in the telling of un-

[1] Muir, *op. cit.*, pp. xviii ff.
[2] *Cit.* Muir, *loc. cit.*

truths, so much as in the manipulation of language in order to allow the truth to become obscured; it gave reality the chance to appear to be something other than itself. The process masks empirical fact and indeed, as this play shows, often makes that a mere tool of the equivocator. Language, which purports to communicate truth and reality, can be perverted by this means from its proper end, and made a weapon of the reason; it can be used to communicate only that kind of 'truth' to which the reason assents.

However, this play also contains a concept of a truth of another sort, one which lies above the level of the reason, and above that of empirical fact and of the language which conditions it. About such a truth, such a reality, there can be no equivocation. Thus, the fact that the King of England can touch for the 'Evil' has the standing of an event which transcends the level of ordinary experience. It is not comprehensible on a rational level, since it reveals

> A most miraculous work in this good king.
> (IV, iii, 147)

and, as we would expect, a super-rational activity such as this draws to itself epithets of blessing, grace, the non-worldly values of heaven, and of the properly prophetic activity of the soul which was noticed in *Hamlet* and *Othello*:

> ... With this strange virtue,
> He hath a heavenly gift of prophecy;
> And sundry blessings hang about his throne
> That speak him full of grace.
> (IV, iii, 156–9)

The 'gift of prophecy' here of course has 'heavenly' characteristics in contrast to the other kind of 'prophecy' in which the Witches indulge, which is equivocal in nature and devilish in purpose. Macbeth's journey from honour to dishonour, from good to evil, quite clearly involves him in a greater and greater reliance on the prophecies of the Witches, and on the empirical conditions on which these depend. In this sense, Macbeth's story tells of a man who comes to depend more and more on the empirically and hence 'apparently' 'true', on what he can see, hear and touch; for, when the physical conditions prescribed by the prophecies are fulfilled, then the remainder of the prediction becomes valid and events follow, or do not follow, automatically. Thus, Macbeth's security depends on empirical grounds as seemingly firm as that Birnam Wood cannot come to Dunsinane, and that no man born of woman can kill him. His life, literally at the end of the play, depends on 'appearances' of this kind, not any 'higher' reality. When the conditions of the prophecies are fulfilled in an equivocal manner, his tragedy lies in that. For him the merely physical and worldly has become 'real', but of an order of reality which cannot be trusted. The play, therefore, implicitly condemns both Macbeth's acceptance of 'fact' of this sort as a basis for action, and his consequent rejection of any higher form of truth. 'Fact', that part of life which the 'lower' reason takes as its province, belongs in a shadowy world, susceptible to equivocal interpretations; true reality inheres in the 'miraculous' world which centres round the King's dispersal of 'Evil'. Perhaps rather more than mere flattery of James I prompted Shakespeare to locate such a world in England.

The play opens with the main traffickers in appearances, the Witches. They speak of time and place and of the 'hurly-burly' which their influence will make of such seemingly stable things. Their meetings will take place under conditions which in themselves suggest disorder and chaos, in 'thunder, lightning, or in rain', and the prospect to which they look forward reflects the same disorder amongst men, 'When the battle's lost and won'. Their role in the 'particular battle' of the play has therefore quite a traditional character. As devilish creatures they will typically disrupt, even reverse the normal order of things, like the Devil, and in so doing will obscure reality.[1] Alfred Harbage points out[2] that everything about the Witches 'reverses the normal'. Instead of calling their pets, their pets call them; they sail in a vessel which is not sea-worthy, a sieve; they fly on an instrument connected literally with the earth, the broom; although aged,

---

[1] Macbeth himself later recognizes their devilishness when he says that he has given his 'eternal Jewel to the common enemy of Man' (III, i, 68–9). Speaking of 'magicians and witches', Burton comments that 'their prince is Satan' (*Anatomy of Melancholy*, 1.2.1.2).

[2] Alfred Harbage, *William Shakespeare: a readers' guide* (New York, 1963), pp. 371–3.

they dance, although women, they have an odd 'manly' quality, they are 'bearded'. In fact a contemporary account of Witches describes them as not only dealers in appearance but, cognately, 'reasoners' to excess:

'Some of these [Witches] owe their fall to their persistent and over-curious temerity in inquiring into and weighing with their native reason those things which necessarily transcend the understanding of all the senses.'[1]

Nashe's comment in his *Terrors of the Night* (1594) hints at similar activities:

'...everything must bee interpreted backward as Witches say their Pater-noster, good being the character of bad, and bad of good.'[2]

As if to echo popular conceptions of them, the Witches chant in unison that line which gives the essence of their intention to invert normality and obscure reality:

> Fair is foul, and foul is fair.
> (I, i, 10)

Another indication of their function in the play lies in the verse itself. The most obvious characteristic of the Witches' verse-style is its incantatory structure. As devilish incantation, their words have a pattern always of rhythm and rhyme, but they never achieve the proper purpose of poetic language, communication. In fact, they seem to have an opposite end in view; they mystify and horrify rather than inform:

> Scale of dragon, tooth of wolf,
> Witch's mummy, maw and gulf
> Of the ravin'd salt-sea shark,
> (IV, i, 22–4)

This has an effect similar to that of the false prophecies in which the Witches also indulge, and they express those in the same sort of verse; it results in a linguistic 'appearance', in which something seems to be taking place, but is not. Their words 'seem' to communicate meaningful information (and they delude Macbeth into thinking as much) but in fact they communicate

---

[1] N. Remy, *Demonolatry* (Lyons, 1595), trans. M. Summers (London, 1930), p. v.
[2] *Cit.* Muir, *op. cit.*, p. 5.

only equivocal and uncertain meanings; their incantatory style 'gives' us the Witches as it underlines their dramatic function.

By contrast – and the scene which immediately follows their first appearance makes such a contrast quickly and effectively – those values against which the Witches pit themselves receive expression in a different kind of verse. With the entry (I, i, 12 ff.) of the King and his attendants, we move from the 'appearance' of poetry (if it can be so described) to its 'reality' in the evenly-lined and majestic rhythm and phrase of the world of order and honour in which Duncan's court resides. In this world we hear of heroism rewarded, deceitfulness punished, and of bravery gaining meaningful victory in a just cause:

> . . . brave Macbeth – well he deserves that name –
> Disdaining Fortune, with his brandish'd steel
> Which smok'd with bloody execution,
> Like valour's minion, carv'd out his passage . . .
> (I, ii, 16–19)

This style is perhaps the most 'poetic' of all dramatic verse-styles, the epic. Within its structure we see, ironically for the last time even though the play has just begun, a Macbeth who is 'brave', who is 'valour's minion', who disdains 'Fortune' and who has all the traditional qualities of true 'manliness'. If the Witches deal in unrealities, this style hints at reality for, in a poetic drama in which poetry constitutes the natural and 'real' language of the characters in the play, then perhaps those who speak most 'poetically' could be said in one sense to be most in touch with reality. The fact that the values of Duncan's court are to be considered 'real' values is hinted at by the 'epic' nature of the verse in which they are expressed; and the nature of the values which the Witches represent is equally hinted at by the ambiguities and the choppy and distorted rhythms in which they express themselves.[1] The way in which the verse spoken by Macbeth himself declines from the style of Duncan's court to that of the starker rhythms which characterize his later as-

---

[1] After all, iambic pentameter was by now the hard-won, but established means of dramatic expression; its achievements were not to be disdained lightly, and its steady motion was a perfect means of indicating 'reality' on the stage. See J. Thompson, *The Founding of English Metre* (London, 1959), pp. 15 ff.

K

sumption of power suggests the extent of the change in his own values and personality.[1]

Nevertheless, into the verse of I, ii, there gradually begins to creep a strain of irony, a hint in the style of something which mocks what the style itself represents, a suggestion of the impending triumph of appearances over its reality. The Sergeant, reporting the battle to Duncan, warns him (immediately after his glowing account of Macbeth's exploits) that

> So from that spring whence comfort seem'd to come
> Discomfort swells. Mark, King of Scotland, mark.
>
> (I, ii, 27–8)

Comfort for Duncan certainly appears to come from Macbeth, but in reality it brings the direst form of discomfort, murder. At this point the nature of the verse changes, and the entry of Ross (I, ii, 46), who 'seems to speak things strange' introduces a different kind of imagery. Ross speaks in gigantic frightening pictures, which most critics notice, changing the atmosphere of the scene from one of reality and security to its opposite. He comes from Fife, where 'foreign' events literally take place, where

> ... the Norweyan banners flout the sky
> And fan our people cold ...
>
> (I, ii, 50–1)

and he brings an account of the disloyalty of a 'traitor', the Thane of Cawdor, and of his downfall. This news ironically shapes the first step which Macbeth will take on his tragic journey, for Duncan promptly accords Macbeth Cawdor's title. Irony abounds here, for with a line whose antithetical structure hints at that of the play itself, Duncan gives utterance to the larger irony that

> What he hath lost, noble Macbeth hath won.
>
> (I, ii, 69)

Macbeth, of course, inherits Cawdor's dishonour as much as his title, and the suggestions of 'losing' and 'winning' as antithetical movements in an enormous battle has the ultimate irony that it recalls the Witches' timing of their own activities; they will meet

---

[1] For example compare the prosodic structure of I, iv, 22 ff. with that of V. v. 17 ff.

again 'When the battle's lost and won'. And so they do, for immediately after Duncan's words, the sound of thunder announces their re-entry. Plainly, this 'battle' has relevance beyond the battlefield, and its motion to and fro prefigures the antithetical struggle between good and evil which is to come.

Macbeth strikes the note of this structural device yet again on his first appearance. The first line he speaks recalls the Witches' reversal of values both in the words he uses, and in their syntax. Meaning and structure combine in them to embody the idea of opposed elements in conflict:

> So foul and fair a day I have not seen.
> (I, iii, 38)

The reversal of the normal order of clauses is traditional enough, but it also emphasizes the line's juxtaposition of opposites in a way which helps to underline the precariousness of such juxtaposing. The distinction between 'fair' and 'foul' is almost blurred, and the word-order itself suggests as much. Banquo's words which follow begin to draw out of this already indistinctive conjunction of good and evil, that ambiguity with which the play will be most concerned. He comments on the essentially deceitful nature of the Witches' physical appearance:

> ...What are these,
> So wither'd, and so wild in their attire,
> That look not like th'inhabitants o'th'earth
> And yet are on 't?
> (I, iii, 39–42)

His eyes, the evidence of his senses, seem to present him with uncertainties which have an equivocal element about them:

> ...You should be women,
> And yet your beards forbid me to interpret
> That you are so....
> (I, iii, 45–7)

The Witches, true to their devilish nature, seem to be something which they are not. More, they have, as has been said, a spuriously 'manly' quality which adds to the effect. Mortal men, like Banquo and Macbeth, cannot in their presence be sure that their senses tell them the truth. A further complexity also pertains in that the audiences of the time would now see and hear part of their own complex response to the play presented on the stage; in performance the sexual status of the Witches would be literally ambiguous in accordance with the convention that the parts of women were taken by boys. Accordingly, at this point, the play deepens and broadens its comment by the use of a mode of dramatic communication of a self-regarding character. In effect, the play points to itself in moments like this, and reminds us of its own nature: that of a dramatic construct. The device recurs in an identical form when Lady Macbeth makes deliberate and (because she is also played by a boy) ironic reference to her own sex, in which we hear her despise her female nature and claim that she wants to change it:

> . . . unsex me here;
> . . . .
> Come to my woman's breasts,
> And take my milk for gall. . . .
> > (I, v, 38–44)

> . . . I have given suck, and know
> How tender 'tis to love the babe that milks me –
> > (I, vii, 54–5)

In both cases the distinction between male and female is deliberately blurred (like that between 'fair' and 'foul') as women on the stage are made to 'appear' to be what off the stage they are, male. So the 'female' Witches have 'male' beards and the 'female' Lady Macbeth wishes to acquire 'male' characteristics. In this she must be considered as more than merely unnaturally masculine on the level of 'character', for she takes on the role of a virtual 'man' in this play in accordance with a larger thematic pattern which has been noticed in other plays. Her aspirations to a spurious 'manliness' are those of Shakespeare's other 'reasoners', and the irony which comes of her being a woman in the first instance heightens the dramatic effect, and makes her 'manliness' that much more spurious. In this role she will frequently urge 'manliness' on the already male Macbeth, and when he falls short of her standards in the matter she will chide him that he is 'unmann'd' (III, iv, 73)

In another role at one remove from the stage, that of a male playing the part of a female, the references made to her sex form part of a complicated dramatic device which has to do with the mode of communication germane to the theatre itself. Since Lady Macbeth's assumption of 'manliness' is analogous to a 'theatrical' kind of illusion in that it disguises reality by appearances (as an actor does when he 'plays' a part) then her role of 'reasoner' in the play may be said to be an extension of her actual existence as a male actor who has the 'appearance' of being female. In performance at such moments, the male 'plays' a female who 'plays' a male; the actor has the tremendously difficult task of 'playing' a character who 'plays' what he is himself. The play supports this view to the extent that 'theatrical' images and situations are often used in it to emphasize that substitution of appearance for reality recounted in the action. In this sense theatricality, the metaphor of the stage itself, becomes part of the play's main conflict. Only towards the end is the process reversed; Birnam Wood moves to Dunsinane in a 'theatrical' way when the soldiers cut and carry branches from its trees, a device which by the conventions of the time might suggest that they 'represented' a wood.[1] By this time many of the play's images and themes have also been reversed, and what at first was used to indicate the triumph of appearance over reality is later given an opposite function; thus the play's antithetical structure goes far beneath its surface. The movement of Birnam Wood is a movement in the direction of reality, for the reality of Macbeth's tragedy will be exposed by its appearance. Only when the devices of dramatic illusion are used in this way, to reveal a reality greater than that of the mere stage (*The Mousetrap* in *Hamlet* has been seen to have exactly this function) do they receive Shakespeare's approval. *Macbeth* itself, of course, achieves this superbly. It exposes appearances by means of dramatic illusion, and is always capable, one feels, of bursting the bounds of the stage and of overflowing into life itself. We are constantly reminded of its relevance to the real world outside the play (and because of the play's royal patronage, of its relevance

[1] So much was this a theatrical convention that it could be satirized as such in the play put on by the 'rude mechanicals' of *A Midsummer Night's Dream*. In another way, it is equally 'theatrical' for, as John Holloway points out, (*op. cit.*, p. 66), 'The single figure . . . pursued by a whole company of others carrying green branches was a familiar sight as a Maying procession, celebrating the triumph of new life over the sere and yellow leaf of winter.'

to its actual audience, amongst whom was James, Banquo's descendant).[1] In this sense, *Macbeth* has a remarkable contact with its own time, for throughout the play there exists a powerful sense of reality elicited by means of art, and only dramatic art of the highest kind can bring this about.

The Witches' prophecies are positive enough: 'Thane of Glamis', 'Thane of Cawdor', and 'King hereafter' (I, iii, 48–50), or so they appear. Nevertheless, Macbeth seems quite aware at this stage of some of the uncertainties involved, and he rightly accuses the Witches of one of their traditionally devilish characteristics, their incomplete knowledge of future events. In this, as in everything, they fall short of divine perfection; they are 'imperfect speakers' (I, iii, 70), and of course, the 'imperfection' of their speech denies it reality. Theirs is an oblique prophecy, able to be fulfilled, certainly, but in a way which allows the apparent to take precedence over the real such as might be expected from that quarter. Aquinas had stated the traditional view when he said that,[2] 'Demons know the future development of events conjecturally, though not absolutely'; that is, that their knowledge of the future may be greater than man's (in conjecture) but must be less than that of the Angels, who

> ... in the truths which they know naturally, ... at once behold all things whatsoever that can be known in them ...[3]

The Witches' prophecy is purely conjectural, and, having delivered it, they vanish appropriately in an atmosphere of 'seeming' and unreality:

> ... what seem'd corporal melted
> As breath into the wind.
>
> (I, iii, 81–2)

Nevertheless, their words draw Macbeth from the reality of the world of war and honour, degree and ceremony symbolized by Duncan's court and the epic speeches of its members, into the half-world of appearance, oracle-utterance and imprecise statement of the demonic powers. Like Othello, he listens to

[1] See H. N. Paul, *The Royal Play of Macbeth* (New York, 1950), *passim*.

[2] Cf. W. C. Curry, *Shakespeare's Philosophical Patterns* (Louisiana, 1937), p. 48.

[3] Aquinas *S.T.*, I. Q. LVIII, A. 3.

these powers and accepts the version of the world which they
offer him. But the powers only indicate the sin; the crime of
committing it lies squarely on Macbeth. His own blind reliance
on the prophecies which the Witches make available to him
causes his downfall; he is his own Iago.

Faced subsequently with the fulfilment of the first prophecy,
Banquo's immediate reaction is noteworthy; it is the quite
proper one of amazement at the apparent truth which has come
from such manifestly suspect sources:

> What, can the devil speak true?
> (I, iii, 107)

The answer to such a question should be 'no', for it is a con-
tradiction in terms for the devil to be able to reveal true reality.
But, as befits their respective roles in the play, Macbeth does not
answer Banquo's question properly; rather his response to the
situation is more complex and, characteristically, he expresses it
in terms of an appearance which hides a reality. He utters the
first of the many metaphors concerning ill-fitting clothes:

> Why do you dress me
> In borrow'd robes?
> (I, iii, 108–9)

The threshold of the play's tale of murder and corruption has
been reached at the moment when Macbeth does not give an
unequivocal answer to Banquo's question. Immediately, and
with some urgency, Banquo advises him of the precise nature of
the danger which he faces as a result. It is that of accepting an
equivocal truth as a real truth, and he links this danger in
particular to the Witches' prophecies. The means by which
Macbeth's ultimate movement from reality to appearance will
be effected are those of equivocation; and as Banquo points out,
these are exactly the means by which the demonic powers create
their world of shadows:

> ... The instruments of darkness tell us truths,
> Win us with honest trifles, to betray's
> In deepest consequence.
> (I, iii, 124–6)

Macbeth's tragedy begins here, for he ignores that warning.

Indeed, he has already begun to accept their equivocal truths as
truth itself, and to embrace them as such, thus involving himself
utterly and hopelessly in that process. His answer to Banquo's
question follows quickly; in his view the devil can speak true, for

> ... Two truths are told,
> As happy prologues to the swelling act
> Of the imperial theme. ...
>
> (I, iii, 127–9)

Appropriately, this momentous statement makes use of a
theatrical metaphor, in which 'prologues' lead to 'swelling acts'
on the appearance-world of the stage.[1]

The see-saw rhythm of the great 'battle' can be discerned in
this speech, the more so because Macbeth begins to equivocate
with himself, and so begins to practise that method by means of
which real truth may be adapted to apparent truth in order to
accommodate his design:

> This supernatural soliciting
> Cannot be ill; cannot be good. If ill,
> Why hath it given me earnest of success,
> Commencing in a truth? I am Thane of Cawdor.
> If good, why do I yield to that suggestion
> Whose horrid image doth unfix my hair
> And make my seated heart knock at my ribs
> Against the use of nature? ...
>
> (I, iii, 130–7)

The antithetical arrangement of the syntax has a positive and
insistent quality suggestive of the play's larger structure.
Macbeth uses 'reasoning' here of the type we have recognized
before in Claudius and in Iago. The facts, the 'real' truths,
undergo 'explanation' in a way which enables the reasoner to get
round them, and even to make them vanish. Supernatural
soliciting cannot be good, and it is certainly 'ill' since it comes

---

[1] There is perhaps a submerged hint in 'swelling' of the notion that
Macbeth's thoughts are the seeds which will bring some event to birth. Iago's
images of 'monstrous birth' in reference to the result of his own machinations
(which have brought 'hell and night' together for the purpose) are recalled
by it. Significantly, the murder of Duncan which initiates Macbeth's own
'imperial theme' is later spoken of in a way which links it with the 'manly'
sexual act which precedes birth. See below, pp. 148 ff.

from sources which are easily recognized as evil, and must therefore be untrustworthy. Further, Macbeth is clearly not so much concerned to consider the Witches' prophecies as involving absolutes of good or evil, as to think of them in terms of values merely relatively opposed one to another in the manner of a formal rhetorical antithesis. In this sense, appearance has already won its victory over reality, for the form of what Macbeth says has taken precedence over the content; he deals now in mere linguistic structures and ignores the moral considerations of the words themselves. In this speech, one sense of the word *good* (i.e. desirable) invades another sense of the word *good* (i.e. moral). Macbeth's becoming Cawdor was *good* since it was both desirable and moral; his becoming King will be *good*, whether moral or not, since it is desirable.[1] He goes on:

> . . . Present fears
> Are less than horrible imaginings.
> My thought, whose murder yet is but fantastical,
> Shakes so my single state of man
> That function is smother'd in surmise,
> And nothing is but what is not.
>
> (I, iii, 137–41)

This touches on two aspects of the appearance-reality structure which have been mentioned before. The future, that area in which prophecies move, has the role of an appearance to the reality of those 'present fears' which now occur to Macbeth. Similarly, as in *Hamlet*, thoughts are seen to stifle acts, 'functions' are 'smothered' by the kind of 'surmise' which looks, illegitimately, into the future for its reality; as a result the potential (i.e. that which lies in the future and is hence only apparent) can destroy the actual (i.e. that which exists in the present and is therefore real). Such a process can only lead to the complete negation of being which Macbeth briefly, and even sadly, recognizes as inevitable, and then ignores until the end of the play. His actions, he seems to know already, will eventually land him in a world where 'nothing' remains, and the subsequent murders will achieve only 'what is not', only appearances. His 'single state of man' is understandably shaken by the prospect, as the political state will be shaken by what follows in the play.

[1] This point is made by Alfred Harbage, *op. cit.*, pp. 374–5.

But, seeing one way, he goes another, and Banquo's apt comment
which uses another metaphor of ill-fitting clothes,

> ... New honours come upon him,
> Like our strange garments, cleave not to their mould
> But with the aid of use.
>
> (I, iii, 144–6)

suggests that Macbeth's journey on the path to complete
destruction will be undertaken by a man tragically blind to the
nature of reality both in himself and others.

Macbeth and Duncan confront each other, therefore, in a
situation of the greatest irony, in which the King takes the
appearance which Macbeth presents to him for his reality, the
garments which Banquo has mentioned for the man they hide.
Cawdor's death has been described in the epic manner, and has
exhibited real values in itself which are the opposite of those
Macbeth's life will uphold; he dies well, to Duncan's lament that

> ... There's no art
> To find the mind's construction in the face.
> He was a gentleman on whom I built
> An absolute trust.
>
> (I, iv, 11–14)

At this point Macbeth enters the stage; the irony is manifest and
powerful, for Duncan's words apply to him. Nevertheless
Duncan greets him as his 'worthiest cousin', and his first words
to the King speak of the traditional, the 'real' values of custom,
duty, service, and order, so glowingly that they seem to want to
instruct in these matters:

> The service and the loyalty I owe,
> In doing it, pays itself. Your Highness' part
> Is to receive our duties; and our duties
> Are to your throne and state children and servants,
> Which do but what they should by doing everything
> Safe toward your love and honour.
>
> (I, iv, 22–7)

But Macbeth who teaches order, plots disorder by the overthrow of these same values; the reality of the situation is

submerged and only implied by the profession of its opposite. So Duncan speaks to Macbeth with metaphors of creation, an activity which the destruction and death implicit in Macbeth's intention ironically threaten:

> ... I have begun to plant thee, and will labour to make thee full of growing. (I, iv, 28–9)

However, in a devilish 'reversal' of normality, this plant will kill the planter, this courtier will disrupt the Court. As an instrument of that kind of evil, Macbeth expresses his purpose aptly in words which speak of cloaking his actions in darkness, of hiding their reality:

> ... Stars, hide your fires;
> Let not light see my black and deep desires,
> The eye wink at the hand; yet let that be
> Which the eye fears, when it is done, to see.
> (I, iv, 50–3)

Lady Macbeth is the major 'reasoner' of this play, and she inspires and furthers those principles on which Macbeth's life will be based from now on.[1] The method by which she does so quickly reveals itself as that of the 'lower' reason, and her manner recalls those of Claudius and Iago. By these means throughout the play she overcomes Macbeth's momentary reluctance to pursue and accept the full rewards, the 'golden round', which, to her limited vision of reality, such actions seem able to attain:

> ... Hie thee hither,
> That I may pour my spirits in thine ear,
> And chastise with the valour of my tongue
> All that impedes thee from the golden round ...
> (I, v, 22–5)

The parallel with other 'reasoners' is just, for her image of pouring spirits into the ear carries connotations of the kind of poisoning in which Claudius was proficient. Possibly, too, it helps to substantiate her functions as an agent of the devil, in the sense that the Serpent's seduction of Eve, like Iago's of Othello,

---

[1] This point is well made by Cleanth Brooks, *loc. cit.*

was also *via* the ear, by means of words, of reasoning.[1] Indeed the 'valour' of her tongue will prove her most valuable weapon in the great 'battle' of the play which she now joins, and it mocks the original bravery of Macbeth in that more glorious battle which preceded the present action; then he was 'valour's minion' in an honourable sense; from now on he will be the minion of Lady Macbeth's 'tongue', the slave of her reason. It has been said that an important part of Lady Macbeth's role as 'reasoner' in this play is her involvement, as part of the play's story and effectively in the play's actual performance, in deceitful appearances. Her prayer to those 'spirits that tend on mortal thought' to 'unsex' her (I, v, 37–8) brings out this aspect of her together with further implications. Some significance may be attached to the fact that she who speaks of physical change should also be concerned with the human mind, with 'mortal thought'. She wants a change to take place in her mind as well as her body and this serves to underline her relationship with traditionally devilish activities. Not only does she wish, in the manner of devils, to reverse the normal order of things in nature and to cease to be a woman, but also as W. C. Curry comments:

'. . . instead of guarding the workings of her mind against the assaults of wicked angels, Lady Macbeth deliberately wills that they subtly invade her body and so control it that the natural inclination of the spirit towards goodness and compassion may be completely extirpated . . . without doubt these ministers of evil do actually take possession of her body even in accordance with her desire . . .'[2]

In other words, she wishes to be possessed by the devil.

Whether we take the point or not, the images which Lady Macbeth characteristically uses exhibit this dual aspect of being concerned both with appearances and with the devil. Her activities, she tells us, must be hidden and made to appear something which they are not, just as the smoke of Hell hides the reality of the light of Heaven:

[1] Already her 'reality' as a 'woman' is half-hidden by her 'male' role as 'Serpent'. By this she takes on the phallic nature of that seducer, and Macbeth assumes a 'feminine' role as the one seduced. *Her* 'manly' urging that *he* should cease to be 'feminine' becomes part of the pattern of appearances which the play weaves.

[2] *Op. cit.*, p. 135.

> . . . Come, thick night,
> And pall thee in the dunnest smoke of hell,
> That my keen knife see not the wound it makes,
> Nor heaven peep through the blanket of the dark
> To cry, 'Hold, hold!'
>
> (I, v, 47–51)

Characteristically, too, the appearance-world of the future which prophecies reveal fascinates her and makes her disdainful of the merely factual present. Her remark to Macbeth that

> Thy letters have transported me beyond
> This ignorant present, and I feel now
> The future in the instant.
>
> (I, v, 53–5)

indicates as much. We have also seen that this represents to a large extent Macbeth's own position, and one which involves both of them in an activity whose end is not only the substitution of appearance for reality, but also the deepest kind of blasphemy. As Aquinas points out, knowledge of 'the future in the instant' properly belongs only to the Angels.[1] Mankind, being of a lower order than that, must initially make use of discursive reasoning; only Angels can acquire their knowledge instantaneously upon apprehending an object. Of course the prophetic vision of the Angels may sometimes be granted to Man in order that he may have knowledge of a higher kind, and this has been seen to happen in other plays. But it is never given in order to allow him to see into the future for the purpose of material gain, such as Macbeth and Lady Macbeth desire. The fact that the English King is later said to be able to see into the future provides an important contrast here. His 'gift of prophecy' is 'heavenly' whereas that in which Macbeth and Lady Macbeth are involved is the reverse of this. To say therefore that she can 'feel the future in the instant' suggests that Lady Macbeth improperly aspires to angelic qualities for the wrong reasons, and as a result she characteristically reverses the proper function of mankind's intuitive faculty. Aquinas's comments on this issue are clear enough:

[1] *S.T.*, I.Q., LVIII, A. 3.

Since it is connatural to our intellect to know things . . . by receiving its knowledge from the senses, it is not natural for the soul to know the future, when withdrawn from the senses: rather does it know the future by the impression of superior spiritual and corporeal causes; of spiritual causes, when by Divine power the human intellect is enlightened through the ministry of angels, and the phantasms are directed to the knowledge of future events; or, by the influence of demons, when the imagination is moved regarding the future known to the demons.[1]

In this latter sense, Lady Macbeth's vision must be demoniacal since it is not divine. Only God, Aquinas says, can see future things as they really are:

Men cannot know future things except in their causes, or by God's revelation. The angels know the future in the same way, but much more distinctly.[2]

— so that for Lady Macbeth to foresee the future, or to attempt to do so, exhibits pointedly that 'influence of demons' which after all she has deliberately invoked. She can hardly claim, as the King of England could, to have had a revelation from God. This 'cult' of the world of the future undoubtedly becomes part of both Macbeth's and Lady Macbeth's sin in the world of the present. In essence it indicates a preference for appearances rather than reality, and naturally enough Lady Macbeth consistently advises her husband to appear to be something which he is not, to hide his evil under a cloak of innocence as the Serpent did:

> . . . To beguile the time,
> Look like the time; bear welcome in your eye,
> Your hand, your tongue; look like th' innocent flower,
> But be the serpent under't.
>
> (I, v, 60–3)

Ironically, she fulfils the latter role herself.

Duncan enters Macbeth's world bringing with him the sense of order, tradition and sanctity which normally accompanies him and his court. These are the values which Macbeth must destroy. They constitute the reality which must be erased, they represent the present which must succumb to his future. Lady

[1] *S.T.*, I.Q., LXXXVI, A. 4.
[2] *S.T.* I.Q. LVII, A. 3.

Macbeth's purpose in this respect becomes quite clear, for she greets the King with words which parody the 'epic' manner which we associate with Duncan; she speaks of 'service', and of 'honour':

> ... All our service
> In every point twice done, and then done double,
> Were poor and single business to contend
> Against those honours deep and broad wherewith
> Your Majesty loads our house ...
>
> (I, vi, 14–18)

– and her voice has the manner, her words the tone, her sentences the structure which we have recognized before. The sinuous, discursive, and almost strangulated voice of Claudius, of Polonius, of Osric, of Iago speaks through her, and it speaks, for all its apparent propriety, of duplicity, of 'double' dealing, in a 'doubled', convoluted manner which syntactically turns in on itself. We hear the same voice from Macbeth, when, minutes later, he reasons his way toward murder:

> If it were done when 't is done, then 't were well
> It were done quickly. ...
>
> (I, vii, 1–2)

It is the 'double'-dealing, 'two-faced' voice of reason.

We hear it in action again, in another mode, when Lady Macbeth presents her husband with arguments which overcome his objections to the murder. She taunts him with the discrepancy between his desire and the act which, she says, makes him less than a man. And in so doing she equates murder (an act which by 'real' standards is bestial, and less than the act of a 'real' man) with 'manliness'; inability to murder becomes, by the same token, something despicable, something 'unmanly':

> ... What beast was 't then
> That made you break this enterprise to me?
> When you durst do it, then you were a man;
> And to be more than what you were, you would
> Be so much more the man.
>
> (I, vii, 47–51)

At the moment Macbeth is only 'potentially' a 'man'; she proposes to force him into 'actual' manhood, or rather into an appearance of manliness, for nothing truly manly can result from what she wants him to do. But in a world where 'manliness' of this sort holds sway, Lady Macbeth is well advised to

> ... Bring forth men-children only;
> For thy undaunted mettle should compose
> Nothing but males.
>
> (I, vii, 72–4)

– and that world of appearances will require from now on such 'men' as Macbeth and his 'manly' wife to

> ... mock the time with fairest show;
> False face must hide what the false heart doth know.
>
> (I, vii, 81–2)

The idea of the 'false face' which hides the real one has a wide provenance in the drama of the time, but in this play it becomes involved in the larger metaphor of the theatre which the action explores. Shakespeare's object seems to be to present a situation in which appearance triumphs absolutely over reality, where images of things entirely replace the things themselves. Hence the play makes much of ghosts, witches, daggers which appear to be real but are not (II, i, 33–47); it underlines and constantly stresses the hallucinatory nature of all that surrounds Macbeth right up to the final hallucination of Birnam Wood, which causes his death. In fact, the climactic act which sets its seal on Macbeth's life, the murder of Duncan, takes place in terms which themselves suggest an 'unreal' area of experience. Lady Macbeth gives the assurance that

> ... The sleeping and the dead
> Are but as pictures; 'tis the eye of childhood
> That fears a painted devil.
>
> (II, ii, 53–5)

Her words refer to painting, to the kind of 'Art' which, by the standards of the time, mocked reality, much as drama could be said to do so; the metaphor is linked in purpose to those of the theatre. Further, it suggests that to do the deed in these terms will bring 'manliness' again; only the child fears a painting. The imagery abounds in these art-terms, and the names of colours; Macbeth says,

> . . . this my hand will rather
> The multitudinous seas incarnadine,
> Making the green one red.
>
> (II, ii, 61–3)

and Lady Macbeth replies,

> My hands are of your colour; but I shame
> To wear a heart so white.
>
> (II, ii, 64–5)

The faces of the grooms are 'gilded' in order, punningly, to establish their guilt.

The murder, then, is done in terms most appropriate to it. A dark act in a dark world, the metaphors of art, of 'manliness', of 'theatrical' and 'devilish' violence surround it. Duncan's reality succumbs to Macbeth's appearance; the real world falls into the hands of these 'artists', these 'actors' who can paint it whatever colour they please, present it in whatever light they desire. The chief 'artist' and 'actor' who has brought this about is Lady Macbeth, she who has drawn attention to herself as an 'actor' throughout the play. She is this drama's 'painted devil'. We have seen her work on Macbeth to this end by means of her use of language. As the metaphors of painting and acting express the climax of this part of the play, so a related climax now follows, expressed in terms of the other major tool of the evil which she represents: words themselves.

The 'porter scene' brings the play's theme of 'equivocation' to its culmination. The setting, in accordance with the Morality-play atmosphere deliberately generated at this point (II, iii) is at 'hell-gate' itself, whilst the topical references to Father Garnet (II, iii, 5 ff.) as an 'equivocator' give a 'local habitation' to its significance. In its far-reaching suggestions, the porter's speech combines particular and universal comments on what has happened in the play, in a way which would bring home very powerfully to the audience the immediate relevance of Macbeth's situation to themselves. The place is Hell, where appearance reigns supreme over reality; it is also a place of death, as the knocking at the door repeatedly reminds us, for that heralds the discovery of Duncan's murder. In a scene often considered to provide 'comic relief', a heightening of tension denies relief of any kind as the drunken ramblings of the 'devil-porter' (II, iii, 18) delay the opening of the gate.

Fittingly, this guardian of Hell speaks of matters which inform the 'devilish' activity of Macbeth and Lady Macbeth, at the very point when their most devilish deed is about to be discovered. So, the porter speaks of equivocation:

> . . . Faith, here's an equivocator, that could swear in both the scales against either scale; who committed treason enough for God's sake, yet could not equivocate to heaven. O, come in, equivocator . . .   (II, iii, 10 ff.)

That this links Garnet with Macbeth as an 'equivocator' and more, one whose equivocation leads to damnation, may now be seen to be an extremely apt comment on this play (especially since James I, whose government had condemned Garnet, was himself watching it). Other dimensions of the play's 'battle' are also hinted at. The deadly conflict between the desire to do something and the performance of the act itself here receives a form of expression deliberately uglier than that which Lady Macbeth had earlier used, with the result that it comments on the essential crudity of her own thinking about the same issue. Hence, the difference between 'desire' and 'performance' of which she makes so much in connection with Duncan's murder is comically (and so powerfully) linked in what the porter says with the difference between another kind of 'desire' and another kind of 'performance'. The link occurs in the references to an act of equivocation common to both in the sense that it creates that false distinction between the two:

> . . . [Drink] provokes the desire, but it takes away the performance. Therefore, much drink may be said to be an equivocator with lechery: it makes him, and it mars him; it sets him on, and it takes him off; it persuades him, and disheartens him; makes him stand to, and not stand to; in conclusion, equivocates him in a sleep, and, giving him the lie, leaves him.
>   (II, iii, 29 ff.)

Lady Macbeth's gibes at her husband have had the central focus of that 'manliness' which the act of murder should have produced in him. The desire for power must be matched with the 'manly' performance of the murder which will give it. The porter here speaks of sexual tumescence, the most literal kind of 'manliness'.

His account of the difference between 'standing to' and 'not standing to' constitutes a vulgar configuration of the difference which Lady Macbeth has suggested between murdering and not murdering; the presence off stage of the murdered Duncan can be felt behind every word which the porter speaks, and this links what he says with what Macbeth has done. In each case the distinction is said to be the same as that between being 'a man' and being, in Lady Macbeth's words, 'unmann'd'. In Lady Macbeth's case equivocation creates the distinction; in that of the porter 'drink', also an 'equivocator', serves the same purpose. What she means by 'manliness', murder, is 'placed' by what the porter means by it, sexual potency. Both kinds are said to lead to a sort of 'lechery'[1] which should be repugnant to the real 'man', for only apparent 'manliness' makes lechery of the sexual act, just as only apparent 'manliness' makes murder a prerequisite of ambition. Murder is to politics what lechery is to love, a moral debasement. The implicit equation which exists here between Lady Macbeth's values and the 'lower' values of the porter therefore serves to put her actions on the level of his function at this moment in the play. He guards the gate of Hell, she operates within it.

The mock-antitheses of the porter's 'argument' also suggest a *pastiche* of the play's own swing between opposite poles, and, like the subtler movement of Macbeth's speeches, draw attention to it. In fact the porter's thinking seems almost to parody Macbeth's in the way that it does that of Lady Macbeth. The cast of mind which sees events of murder or of lechery in simple antithetical terms as either 'making' or 'marring', 'setting on' or 'taking off' and finally as 'equivocating' the victim into 'a sleep' is common to both of them. The expression which these things receive from the mouth of the porter comments in its own way on what Macbeth has done. His action is as crude, and as 'devilish' as the porter makes his own sound. Macbeth, on such a level, is as ridiculous a fool as this man.

However, since we are in 'Hell', reality does not emerge. Duncan's murder appears to be something other than itself and Macbeth can conceal the reality of what has been done and 'put on manly readiness' (II, iii, 132) as part of his deceit. Nevertheless, the normal state of nature has been disrupted, and we are

[1] The sexual undertones of murder by 'stabbing' need no comment.

left in no doubt of this, for its reality has been submerged in the
unreality of unnatural events:

> . . . strange screams of death,
> And prophesying, with accents terrible,
> Of dire combustion and confus'd events
> New hatch'd to th' woeful time; the obscure bird
> Clamour'd the livelong night. . . .
>
> (II, iii, 54-8)

The 'time' has indeed become 'woeful' and aptly, in the play's
terms, accompanied by 'prophesying', one of the activities which
have led up to it, and which have produced in place of reality
that obscurity which the 'obscure bird' represents.

Hence, the reality of Duncan's death can now be seen only
incompletely through the carefully woven veil of appearance
which Macbeth has cast over the event. Once again art-terms
are employed to this end with the irony that they too are
equivocal. Duncan has in a sense been 'equivocated' to 'sleep';
now Macduff uses just that word to speak of his death in an
image of 'counterfeiting':

> Shake off this downy sleep, death's counterfeit,
> And look on death itself. Up, up and see
> The great doom's image!
>
> (II, iii, 74-6)

The irony touched on by Macduff's use of the equivocation
implicit in the contrast between 'death's counterfeit' and 'death
itself' is increased by the greater irony of Macbeth's mock sorrow
over Duncan. As an appearance of sorrow it has the desired
effect, but as a real statement which describes the future course
of the play (in the manner of 'dramatic irony', of a subtlety of
equivocation of which even Macbeth himself is unaware) it is
most exact; as he says,

> Had I but died an hour before this chance,
> I had lived a blessed time;
>
> (II, iii, 89-90)

Certainly from now on Macbeth can have little access to
'blessing'; he is damned. The enormity of his crime is signalled
by the implication that we have witnessed much more than the
death of a King. There has been a greater crime, and a more

general dissolution of values, for 'All is but toys; renown and grace is dead' (II, iii, 92). Macbeth has murdered reality itself; that which remains is worth nothing. This theme gathers momentum for the banquet scene. Lady Macbeth's concern is to put on a show of physical well-being, and Macbeth will agree to her suggestion, as to the life of appearance to which he now finds himself committed. Their decision to

> ... make our faces vizards to our hearts,
> Disguising what they are.
>
> (III, ii, 34 f.)

is nevertheless a momentous one. Macbeth has by now fully embraced this way of life. He shies from a reality not of his own making and consequently wishes to cut 'that great bond' which keeps him pale. The bond is that between man and the real world, the 'law' which nature enforces on the world and on man.[1] It involves reality itself, and the bond keeps him pale because it makes him unable fully to impose his own version of reality on the world around him. Hence, whilst he longs to be

> Whole as the marble, founded as the rock,
> As broad and general as the casing air ...
>
> (III, iv, 22–3)

– news such as that of Fleance's escape can make him

> ... cabin'd, cribb'd, confin'd, bound in
> To saucy doubts and fears....
>
> (III, iv, 24–5)

because it speaks of a real world which lies beyond his grasp and which he cannot control. This will be the pattern of his experience from now on.

The murderer therefore rightly terms Banquo's death a 'death to nature' (III, iv, 28) since a law of nature has been violated. The appearance of his ghost at the banquet has the added irony

---

[1] W. C. Curry comments: 'Macbeth . . . recognizes that the acts of conscience which torture him are really expressions of that outraged natural law, which inevitably reduces him as an individual to the essentially human. This is the inescapable bond which keeps him pale.' (*Op. cit.*, pp. 127 ff.). In the sense that the law of nature is only perceived by man's 'right' use of reason (Cf. Hoopes, *op. cit.*, p. 123) Macbeth's reason is here categorized as the 'wrong' sort.

that it disrupts a situation which is apparently 'real' and 'natural'. Macbeth presides by now over his own version of Duncan's 'real' court, where tradition and ceremony signal poetically that set of values to which he aspires. As Lady Macbeth says, '... the sauce to meat is ceremony' (III, iv, 36) and the guests sit down in their 'own degrees' (III, iv, 1) in surroundings which purport to be in accordance with the principles of social order. Macbeth, called 'your Highness' (III, iv, 39), sits at the 'head' of an 'ordered' table, at which food, itself suggestive of order, propriety, health and 'reality', is ceremonially taken.[1] Ironically, Macbeth speaks of Banquo as the last, missing element which would make the hierarchical order of the occasion perfect:

> Here had we now our country's honour roof'd,
> Were the grac'd person of our Banquo present . . .
> (III, iv, 40–1)

However, Banquo's real presence proves to be of a spiritual sort which undermines Macbeth's claims to the 'grace' of Duncan's position, and the scene reaches a climax when he discovers the ghost's presence by suddenly becoming aware that there is literally no room for him within this ordered structure:

> *Ross*   ... Please 't your Highness
>   To grace us with your royal company.
> *Macbeth* The table's full.
> (III, iv, 44–6)

Banquo's ghost, like the ghost of *Hamlet*, brings reality to a world of appearances, whilst being itself beyond the world of the flesh. Accordingly, like Gertrude, Lady Macbeth cannot perceive it, for she sees nothing beyond the fleshly. The ghost does not exist for her, as reality does not. As she says,

> ... When all's done
> You look but on a stool.
> (III, iv, 67–8)

and she taunts her husband, predictably by now, with the familiar gibe about his 'manliness', 'Are you a man?' (III, iv, 58) and goes on to express her view of the situation in those terms of art which we equally expect from her:

---

[1] See G. Wilson Knight, *op. cit.*, pp. 140 ff.

... O proper stuff!
This is the very painting of your fear. ...
(III, iv, 60–1)

In her world, the 'stool' represents reality, and anything else
must be unreal; whatever she can see, hear, and touch encloses
her completely and she judges by these standards. Macbeth who
finds himself unwillingly in contact with reality of a higher sort
becomes for her simply, '... quite unmann'd in folly' (III, iv, 73).
She thinks him less than a 'man' when, paradoxically, he
experiences the visitation of the superhuman. As a result such
'manliness' becomes the theme of his protest against a reality
which lies beyond the evidence of the senses. To 'be a man'
requires him to live in *this* world, the world of empirical fact; it
is a world with which he can deal:

> What man dare, I dare.
> Approach thou like the rugged Russian bear,
> The arm'd rhinoceros, or th' Hyrcan tiger;
> Take any shape but that, and my firm nerves
> Shall never tremble.
>
> (III, iv, 99–103)

And, when the spiritual presence retreats, this world can re-
assert itself, and lay claim to 'reality', to normality, and to the
'manhood' inherent therein:

> Why, so; being gone,
> I am a man again.
> (III, iv, 107–8)

Manhood then, like its analogue, the reason, depends on
empirical experience for its very existence, and on the view that
all life, 'all that is' in Gertrude's words, can be accounted for, and
'explained' in those terms. However, as Macbeth finds out, such a
view results in illusion; his tragedy is that of an empiricist who
discovers that life involves more than matter. He may perhaps
be prepared to 'jump the life to come' as he has told us; nevertheless he finds that this present life has its non-physical, non-
rational side too. The 'order' of the banquet breaks up in disorder as the guests hurriedly disperse. Lady Macbeth urges
them:

> Stand not upon the order of your going,
> But go at once.
>
> (III, iv, 119–20)

Appearance has, for once, been dispelled by reality.

However, the 'battle' is joined again almost immediately, for in the scene which follows (III, v), the Witches meet Hecate and plan the next stage of their operation: their purpose, we learn, will be to dispel reality for Macbeth once and for all. They intend to

> ... raise such artificial sprites
> As, by the strength of their illusion,
> Shall draw him on to his confusion.
> He shall spurn fate, scorn death, and bear
> His hopes 'bove wisdom, grace, and fear;
> And you all know security
> Is mortals' chiefest enemy.
>
> (III, v, 27–33)

The 'security' which they offer will be of the sort enjoyed by the empiricist, the certainty about reality which Macbeth later exemplifies in his incredulity that the world could ever be otherwise:

> ... That will never be.
> Who can impress the forest, bid the tree
> Unfix his earth-bound root? Sweet bodements, good!
>
> (IV, i, 94–6)

In Macbeth's case, this kind of security will indeed be his 'chiefest enemy', for Birnam Wood will move, eq̇uivocally, to cause his downfall.

Thus, the apparitions which the Witches presently (IV, i, 69 ff.) cause to appear before him mock his desire for empirical reality, since they are themselves 'illusions', the apt product of devilish cunning, and they naturally prophesy the future for Macbeth in an entirely equivocal manner. By now, however, he has advanced too far in that direction to grasp fully the realities hinted at by the 'Show of eight Kings', and he dismisses the Witches angrily, and with words which are highly ironic:

> Infected be the air whereon they ride;
> And damn'd all those that trust them!
>
> (IV, i, 138–9)

He has pronounced sentence on himself, and on the world which he has created around himself. That world consists entirely of apparent values, not real ones; as the pathetic figures of Lady Macduff and her child remind us, mercy and justice are absent from it. Her description is accurate and poignant:

> I am in this earthly world, where to do harm
> Is often laudable, to do good sometime
> Accounted dangerous folly.
>
> (IV, ii, 74–6)

It is a world in which real values are reversed, and perverted; the only 'reality' lies in the hands of the murderers who now seize her child.

The first note of hope, of a restoration of reality and of true moral values is struck in the scene (IV, iii) in which Malcolm and Macduff meet in England. Recounting the sorrows of Scotland which 'strike heaven on the face', and in an atmosphere charged with uneasy mistrust, Malcolm can nevertheless still speak of Grace, and say that whatever appearances may prevail, reality must eventually emerge. The image he uses to embody this idea is that of Lucifer, the Devil/Angel who first reversed the normal order of things by literally 'striking heaven on the face', and who originally substituted the apparent for the real:

> Angels are bright still, though the brightest fell.
> Though all things foul would wear the brows of grace,
> Yet grace must still look so.
>
> (IV, iii, 22–4)

A flash of light thus illuminates a dark setting and from this point events in the play move swiftly, with a new force. The force is that of 'good', and the 'battle', which before had gone the way, at almost every turn, of evil, now swings in a different direction. Indeed, from now on, appearances will themselves be 'reversed' in purpose and will be used to help bring about the eventual victory of good. So Malcolm pretends, 'appears', to be on the side of evil, in order to test Macduff's mettle, and thus in talking about himself, reveals the full extent of the 'real' evil of Macbeth (IV, iii, 37 ff.).

By contrast with the 'supernatural soliciting' in which Scotland's King is involved, the English King is spoken of, as has been said, in terms which refer to his ability to remove 'the evil' (IV, iii, 146) by his 'most miraculous work'. Where Macbeth involves himself in false, devilish prophecies, the English King has 'a heavenly gift of prophecy' (IV, iii, 157) with which he 'solicits heaven' (IV, iii, 149). This King is in touch with reality, in the proper 'angelic' manner fitting to a divinely appointed monarch. He exhibits the opposite in every respect of Macbeth's appearance of the same virtue.

Similarly, Lady Macbeth's sleep-walking, an 'appearance' of life (she appears to be awake, alive, but is not) now reveals her own reality; she is spiritually possessed of the Devil, rather than physically sick; she needs 'the divine' rather than 'the physician' (V, i, 72), and her speech, now non-rational, 'mad' in the sense that Ophelia's was, tells truth for the first time in its own way (V, i, 30 ff.). As the tide begins to turn firmly against the way of life which she and her husband have chosen, a kind of finality invests descriptions of Macbeth; an image of ill-fitting clothes aptly describes his 'appearance' of Kingship:

> ... Now does he feel his title
> Hang loose about him, like a giant's robe
> Upon a dwarfish thief.
>
> (V, ii, 20–2)

This is all he has come to. He set out to be a 'man', he has become a dwarf. The way of life which he has adopted, the 'outward' way of the world, which was to have bettered Duncan's 'real' values of tradition, honour, love, obedience has led merely to an appearance of these things, and this tragic knowledge draws the play to its conclusion:

> I have liv'd long enough. My way of life
> Is fall'n into the sear, the yellow leaf;
> And that which should accompany old age,
> As honour, love, obedience, troops of friends,
> I must not look to have ...
>
> (V, iii, 22–6)

The soldiers cut the branches of Birnam Wood; once again, appearances take the side of the forces of good; the 'battle' is all but over before it begins.

The downfall of Macbeth's world takes place, finally, on another battlefield, that of the mind. In his last great soliloquy he reveals himself perhaps more fully than at any other point in the play. He has, as has been said, based his life on the principle that the Witches revealed reality to him and that the material world which they offered as a prize was worth having. But nothing, the play argues, could be further from the truth, and from reality. Life has no meaning for Macbeth at the end of the play and neither has time, nor eternity. He inhabits a kind of materialistic void in which the future on which he had based so much, for which he had sacrificed everything, has become but a successive progression of meaningless 'tomorrows':

> To-morrow, and to-morrow, and to-morrow,
> Creeps in this petty pace from day to day . . .
>> (V, v, 19–20)

The 'valour's minion' of Duncan's court faces a life in which the values which he then held have long since vanished, a life which consists solely of an arid 'petty pace' from one moment to the next, leading nowhere, except to a 'dusty death'. Such a life is a mere shadow, an appearance, not a reality. In a final 'theatrical' image which suggests exactly this, it becomes

> . . . a walking shadow, a poor player,
> That struts and frets his hour upon the stage,
> And then is heard no more;
>> (V, v, 24–6)

As such, it has no meaning, no significance:

> . . . it is a tale
> Told by an idiot, full of sound and fury,
> Signifying nothing.
>> (V, v, 26–8)

Yet in another sense, the story of Macbeth's life has a great deal of significance for, as the full reality of the Witches' prophecies reveals itself, he begins for the first time to realize the extent of his involvement with evil; he begins

> To doubt th' equivocation of the fiend
> That lies like truth.
>> (V, v, 43–4)

and the point of his tragedy lies in that. Equivocation, the rational juggling with meanings which has been seen to characterize the method by which the powers of evil work, is roundly condemned both in its particular manifestation here, and in a larger sense. Macbeth had sought, by such means, to achieve that worldly 'manliness' to which Lady Macbeth so often urged him, to turn his 'potential' power wrongly into an 'actual' force for evil. The irony of his end lies in that the equivocal nature of what the Witches promised has achieved exactly the reverse of this; it has 'unmann'd' him, and he is killed by a real 'man' whose birth was 'rationally' impossible, but whose reality and manliness is undeniable. Macbeth in fact, at the end of the play, has ceased to be a 'man'; he has become a dwarf, a 'bear' (V, vii, 2), a 'hell-hound' (V, viii, 3), finally a 'monster' and a 'coward' (V, viii, 23 ff.). Just before his death, when he discovers the truth, he makes exactly this point, linking his lack of 'manliness' with his deception by the equivocation of the Witches:

> Accursed be that tongue that tells me so,
> For it hath cow'd my better part of man;
> And be these juggling fiends no more believ'd
> That palter with us in a double sense,
> That keep the word of promise to our ear,
> And break it to our hope!
>
> (V, viii, 17–22)

The ending of this theme, with its reference to the mental 'battle' that has throughout been part of this 'special battle in a universal war' marks virtually the end of the play. Clearly, and the antithetical structure of the play adds to this impression, this 'battle' has great significance in the pattern of Shakespeare's tragedies. It embodies a struggle in which the mind is the battle-field, and the possession of the mind by good or by evil the issue over which it is fought. To a large extent it has taken place in terms of the 'devilish' nature of equivocation, which opposes the 'divine' nature of reality and truth (just as, on a 'localized' level, the 'devilish' Roman Catholic priest could be said to be politically subverting, in some eyes, the 'divine' order of James's government. Macbeth, who almost prevents James's forebears from fulfilling their divine destiny, must be, of course, the villain of the piece on this as other levels). Of all the tragic protagonists in these plays, Macbeth fares worst. His sin is perhaps blacker, his fate harder. As a portrayal of a man deluded by appearances he has no equal, and there can be no doubt that this comprises the main burden of the play. It is as an analogue of the use of reason of the 'lower' sort, in a material world and for material gain, that appearance gradually takes precedence over reality in Macbeth's mind, and the chief user of that kind of reason has been seen to be Lady Macbeth. The solution to Macbeth's problem, however, does not lie in a withdrawal from the world, or from the reason, any more than it did for Hamlet or for Othello. Rather, in considering such a situation, Shakespeare seems to be moving towards the view that a compromise of sorts is necessary, coupled with an active faith in a higher form of thinking which leads to God. For the moment, order in *Macbeth* is restored, and reality enthroned, by supernatural sanctions and 'the grace of Grace' (V. viii, 72) with all the implications that such events have for a faith in a higher order of reality. In *King Lear*, this affirmation will be even more powerfully expressed.

6

'KING LEAR'

He will not believe a fool.
(I, iv, 134)

'KING LEAR' represents the peak of Shakespeare's achievement
in the tragic period. Its perfect structure and its sense of 'sum-
ming up' within that perfection much that had gone before
combine to produce an effect both of completion and of re-
crudescence. The plays which precede it seem to 'move towards'
King Lear, and their themes undergo a re-statement there, their
problems a resolution. The play brings to a conclusion the cycle
which *Hamlet* began, and contains a final statement of the issues
with which that relatively early work concerned itself. That
statement also comprises a first step in the direction of the later
plays. *King Lear* therefore constitutes a 'climactic' point in the
Shakespearean canon and its construction presents us with the
sort of 'still' perfection such a point should have. Accordingly,
the play argues no 'case' in the manner of its predecessors. It does
not 'move' discursively as the other plays do, but stands almost
mute and immobile, a 'brute fact' in itself and almost beyond the
scope of any analysis.

Nevertheless, an attempt at an analysis must be made, and it
should perhaps begin by a consideration of one aspect of that
structural perfection itself: the interaction noticed by all critics
between the play's two 'plots', the 'Lear' plot and the 'sub-plot'
of Gloucester. To call them such of course violates the play's
unity; *King Lear* has only one 'plot' composed of two elements.
And in so far as the story of Gloucester is a 'version' of the story of
Lear, as well as part of it, no 'sub-plot' exists in this play. Its two
tales simply constitute parts of a greater whole.[1] The Gloucester

[1] Cf. Nicholas Brooke, *Shakespeare: King Lear, Studies in English Literature*
No. 15 (London 1963), p. 16.

'plot' presents the Lear 'plot' in another mode, it particularizes and exemplifies the gigantic 'thesis' which Lear's story unfolds.

Much of the play's organic perfection lies in that arrangement, but the interaction of its elements also serves a larger purpose. *Hamlet* has presented us with a diffused dichotomy between reason and intuition and between appearance and reality. In the 'problem plays' those matters have been dealt with separately, and the subsequent tragedies have followed a related pattern. *Othello* has examined the dichotomy between reason and intuition in particular, and *Macbeth* has performed a similar examination of that between appearance and reality. *King Lear* finally completes the task for which *Hamlet* was unsuited, and examines both aspects of the conflict at the same time by means of its structural duality. The 'Lear' plot treats the dichotomy of reason and intuition, as the 'Gloucester' plot treats its analogue, that of appearance and reality. What Lear suffers in terms of one, Gloucester also suffers in terms of the other. Where Lear struggles with himself and a world in the grip of reason, Gloucester struggles with himself and a world in the grip of appearance. At the end of the play, and in solution of a problem of dramatic construction which *Hamlet* had created but failed to solve, these two threads are drawn together, the 'plots' coalesce, the 'themes' conjoin, and a conclusive treatment of what has by now become a single issue makes them aspects of the same dilemma. Significantly, perhaps, *King Lear* is the only one of these plays to be set in Britain. It is as if, in its statement and its solution, that dilemma seemed to Shakespeare to have a personal and a national importance to which its setting in a period before Britain became a nation gives an ironic and (as the Fool will later be seen to point out) a prophetic note.

Lear's story tells, even superficially, of a conflict between two opposed ways of looking at the world. His initial and perverse embracing of one of them is followed by a painful and difficult rejection of it. His consequent madness and gradual movement towards an acceptance of the other comprises the 'plot', the events which that part of the play narrates.

The poles between which Lear makes his tragic journey cannot be simply 'labelled' but they invite consideration as representative of the opposition between the 'higher' and the 'lower' reason. In fact, the play yields quite easily to such a view, and it offers the further satisfaction of fulfilling a pattern which might now be expected. So clearly does that 'shape' occur and recur that it could almost be called Shakespeare's 'signature' to the plays of this period.

Goneril and Regan constitute one pole which could be broadly characterized as 'rational'. The mode of thinking and the consequent value-judgements exhibited by an at first sight oddly assorted couple, Cordelia and the Fool, characterize its opposite; if Goneril and Regan embody reason, Cordelia and the Fool embody intuition. Such an opposition clearly informs the play's totality to the extent that many other dichotomies could also claim to be embodiments of it; that between 'court' and 'country' is a common configuration. Nevertheless, the conflict between a rational way of looking at the world and an intuitive way is fundamental, seems effectively to preponderate, and could be said to constitute the 'matrix' on which the play's other, cognate, oppositions depend and out of which they spring.

Lear's journey, from his acceptance of Goneril and Regan's view of life to his rejection of it in favour of the 'foolish' way of Cordelia and the Fool can thus be said to involve an initial acceptance of the way of life and the values of the reason, followed by a rejection of these in favour of the way of life and the values of the intuition. As in the preceding plays, the tragedy seems to lie, not in the initial choice or in the experiences consequent upon it, but simply in the fact that a choice exists at all. Tragedy inheres in the total situation and is implicit in the nature and extent of the division which Lear brings about on all levels, familial as well as moral. His dilemma lies in the resolution of the dichotomy, not in the choice of one side over the other. Lear's ultimate realization that the choice can be avoided by means of a kind of faith on the part of the chooser, provides an answer to it which Shakespeare at least seems to find satisfactory.

The conflict springs from Lear's proposed division of his kingdom between his daughters. The view of life which manifests itself in such an act is completely 'rational' and materialistic. From the very beginning, Gloucester lays stress on the mathematical 'equality' which the partition of that most material entity, land, demands. We learn that 'equalities' have been 'weigh'd' (I, i, 5 ff.) in this case, and that exact computation has been its first principle. Yet, moments later, Lear speaks of 'love' in this very connection, and claims that he does so in order that

> ... we our largest bounty may extend
> Where nature doth with merit challenge.
>
> (I, i, 51–2)

The moral enormity which this masks begins the play and sparks the tragic situation. Quite simply, Lear postulates an equation in which so much love is said to 'equal' so much land. His implication is that love can be weighed, measured, assessed in terms of physical and monetary 'values'.[1] As a result, 'love' is equated with finance; so much love will be rewarded by so much money. Though at first this idea seems simply imponderable, if not preposterous (as Alfred Harbage notes, 'the non-negotiable is being negotiated'),[2] it may perhaps also be categorized as 'rational', for Lear's equation presupposes that love can be 'reasoned' about and that its values can in some way be mathematically 'computed'. Polonius' views, which made love a matter of semi-scientific inquiry, are echoed here, and in a striking violation of the convention (which still forms part of the modern experience) that 'love' and 'money' are totally opposed in terms of the values both represent, Lear's proposition recalls Iago's 'rational' account of love which he urges on Roderigo with the repeated injunction: 'Put money in thy purse' (*Othello*, I, iii, 340 ff.).

Nevertheless, both Goneril and Regan readily accede to Lear's view of love, and their answers to his question reveal them as willing supporters, indeed proponents, of the course he has adopted. Notably, both respond to his question in that 'rational' voice which has been heard in other plays. Goneril, not surprisingly, presents a fairly precise account of her love, and a carefully tabulated 'catalogue' in the manner of an 'estimate' of its 'worth':[3]

---

[1] Because of a pun on the word 'love', Lear's equation also carries connotations of a deeper betrayal of spiritual values. *Vid.* my article 'Love in *King Lear*', *Review of English Studies*, Vol. X., 1959, pp. 178–81.

[2] *Op. cit.*, p. 401.

[3] *Vid.* my *art. cit.*

> Sir, I love you more than word can wield the matter;
> Dearer than eyesight, space, and liberty;
> Beyond what can be valued, rich or rare;
> No less than life, with grace, health, beauty, honour;
> As much as child e'er lov'd, or father found;
> A love that makes breath poor and speech unable:
> Beyond all manner of so much I love you.
>
> (I, i, 54–60)

If what she says here were true, if her love really were 'more than word can wield the matter', then she should, in reality, say nothing. Cordelia's 'aside',

> What shall Cordelia speak? Love, and be silent.
>
> (I, i, 61)

makes exactly this point. But reality, typically, is not in question, and Goneril's speech provides a good example of the rational construction of an appearance which in its own terms is self-denying. Like the language used by the Witches in *Macbeth*, her words have an equivocal quality which suit her and her sister's role in the play. After all, Goneril begins by asserting that her love lies 'beyond' value so that it cannot be assessed, and yet she ends by hinting at its comparability with things of value. Her love is 'no less than' and 'as much as' entities like 'grace, health, beauty, honour' (themselves an oddly assorted group). Finally, she claims that her love ranges 'beyond all manner of so much' and that it makes her 'speech unable' to express its extent. Nevertheless she proceeds to express its extent most forcefully and to good advantage for, as a result, Lear is enabled to 'compute' the amount of land she has earned for herself by such means. Goneril has thus managed to present her father with something which is essentially measurable, whilst protesting its immeasurability. She has created an appearance which cloaks a reality and she gains, financially, as a result. As an instance of what Cordelia aptly calls the 'glib and oily art' (I, i, 224) her speech could hardly be bettered, and the point which the play makes here could not be better made. Real love, such as Cordelia's, is not susceptible to rational analysis and measurement. It cannot be put into mere words. Whilst Goneril pretends to take this point, she speaks nevertheless in a way, and for a purpose, which 'devilishly' reverses it.

Regan is left to emphasize and reinforce Goneril's argument, and she does so by adding to her sister's account of her 'love' the unmistakable and ironic colouring of money itself; her metaphor is of coinage:

> I am made of that self metal as my sister,
> And prize me at her worth. . . .
>
> (I, i, 68)

she uses an image of a negotiable instrument to express an emotion whose scope supposedly lies beyond that of financial transaction. Regan is plainly concerned with the 'worth' of her own and her sister's love in the sense of its financial value, and her account of such a love consequently becomes even more immoderate than that of her sister:

> . . . she comes too short, that I profess
> Myself an enemy to all other joys
> Which the most precious square of sense possesses,
> And find I am alone felicitate
> In your dear Highness' love.
>
> (I, i, 71–5)

Nevertheless, in raising her love to such heights, Regan cannot speak of it on a level much above that of the 'other joys' which the five senses bring. She thus strikes a mundane note which unwittingly reveals both her sister and herself.

Only Cordelia still resists the impropriety of Lear's design on its own terms. Love for her remains inexpressible in reality so that, unlike her sisters, she will not 'appear' to express it. Indeed, she implies that this cannot be done; love cannot be 'weighed' in words:

> . . . I am sure my love's
> More ponderous than my tongue.
>
> (I, i, 76–7)

Hence, when Lear questions her in a manner which openly reveals his equation between love and money, and invites her to compete on this level,

> . . . what can you say to draw
> A third more opulent than your sisters? Speak!
>
> (I, i, 84–5)

her case needs no argument. She has already denied that 'speech' can contain her affection; consequently she can only say 'Nothing, my lord' (I, i, 86). Lear counters her reply with a more emphatic statement of his equation. If a sum of money must be computed in accordance with the amount of love offered, 'no' love will produce (and there is a half-suggestion here of usury, of money 'coming' of money) 'no' money: 'Nothing will come of nothing' (I, i, 89). And, insensitive to the difficulty which faces his daughter, he commands her to 'Speak again'.

Cordelia's reply simply re-states her position. Words from the mouth cannot express the truth of the heart:

> ... I cannot heave
> My heart into my mouth
> (I, i, 90–1)

– and the only aspect of love which she can so express is the simple civil requirement which, as 'law', and a product of the 'computing' reason, may legitimately be put into words:

> ... I love your Majesty
> According to my bond; no more nor less.
> (I, i, 91–2)

She elaborates her point of view further when Lear urges her not to 'mar' her 'fortunes' by her attitude:

> You have begot me, bred me, lov'd me; I
> Return those duties back as are right fit,
> Obey you, love you, and most honour you.
> (I, i, 95–7)

– and she offers this, quite legitimately, as the only possible comment which, in the circumstances, can be made on her sisters' protestations. They have spoken improperly, not she:

> Why have my sisters husbands, if they say
> They love you all?
> (I, i, 98–9)

These words are often considered silly or priggish; they are nothing of the sort. They constitute the only answer Cordelia can honourably make in her situation, and they are meant, surely, to reflect great credit on her. Called upon to 'speak', she has recognized the impropriety involved in Lear's plan and in the consequent reduction of love to the level of linguistic protestation, where it becomes a mere tool of the reason. Forced to say something, she has said all that can be put 'into words' about love. The rest lies on a higher non-linguistic level, and remains ineffable. What Cordelia does say offers a frank and perfectly acceptable statement about the duty and obedience which a girl should properly owe to her father. As such, her statement on this level would have the full approval of a Jacobean audience (as would the implication about love's inexpressible nature on another level). By denying reason access to the higher world of love, Cordelia should win our applause, as Shakespeare intended, and our recognition that she stands for that higher world itself, a world to which access is gained only by means of a reason higher than that which we have hitherto seen displayed.[1]

Lear's inability to comprehend this principle leads him to take the first step in his journey. He mistakes Cordelia's replies for false pride and rejects the values which she has to offer him. In siding with Goneril and Regan, he attaches himself the more firmly to those principles and that way of life which we have seen reason to involve. He has had the opportunity to choose, to 'believe in' something of a different order, and he has not made use of it. Kent, who states Cordelia's case even more simply than herself (I, i, 150 ff.) is cast out, and Lear swears (significantly by those very creatures who, in *Macbeth*, have been seen to deal only in appearances: by '. . . the mysteries of Hecat and the night' (I, i, 109)) that he will throw off the reality of his position as King and father, 'disclaim all my paternal care' and retain only 'the name and all th'addition to a King' (I, i, 135 ff.). He will embrace a world of false rational values, of appearances, of worthless 'names' of the sort that a previous King had denounced in *All's Well That Ends Well*. He has become, metaphorically, blind to an extent where Kent's plea, 'See better, Lear' (I, i, 157) is made with considerable urgency. But Lear is unmoved. It will take madness, the loss of the reason which now blinds him, to make him 'see' again.

The union of Cordelia and France indicates an acceptance of her intuitive values by a sympathetic mind open to conviction

---

[1] She achieves this by means of a 'legitimate' use of reason, of course; hers is the *recta ratio* noticed in Desdemona.

by 'faith'. France cannot believe that her 'offence' could be 'unnatural'. As he says, most appropriately:

> . . . Love's not love
> When it is mingled with regards that stand
> Aloof from th'entire point. . . .
>
> (I, i, 238–40)

Cordelia has been pre-eminently concerned with the 'entire point', the 'whole' of love. France's denial that any guilt can be rationally apportioned to her indicates the nature of their roles in the play's scheme:

> . . . which to believe of her
> Must be a faith that reason without miracle
> Should never plant in me.
>
> (I, i, 221–3)

His mind lies open more to faith and miracles than to reason of the 'lower' kind, and he accepts Cordelia on her own terms where the lesser Burgundy demurs.

Significantly, Cordelia also has strong links with the Fool throughout the play. After her banishment, we learn that

> Since my young lady's going into France, sir, the fool hath much
> pined away. (I, iv, 72)

and this relationship between them receives many comments as the play progresses. Lear, naturally, finds it uncomfortable to be reminded of his daughter, though he has noticed the event too; he growls, 'No more of that; I have noted it well' (I, iv, 73). Clearly, their relationship should be considered close and affectionate on the level of the plot, and some critics have found it odd that Cordelia and the Fool never appear on the stage together (a fact which in its day has given rise to the critical fatuity which argues that they are one and the same person: the Fool is Cordelia in disguise).[1] However, the fact that they do not appear together is capable of a more provocative interpretation. On the level, not of 'fact' but of function, Cordelia and the Fool can be said to be the same 'character'. They fulfil identical roles in the play's thematic construction, and when one appears on the stage,

---

[1] There is of course some likelihood that a company problem of casting meant that the two characters would be played by the same boy.

there is no need for the other to be there. Indeed, Lear's initial reaction to his daughter's position could be well expressed by saying that he finds her extremely 'foolish', and the paradox of Lear's stupid 'sanity' at the beginning of the play compared with Cordelia's 'wise foolishness' in reply to it provides a large part of the irony which those first scenes generate.

The Fool himself combines the wit of the Court with the traditional rustic role of Fool. He thus bridges the gap between court and country, as that between reason and its opposite, by being above reason of Lear's sort. He deals in a kind of pure intellection, which, whilst seeming to give rise only to nonsense, elicits great truths in the manner of the non-rational Ophelia and the 'foolish' Hamlet. Thus his words, unlike those of Goneril and Regan, and like those of Cordelia, have no overt worldly concern, but are the product of an intuitive irrationality which attains a reality above the level of the Court.

Cordelia's 'reality' has a grounding in reason, as we have witnessed in her statement about her filial duties, and in this respect she resembles Desdemona. In the person of the Fool, nevertheless, Cordelia's ability to rise above the level of mere reasoning exhibits itself abstractly in action, by means of a character whose function is 'de-personalized'. The Fool rises 'above' the plot, having no direct influence on it, and only a tenuous connection with the continuous story. This places him very much in the position of a chorus, but it would be dangerous to ascribe such a positive role to the Fool. In effect, he makes certain that the theme for which Cordelia acts in the story is maintained when she is off-stage.

His role of Fool strengthens the 'intuitive' aspect of the play's structure for two reasons. First, as a character who represents a rejection of the values of the reason, he brings to this play echoes of other Fools in other plays who perform similar functions,[1] and he adds to that 'pole' of the play the simplicity of nature's 'natural', which acts as a force of positive good when pitted against the 'non-natural' and 'civilized' rationalism of a morally debased Court. The play thus elaborates and extends a traditional conflict between Court and Country by means of metaphors and situations in which 'courtly' values are depicted

---

[1] Cf. Enid Welsford, *The Fool* (London, 1935), pp. 245 ff., and R. H. Goldsmith, *Wise Fools in Shakespeare* (East Lancing, 1955), *passim*.

as rational and materialistic, and so opposed to those of the 'country' which are intuitive and, in a related sense, 'natural' or 'foolish'.

Second, what the Fool says, despite its apparent irrationality (though indeed, in the play's terms, because of it), evinces reality and truth where what the Court says (in the persons of Goneril, Regan and later Edmund) leads to appearance and untruth. Typically, the Fool's words are couched in non-rational forms. They shape themselves in non-sequiturs and witty paradoxes which give in part the key to his role. He enacts a paradox on the stage for, when the King shows himself to be a fool, then the Fool has good claim to be King. One of the necessary paradoxes of the intuitive faculty is thus acted out. Non-rational, intuition proves itself a better guide to reality than the reason. This aspect of the Fool's function in the play links him most closely with Cordelia. Indeed, Lear ultimately recognizes and states that link himself at the end of the play when, over the body of the dead Cordelia, he laments that '. . . my poor fool is hang'd' (V, iii, 305). The reference has puzzled many critics, but we need not ask to whom Lear refers here. He speaks of one composite character, that of Cordelia *and* the Fool who, the play implies, have one and the same function and represent one and the same set of values. Thus Lear's ultimate recognition that the Fool is 'no fool' but that on the contrary he possesses the kind of 'learned ignorance' which leads to a firm intuitive grasp of reality, reveals not only an aspect of his own purgation but also serves to indicate his final acceptance of the propriety of Cordelia's response to his initial question.

Before this point is reached, the way in which the Fool attains and expresses his intuitive truths should be examined. He is concerned, traditionally, to depict Lear's true position to him, to show him the reality of what he is doing. Thus he continually presents Lear with his own image expressed in the 'non-rational' mode of jingles, rhymes, folk-lore and song. He will speak, for example, of values which exist above the level on which they can be 'known' or 'shown', and which outstrip mathematical computation because they lie beyond it:

> Mark it, nuncle:
> Have more than thou showest,

Speak less than thou knowest,
. . . .
And thou shalt have more
Than two tens to a score.
(I, iv, 117–26)

He will mock, in the same manner, Lear's angry threats to
Cordelia, and point out the crime Lear has committed in
equating the value of land with that of love:

Fool Can you make no use of nothing, nuncle?
Lear Why, no, boy; nothing can be made out of nothing.
Fool (*to Kent*) Prithee tell him, so much the rent of his land
comes to . . .   (I, iv, 130–3)

His comment to Kent contains a phrase which comprises a 'non-
rational' summation of Lear's position, and which in its implications aptly suggests the movement of the whole play:

. . . He will not believe a fool.
(I, iv, 134)

Lear's tragedy lies here. The 'fools' of the play, Cordelia and this
boy, offer him truth and reality on a level beyond that of the
reason, but Lear will not accept it, preferring something less.

The Fool continues to elicit the truth in his own way. He even
'acts it out' for Lear:

That lord that counsell'd thee
To give away thy land,
Come place him here by me –
Do thou for him stand.
The sweet and bitter fool
Will presently appear;
The one in motley here,
The other found out there.
(I, iv, 139–46)

The two 'fools', the one in motley who sees the truth, the other
wearing the crown who is blind to it, confront each other, and
the point is visually made. Lear, rational, is foolish; the Fool,
irrational, is wise. But Lear characteristically does not see
beyond the literal meaning of the words themselves. He loses his
temper and shouts:

Dost thou call me fool, boy?
(I, iv, 147)

Only Kent understands such events and can see that 'This is
not altogether fool, my lord', but he is quickly silenced.

Sometimes the Fool's analysis of Lear's situation becomes
practically explicit:

Thou hadst little wit in thy bald crown when thou
gav'st thy golden one away.
(I, iv, 158 ff.)

At other times it lies far from that, couched in obscure forms, in a
kind of 'meaningful' nonsense which looks forward to Lear's own
excursions into this same sort of 'mad' language later, when he
too will be discerning reality by its means. Whatever linguistic
forms the Fool uses, the effect is the same: to expose the sham
values which surround Lear in his alliance with Goneril and
Regan. And indeed, when the time comes for that alliance to be
broken, when Lear, shocked and angry at the treatment Goneril
affords him, and feeling that his very identity is at stake, so much
has that been based on his expectations of the way of life he has
chosen, cries out in anguish

Who is it that can tell me who I am?
(I, iv, 229)

– only the Fool can answer him with the perfect truth, which
indicates how far the reality of Lear has been replaced by an
appearance of itself: 'Lear's shadow' (I, iv, 230).

Lear's purgation from the taint of the world he has created by his
own action is a gradual and a painful one. It begins when he
discovers that that world cannot provide him with the kind of
sustenance he needs. What on one level manifests itself as a
physical denial of comfort, shelter, and protection, indicates on
another the inability of such a barren place to provide for the
total 'needs' of the whole nature of man. Goneril rejects her
father on 'rational' grounds, arguing a case in which Regan later
supports her, which parallels and comments on Lear's own
position at the beginning of the play. Then, supremely rational,
he was prepared to compute his daughters' love in terms of land
and money. Now, ironically, the tables are turned, and his own

'needs' undergo computation in exact mathematical terms. He has a hundred knights, but Goneril assesses his 'need' at half that, and will only allow him fifty (I, iv, 294 ff.). Later, Regan advises Lear that he should be rational in these matters, that he

> . . . should be rul'd and led
> By some discretion . . .
>
> (II, iv, 146–7)

and that Goneril is one of 'those that mingle reason with your passion' (II, iv, 233); she cuts the number to twenty-five, at which Lear wryly parodies his former calculation of love's 'value' with his comment to Goneril:

> Thy fifty yet doth double five and twenty,
> And thou art twice her love.
>
> (II, iv, 258–9)

Then both Goneril and Regan together reduce the number to nothing (II, iv, 260 ff.). Lear, by their computation, 'needs' no knights, and their assessment shows his mathematical accounting of spiritual values distorted, burlesqued, and turned on its perpetrator; the world Lear has created now calculates in his way on the level of the reason, and he comes at length to realize this. He puts his own case well in terms similar to those in which Cordelia had formerly put hers: 'Need', like 'love' which forms part of everyone's needs, cannot be 'reasoned' about:

> O, reason not the need! Our basest beggars
> Are in the poorest thing superfluous.
> Allow not nature more than nature needs,
> Man's life is cheap as beast's. . . .
>
> (II, iv, 263–6)

Unfortunately, his argument, like Cordelia's, falls on deaf ears, and the speech finishes on a note of hysterical anger:

> I will have such revenges on you both . . .
> (II, iv, 278)

But the point has been made. Elements exist in man, his 'needs' express it well, which cannot be made susceptible to reason and to rational analysis, or to the sort of assessment in which Lear himself has indulged. Such an 'accounting' reduces man to the level of a beast. The recognition on Lear's part that there is more to man than reason allows signals the beginning of his break from the world where reason rules. He does not find it easy to accomplish, and he rightly fears the consequences. During the scenes which lead up to this point, he rages, curses, and storms about the stage. He has been caught in a trap of his own design and his anger, as a result, takes on the colour of frustration. He turns at one point to 'Nature' as a 'Goddess' in order to curse Goneril:

> Hear, Nature, hear; dear goddess, hear.
> (I, iv, 275)

and only evokes in our minds Edmund, who also allies himself with the 'Goddess' of the material world. His own (unrecognized) chief ally, Kent, has been thrown into the stocks, and this leaves Lear with only one means of escape from a world in which the rational and estimable provide the only standard of truth and reality. The means are those which Hamlet deliberately chose, but Lear has them forced upon him. They offer the last refuge from reason, and they involve its total abandonment.

Naturally, Lear shies away from such a conclusion and clings as long as possible to the rational world: 'I prithee, daughter, do not make me mad' (II, iv, 217). Yet, when the inevitable has to be faced, he finds that he already has a most suitable companion by his side. He goes into madness accompanied, appropriately, by the Fool (II, iv, 285). In fact, before he has reached this pitch, the Fool has already promised him that he will accompany him on his tragic journey away from the kind of rational 'wisdom' which Goneril and Regan exhibit:

> That sir which serves and seeks for gain,
> And follows but for form,
> Will pack when it begins to rain,
> And leave thee in the storm.
> But I will tarry; the fool will stay
> And let the wise man fly. . . .
> (II, iv, 76–81)

Lear's retreat from the Court to the heath, 'To be a comrade with the wolf and owl' (II, iv, 209) should be regarded, then, as rather more than a mere 'return to nature', a simple rejection of 'Court' for 'country'. Certainly Lear does reject 'Court' values, for these are what Goneril and Regan profess, and they are interestingly similar to those Claudius and Macbeth have been seen earlier to profess in their Courts (significantly, none of these is rightfully at the head of the Court concerned). Certainly, too, Lear finds real values only against the background of those of Nature herself. He recognizes the shallowness of a civilization which has grown too far away from that yardstick. But this particular notion is treated more fully by Shakespeare else-where.[1] *King Lear* on the other hand seems to have an added depth, whereby Lear not only rejects the Court and the civiliz-ation of which it is the apogee, but also the kind of thinking which characterizes its members. Hence, as he rejects the 'Court' for the 'country', so he must reject the Court's reason in favour of another kind of thinking which is proper to the country. In terms which the play punningly explores, Lear's return to nature will be accompanied by a way of thinking which parallels that of the 'natural', the Fool. He will reject reason for its 'natural' and 'foolish' counterpart, manifested in a kind of sagacious madness; in effect for a way of thinking which is non-rational, and intuitive.

Accordingly, Lear's initial madness differs noticeably from its later manifestation. At the beginning he is tortured, restless, experiencing the pangs which Hamlet also felt of a man turning from the 'outward' and rational life to the 'inward' life of intuitive knowledge. This constitutes the purgation proper, and the play depicts it as a cosmic event, the tortured elements echoing Lear's mental torture, the agony of his mind reflected by the world's agony. At the end of this period of toil, anger, and despair, Lear's new, purged madness emerges to link itself ecstatically with the 'foolishness' of Cordelia. The crisis over, the purged Lear will achieve unity with the intuitive world he once rejected.

His last words, then, before the storm-scene, 'O fool, I shall go mad' (II, iv, 285) are sufficient preparation for the sight of him next, on the heath, raging with the elements. Here we see the initial overthrow of reason in Lear's mind. Here he

> Strives in his little world of man to out-scorn
> The to-and-fro conflicting wind and rain.
> (III, i, 10 f.)

[1] Notably in *Timon of Athens*, that most *Lear*-like of plays.

He struggles for control whilst craving for destruction; he wants
to get rid of the world and worldly things which have hurt him so
much:

> ... And thou, all-shaking thunder,
> Strike flat the thick rotundity o'th'world ...
> (III, ii, 6–7)

And he wills such destruction to the very heart of matter itself:

> Crack nature's moulds, all germens spill at once,
> That makes ingrateful man.
> (III, ii, 8–9)

The Fool wisely adds a practical comment to this which directly
contrasts the 'Court' with the 'country' of the heath, and hints
that the former is the lesser evil on such a night:

> O nuncle, court holy water in a dry house is better
> than this rain-water out o'door.
> (III, ii, 10–11)

But Lear has begun to see the difference between the two; the
'country' is blameless, not tainted with his crime:

> I tax not you, you elements, with unkindness;
> I never gave you kingdom, call'd you children ...
> (III, ii, 16–17)

He even begins now to acquire a Christian kind of patience
which suggests that of Cordelia herself, who, faced with a
different kind of storm, met it with silence, and said 'nothing'.

> No, I will be the pattern of all patience;
> I will say nothing.
> (III, ii, 37–8)

He understands that above the level of the Court's reasoning,
reality will reveal itself, crimes will be punished which before
were concealed, a universal judgement will unveil the 'seeming'
world of appearance:

> ... Tremble, thou wretch,
> That hast within thee undivulged crimes
> Unwhipped of justice. Hide thee, thou bloody hand;
> Thou perjur'd, and thou simular man of virtue
> That art incestuous; caitiff, to pieces shake,

That under covert and convenient seeming
Hast practis'd on man's life. Close pent-up guilts,
Rive your concealing continents . . .

(III, ii, 51–8)

– and a new vision of man's 'needs' seems to come with his tentative acceptance of and real pity for the Fool:

The art of our necessities is strange
That can make vile things precious . . .
Poor fool and knave, I have one part in my heart
That's sorry yet for thee.

(III, ii, 70–3)

Lear's gradual movement towards full acceptance of the values represented by the Fool and Cordelia begins here, and the Fool heralds it by the utterance of a 'prophecy':

. . . I'll speak a prophecy ere I go.
When priests are more in word than matter;
When brewers mar their malt with water;
When nobles are their tailors' tutors;
No heretics burn'd, but wenches' suitors;
When every case in law is right;
No squire in debt, nor no poor knight;
When slanders do not live in tongues;
Nor cutpurses come not to throngs;
When usurers tell their gold i'th'field;
And bawds and whores do churches build –
Then shall the realm of Albion
Come to great confusion . . .

(III, ii, 80–92)

Macbeth has indicated that prophecies can be devilish, can equivocate about the future and disguise the reality of the present. But in that play 'heavenly' prophecies also existed whose purpose was the reverse of that, and the Fool's 'prophetic' statement, cast in traditional 'merlinesque' form, is of that sort. It reveals a faith in an ordering of the world and of man's activities in it which lies beyond the comprehension of the limited reason, and it argues implicitly against an acceptance of a rational and (by the reason's standards) normal expectation of what life should be like.[1] Hence, if reason ever did prevail, if a time ever came 'When priests are more in word than matter', or 'When every case in law is right', then the result for the world, for 'Albion', would simply be 'confusion'. The world is not designed in accordance with man's reason, and his vision of rational perfection (which the 'conditions' of the prophecy prescribe) would not lead to perfect order, but to its reverse. The world is designed to run along rational lines, certainly, but they are of an order of reason far higher than that which man possesses. What man thinks of as 'right' may well be wrong in the light of a superior view of rightness. Significantly, the Fool strikes this note of 'divine irrationality' at the point in the play where Lear deserts human reasoning for a higher kind. The rest of the play will develop the prophecy's implications more fully and, in its ending, make it the basis of a tentative solution to some of Lear's (and mankind's) problems. For the moment, the Fool's concluding words express a huge irrationality in terms of time, space, and personality, as if to set an impersonal seal on the 'philosophy' which has been put forward:

> This prophecy Merlin shall make, for I live before his time.
> (III, ii, 95)

They offer a 'prophetic' statement about a prophecy, just as what has been said gives an 'irrational' account (which forms part of the merlinesque tradition; the prophecy should typically be obscure, obtuse, on one level meaningless) of a viewpoint which is not itself 'rational'. The prophecy has (also traditionally) been directed towards 'Albion'. It has the ring of *de te fabula*, and its paradoxes reach to truth in the way that Hamlet's 'mad' statements have been seen to do.

Shortly afterwards, Lear, Kent, and the Fool encounter Edgar in the 'hovel' scene. The 'plots' of the play merge on the stage, each illuminating and being illuminated by the other in a complementary unity as the action reaches its conclusion. This scene (III, iv) constitutes a kind of climax, then, a point at which the play's action is 'frozen' for a moment at its peak before the descent into resolution begins. By now, Lear has fully rejected

---

[1] A fuller account of the merlinesque 'prophetic' tradition and its relation to this passage is given in my article, 'The Fool's Prophecy in *King Lear*', *Notes and Queries*, n.s., Vol. 7, No. 9, 1960, pp. 331–2.

the Court-world of reason, and, on a social level, the cruelties which it prescribes. His purgation continues as he expresses his pity for the poor amongst his subjects in images which hint at depuration:

> Poor naked wretches, wheresoe'er you are,
> That bide the pelting of this pitiless storm,
> . . . .
> . . . . O, I have ta'en
> Too little care of this! Take physic, pomp; . . .
> (III, iv, 28 ff.)

When he meets Edgar, he meets in effect one of these 'poor naked wretches', with the result that Edgar fulfils a thematically satisfying role at this point. However, on another level, since Edgar is also disguised as a madman, their meeting is one of like minds on cognate planes. The fusing of the play's two stories, structurally so perfect here, is also beautifully contrived in another dimension, for Lear, the Fool and Edgar are all 'non-rational', each in his own way, and are involved in a process of withdrawal from a world whose rational values have driven them to this pitch. Certainly Lear's madness is real, Edgar's feigned, the Fool's 'professional', but the resultant climate on the stage of 'wise' irrationality, with the consequent utterance on the part of all the participants of non-rational truths, and their subsequent revelation to each other of the reality of what they are and of what has happened to them, serves to make this scene a focal one. Its 'madness', its use of the 'higher' reason, balances beautifully the awful 'sanity' and use of the 'lower' reason which characterizes the scenes at Court. Edgar is to Gloucester what Cordelia is to Lear, and Lear's whole-hearted acceptance of Edgar as a person whose situation reflects his own suggests that symmetry:

> Didst thou give all to thy daughters? And art thou come to this?
> (III, iv, 48f.)

Like the story of Lear, Gloucester's story tells of a conflict between two opposed ways of looking at the world, symbolized by his children. As in the case of the polarities of the Lear story, precise 'labelling' is unsatisfactory, but the play's presentation of the situation suggests a similar, related opposition. For example, an examination of the way in which Edmund and

Edgar speak and act reveals that the dichotomy between them is an analogue of that between Goneril and Regan on the one hand and Cordelia on the other (and indeed, in the battle which enacts the ultimate opposition of these factions, this is how the alliances are formed. Edmund sides with Goneril and Regan, and Edgar joins the camp of Cordelia, France, and their followers).

Thus Edmund, whose illegitimacy provides the source of his actions on one level, is characterized as one who 'illegitimately' masks reality by appearance. He makes his 'legitimate' brother appear to be evil when he is not, and thereby makes him appear to be 'unnatural' (I, ii, 74) whilst gaining for himself the reward of the epithet 'natural' (II, i, 84) and the promise that he will be made 'capable' of all that a legitimate son should have. By contrast, Edgar constantly strives to preserve his own reality and is thereby constrained, paradoxically, to remove himself from the court to a more 'natural' place, the heath, and to submerge his identity in that of a 'natural' (in the sense of 'foolish') character, Poor Tom. Where, in the Lear story, intuition is characterized by two persons who have a single function, Cordelia and the Fool, here reality is similarly expressed. If Cordelia and the Fool are thematically the same, Edgar and Poor Tom are literally the same. And since the Gloucester story deals with the distinction between reality and appearance, the changing of Edgar to the character of Poor Tom occurs visually on the stage; we see it happen. The paradox lies in the fact that Edgar has to stoop to disguising himself, to becoming an 'appearance', in order to preserve his reality, just as Cordelia may be said to be forced to appear perversely rational, in her account of her love for her father, in order to preserve the values of her intuitive faculty.

Gloucester's journey, from his initial acceptance of Edmund's version of reality to his final acceptance of that of Edgar-Poor Tom, parallels Lear's journey exactly. When the two stories fuse in the hovel scene, Edgar's 'madness' has the same function as that of the Fool, for it serves eventually to lead Lear and Gloucester to the literal 'end' of their journey; to the non-rational 'real' world of the camp of Cordelia and France at Dover, the very edge of England. Reality and intuition have at least a foothold in the country to which, embattled as it is, its supporters rally. In the course of the journey, where Lear has to go mad in order to achieve a higher sanity, Gloucester must be blinded in order to be able to 'see' more clearly. As he says, 'I stumbled when I saw' (IV, i, 20).

Edmund's dealing in appearances involves him in most of the typical manifestations of that activity which have been noticed in other plays. Like Goneril and Regan, and like Iago, he makes much of a feigned reluctance to speak at first. He parodies Cordelia's reply to Lear with a 'Nothing, my lord' (I, ii, 31) of his own when questioned by Gloucester. But he utters these famous words for a very different purpose. Gloucester, of course, should not escape his share of the blame for what follows. Like Lear, he has himself deliberately created that which later tries to destroy him. He has already told us (I, i, 20 f.) that 'there was good sport at [Edmund's] making'. He seems quite unrepentant over the circumstances of Edmund's conception and birth, and he even makes the matter an occasion for levity in his conversation with Kent. Edmund, however, is very serious about what is involved. His 'goddess', he claims, is Nature, and he binds his services to her law (I, ii, 1 ff.), but for reasons of which only Macbeth could approve, and with a series of equivocal jugglings of the word 'Nature' itself which recalls the activities of the Witches in the same play.

Like that of Claudius, his reasoning has logical validity, but it does not lead to the truth, for he tries to make the point that his allegiance to the 'law' of nature justifies his own position as a 'natural' child of Gloucester:

> . . . Wherefore should I
> Stand in the plague of custom, and permit
> The curiosity of nations to deprive me,
> For that I am some twelve or fourteen moonshines
> Lag of a brother? Why bastard? Wherefore base?
> (I, ii, 2–6)

We may sympathize with this, but a Jacobean audience would not. Because 'nature' is good it does not follow that 'natural' children are better than those legitimately got. The chief virtue of being 'natural' has been seen to lie more in the word's sense of 'foolish'. To presume to virtue on the basis of the word's other sense of 'illegitimate' becomes itself an illegitimate presumption. The form of Edmund's argument thus fulfils what its content denies, and his manipulation of the idea of 'natural' is an example of equivocation of a type we have seen roundly condemned elsewhere. It constitutes, as *Macbeth* showed, a means by which appearance may be substituted for reality. Edmund goes on to argue further that the creation of bastards will

> ... in the lusty stealth of nature, take
> More composition and fierce quality
> Than doth, within a dull, stale, tired bed,
> Go to th' creating a whole tribe of fops
> Got 'tween asleep and wake...
> (I, ii, 11–15)

Here again, 'nature' is summoned equivocally in support of his argument, with the implication that it involves something 'free' and 'strong' rather than those qualities which the Jacobeans more usually admired in the concept. To them, the word had another sense: that of nature controlled and directed to the good of society.[1] Typically, Edmund implicitly extols the 'manliness' which went to his own creation, in the manner in which the 'reasoners' of these plays often argue that sexuality inculcates that quality.[2] Further, what he argues here proves to be a wholly material explanation and 'assessment' (of a sort which almost recalls that of Lear earlier) of matters which in reality involve moral issues. 'Legitimacy' has to do with ethics, not physiology, and Edmund exhibits a Polonius-like rationality when he causes one frame of reference 'illegitimately' to invade the other, and speaks of matters which are not capable of being 'scientifically' analysed as if they were.

[1] Caliban is 'natural' in Edmund's sense here, and has the same 'free' sexual proclivities to which Edmund lays claim through his forebears. Shakespeare seems positively to condemn this sense of 'nature' in *The Tempest*. Cf. Frank Kermode, ed., *The Tempest*, Arden edn. (London, 1954), Introduction, pp. v ff.

[2] Just as Goneril, Regan and Edmund all urge 'manliness' on each other by statement or by implication, the more 'irrational' Lear and Edgar become, the more child-like (and so 'unmanly') is their language and behaviour. The child, of course, traditionally has the innocence which the man lacks, and Huntington Brown's suggestion that the Fool was in fact a part designed for a boy gives this idea more support: *vid.* his 'Lear's Fool, a Boy not a Man', *Essays in Criticism*, Vol. XIII, No. 2, April, 1963, pp. 164–171. It is perhaps worthy of note that Lear's irrationality is described by him as something specifically 'unmanly', because 'feminine'; it is *hysterica passio*, the 'mother'.

The climax of this statement of his own role in the play comes when he dismisses the principle of legitimacy altogether as a mere word: 'Fine word, legitimate!' (I, ii, 18). To do as much suggests that the concept does not exist; legitimacy is merely *flatus vocis*. By this argument, illegitimacy does not exist either. Thus, to his own satisfaction, Edmund disguises what he really is, a bastard, and so celebrates a consequent (and almost sexual) triumph of appearance over reality:

> . . . Edmund the base
> Shall top th' legitimate. I grow; I prosper.
> Now, gods, stand up for bastards.
>
> (I, ii, 20–2)

In this world of appearance the Gods 'stand up for' (there is a hint of 'manly' tumescence here) the 'apparent' son of Gloucester, and, Edmund hopes, will help him to topple the 'reality' inherent in Edgar's legitimacy.

Thus Gloucester finds himself caught, like Lear, in a trap of his own design. In the manner of Iago, Edmund presents him with evidence which 'proves' Edgar to be 'unfaithful'. Like Iago, Edmund provides 'testimony' (I, ii, 79) against a love which is really true in order to make it appear false. And although Gloucester can lament that such eventualities are not capable of rational explanation, and can give personal preference to explanations of another kind as Horatio did;

> These late eclipses in the sun and moon portend no good to us. Though the wisdom of nature can reason it thus and thus, yet nature finds itself scourg'd by the sequent effects: love cools, friendship falls off, brothers divide . . .   (I, ii, 100 ff.)

– Edmund nevertheless leaves us in no doubt that what has happened has been brought into being by much more mundane causes. He mocks at Gloucester's non-rational account of the situation's origins, and offers us one whose basis is the reverse, and firmly grounded in a 'lower' kind of reasoning:

> This is the excellent foppery of the world, that, when we are sick in fortune, often the surfeits of our own behaviour, we make guilty of our disasters the sun, the moon, and stars; as if we were villains on necessity; fools by heavenly compulsion . . . Fut, I should have been that I am, had the maidenliest star in the firmament twinkled on my bastardizing.   (I, ii, 118 ff.)

Edmund's words strike a 'modern' note of rational explanation which we have heard before. He claims, as Parolles did, to be his own creation, 'simply the thing I am'. What he does, he does for his own reasons, and because of his own reasoning. He is a product of that, and, as a maker of his own reality, an 'actor' (like Lady Macbeth) in his own 'play', it is fitting that he should arrange a little 'play' with Edgar in it, the mock sword-fight, which will present his own version of reality to Gloucester. His speech therefore takes on 'theatrical' metaphors, as did Lady Macbeth's, and for the same reason. As Edgar enters, Edmund comments,

> Pat! he comes like the catastrophe of the old comedy.   My cue is villainous melancholy, with a sigh like Tom o'Bedlam.
>
> (I, ii, 128 f.)

– thus forcing Edgar into a role in his own version of reality, and ironically hinting at his later 'real' role of Poor Tom. Edgar himself becomes unwittingly duped – though he significantly, albeit jokingly, accords Edmund the 'scientific' title of 'sectary astronomical' (I, ii, 143) when he hears him mock Gloucester's reading of the 'portents' in the elements – and Gloucester is led to believe that he has witnessed valid evidence which 'proves' Edgar's guilt, for Edmund had promised him 'better testimony' and a measure of 'auricular assurance' (I, ii, 77 and 88) (the terms carry a sinister echo of Iago's 'ocular proof'). Edmund's purpose is finally achieved when, as a result of such 'proof' he is accorded the privileges and status of a 'legitimate' son, whilst Edgar is denounced as if he were the bastard; appearance has triumphed over reality.

The only escape open to Edgar, as to Lear, lies in a retreat to a world the reverse of that in which 'proof' dictates what is true and what is real. Accordingly, he must divest himself, literally, of the trappings of that world, and put on the poverty and the 'foolishness' of Poor Tom. He retreats, like Lear, from the Court-world of appearance to the Country-world of reality. His 'mad' speech hints at the essence of his situation, for he has indeed been pursued by a 'foul fiend', a description of Edmund which aptly touches on his devilish nature and, again, links him with the rational 'devils' of other plays. Thus, Lear's recognition of the similarity of their positions,

What, has his daughters brought him to this pass?
Could'st thou save nothing? Would'st thou give 'em all?
(III, iv, 63-4)

– also establishes the cognate nature of what has happened to
both of them. The 'foul fiend' which pursues Edgar-Poor Tom is
appearance, and it is analogous to the same devilish force which
has harried Lear, reason. Lear's greeting of Edgar links these
two, brings Gloucester's story into the ken of his own, and
proclaims them complementary. They remain so until the end of
the play.

The sight of Edgar brings about a new phase in Lear's purgation,
one which, as might be expected, takes the form of his being
made more aware of the essential reality of man, stripped of all
his 'courtly' borrowings. The apparent 'manliness' to which
reason urges its proponents here suffers dismissal and replace-
ment by a consideration of man's reality so stark as to be almost
shocking. Viewed by this new clear sight, man becomes a poor
thing indeed, who covers his reality with an appearance of
ceremony and pomp:

Is man no more than this? Consider him well.
Thou ow'st the worm no silk, the beast no hide,
the sheep no wool, the cat no perfume.
(III, iv, 100 ff.)

The almost-naked Edgar causes Lear to recognize his own merely
human status, and involves him finally, in his madness, in an
acceptance of the 'reality' of man himself:

Ha! here's three on's are sophisticated! Thou art the thing itself:
unaccommodated man is no more but such a poor, bare, forked
animal as thou art. Off, off, you lendings! Come, unbutton here.
(III, iv, 104 ff.)

He tears off his own clothes in a symbolic rejection of the 'lendings' of appearance, just as his madness has required a stripping-
away in his mind of the 'garments' of reason. At this point
Gloucester enters (III, iv, 109), confronting Lear but unrecognized by him, and the fusion of the two plots is completely
effected.

Before his exit, Lear recognizes truth in the 'mad' ravings of

Edgar. He refuses to be separated from him, calls him a 'philosopher', and, mocking the rational world he has left behind, will talk of 'causes' with him (III, iv, 150 f.). To Lear, Edgar is a 'learned Theban', a 'good Athenian' (III, iv, 153 and 176) and he clearly respects the non-rational import of his words which, in their own way, suggests some truth, some horror (pertaining particularly to Britain) which lies far beyond the capacity of the reason to state, but which oddly conveys much of the darkness, absurdity, and tragedy of this part of the play:

> Child Rowland to the dark tower came,
> His word was still 'Fie, foh, and fum,
> I smell the blood of a British man.'
>
> (III, iv, 178–80)

Looking at Lear, formerly a British King, now simply a British man, we may feel that, intuitively on our part, we know what he means.

The pace of the play now quickens considerably. Edmund's plotting, his joining with Goneril and Regan (the 'love' which exists between them becomes a grotesque parody of that which all three have professed to their parents) parallels the joining of forces between Lear, Edgar, and the Fool. The alliances take shape, and the way is prepared for the final version of that 'battle' between these enemies of which *Macbeth* was so graphic a chronicle. On his side, Lear has by now accepted 'foolishness' completely, and he accords it the highest of values. He joyfully accepts the 'madman' as 'King' where before he had threatened to strike the Fool when he suggested the same idea:

Fool Prithee, nuncle, tell me whether a madman be a gentleman or a yeoman?
Lear A king, a king! (III, vi, 9–10)

– and Edgar, now termed a 'learned justicer' (III, vi, 21), is enlisted as one of Lear's new 'hundred' knights (III, vi, 78) an army of 'fools' which has the reverse function of that army which Goneril and Regan unmercifully reasoned away. Lear's 'needs' are supplied by the non-rational now, and the march towards Dover begins.

Gloucester's purgation takes the form of blindness. Deceived by the 'auricular assurance' which Edgar gives him, his perception of reality is accompanied by his loss of that sort of sight. As in the case of Lear, his first reaction takes the form of bitter anger:

> As flies to wanton boys are we to th' gods –
> They kill us for their sport.
>
> (IV, i, 37–8)

– and not until after the climax of his attempted suicide is the purgation complete, and Gloucester freed from the taint of his sin. Nevertheless, his momentary cynicism receives its answer in Albany's pronouncement after Cornwall's death. Albany calls Goneril a 'devil' and a 'monster' (IV, ii, 59 ff.) – and whilst he does so, she hurls insults at him whose burden is that he is a 'milk-livered man', whom she mocks typically, 'your manhood – mew!' (IV, ii, 68); characteristically, she thinks of Albany as 'unmanly'. She is a devil who has only the 'appearance' of a woman, like Lady Macbeth:

> . . . thou art a fiend,
> A woman's shape doth shield thee.
>
> (IV, ii, 66–7)

He greets the death of her ally Cornwall as a manifestation of divine justice:

> . . . This shows you are above,
> You justicers . . .
>
> (IV, ii, 78–9)

– thus balancing Gloucester's despair.

Gloucester's leap from the cliff constitutes, metaphorically, a leap from appearance to reality. At this stage he can still be deceived, and is so by the cliff itself. However, at this climactic point of his purgation, he kneels down and renounces 'the world' (IV, vi, 35) in a way which makes his leap only metaphorically necessary. It becomes a ritual act, almost, of withdrawal from the world of appearances by means of a last, benign 'appearance'.

Subsequently, his character changes. He becomes resolved, strong, certain of himself. He has regained contact with reality, and his former bitterness has gone:

> ... Henceforth I'll bear
> Affliction till it do cry out itself
> 'Enough, enough' and die. ...
> (IV, vi, 75–7)

He can now accept Edgar's advice to him to 'Bear free and patient thoughts' (IV, vi, 80). Thus, by means of a 'theatrical' metaphor (and, as in the case of *Macbeth*, 'theatrical' effects are seen to take the side of reality now, as the tide turns the other way) whereby Gloucester leaps from a 'stage' cliff, on the stage, reality triumphs over illusion through a dramatic exploitation of that illusion itself. Gloucester now confides to Edgar, who describes to him his own former appearance as Poor Tom, that

> ... That thing you speak of
> I took it for a man ...
> (IV, vi, 77–8)

But he can now distinguish true 'manliness' from false.

At the point when Gloucester is finally purged, he encounters Lear again, flower-bedecked, face to face (IV, vi, 80 ff.). The victim of appearance meets the victim of reason, one now blind, the other mad. As Edgar says, they are a 'side-piercing sight' (IV, vi, 85) – with all the force of the connotation of Christ's side pierced by a spear which that has. Both have, in their own way, been 'crucified', and Lear's comment that 'Nature's above art in that respect' (IV, vi, 86) is very apt. What we now witness, with Edgar, is 'natural' in every respect. It is real, intuitively, 'foolishly', 'naturally' so, just as the crucifixion was more real than its representation in art, the crucifix. Again, as in the case of *Macbeth*, what we now see on the stage overwhelms 'art', the appearance to nature's reality.

The idea of a divine 'irrationality' (which Christ's death suggests) is developed for the rest of the play. To Gloucester's newly-acquired 'sight', Lear adds intuitive 'irrational' understanding. He knows he is not 'everything', and they that told him so are 'not men o' their words' (IV, vi, 104). He knows that all power is relative, and that its source lies in mere social convention, for 'a dog's obey'd in office' (IV, vi, 157). True 'manliness' does not lie in that. No longer, in contrast to his position at the beginning of the play, does he insist on rational computation in the matter of love or of justice. Now, 'every inch a king', he has learned, as Angelo did, that rational justice must be tempered with divine mercy:

> Thou rascal beadle, hold thy bloody hand.
> Why dost thou lash that whore? Strip thy own back;
> Thou hotly lusts to use her in that kind
> For which thou whip'st her . . .
> (IV, vi, 160–3)

Money, that by which he formerly assessed love, he now denounces as an appearance behind which vice hides itself, a veil which justice cannot pierce:

> Robes and furr'd gowns hide all. Plate sin with gold,
> And the strong lance of justice hurtless breaks. . . .
> (IV, vi, 165–6)

True reality lies, rather, in the enormous 'irrational' love which Lear feels for all mankind, and which manifests itself in a gigantic all-embracing mercy:

> None does offend, none – I say none. . . .
> (IV, vi, 168)

None have offended and yet – and the play ends with this ultimate irrationality – all, even the innocent, suffer. The 'irrational' ending of the play which has puzzled some critics must be regarded in this light. What Lear implies in these scenes lies, as Edgar comments, far above the normal level of the reason. It is 'mad' certainly, but contains a disturbing degree of truth whose composition is of

> . . . matter and impertinency mix'd!
> Reasons in madness! . . .
> (IV, vi, 175–6)

In effect, Lear reveals that balanced way of thinking, that combination of *ratio superior* and *ratio inferior* which Shakespeare seems to have been advocating throughout his plays. In his 'madness' he exhibits the right amount of reason. His 'lower' reasoning is balanced by that of a 'higher' order, intuition. The combination of 'reason in madness' leads him to those enormous truths which we have heard him utter. In his stage 'madness' he arrives at tremendous sanity; by means of the artificial dramatic

art he has become 'natural'. He has finally, in the play's metaphor, 'believed in' a Fool, and has accepted the 'foolishness' of
Cordelia for what it is, a road to reality. With the Fool vanished
from the stage, and Cordelia not yet reached at Dover, Lear
becomes, literally, a 'fool' himself:

> ... I am even
> The natural fool of fortune.
> (IV, vi, 191–2)

His journey is virtually over.

Cordelia's camp, the journey's end, therefore becomes a place
of holiness and sanctity. These are the terms in which she herself
is described throughout the latter part of the play, and they
'surround' and 'place' her as they did in the case of Desdemona.
We are told that

> ... There she shook
> The holy water from her heavenly eyes ...
> (IV, iii, 29–30)

In her presence, Kent can re-assert an 'old' way of looking at the
heavens which we have heard Edmund earlier despise:

> ... It is the stars,
> The stars above us, govern our conditions. ...
> (IV, iii, 32–3)

Lear, on his arrival at this place, calls Cordelia 'a soul in bliss',
says to her 'You are a spirit, I know. Where did you die?' She
brings him 'restoration' and 'medicine', and begs his 'bene-
diction' over her (IV, vii, 26 ff.). The camp, then, presents
'heaven' on the stage, and here Lear's madness undergoes a
significant change of pitch: the 'great rage ... is kill'd in him'
(IV, vii, 78 f.) and he finds peace. Here, too, Gloucester attains
a new quietness, blesses his son, 'Grace go with you, sir!' and
Edgar himself expresses the sort of philosophy which such a
place requires. He speaks of a point of view which accepts that
the world of men is not 'rationally' created, for the momentous
irrational event of death overshadows it. In these circumstances,

> ... Men must endure
> Their going hence, even as their coming hither:
> Ripeness is all.
> (V, ii, 9–11)

This involves not simple stoicism so much as an acceptance of a divine 'plan' for the world which, by the light of man's limited view, often seems 'irrational'. God and events move in mystery, not according to human reason. What appears to be irrational in fact reveals God's way with the world, God's providence.

The ending of the play supports this notion very well. Lear's remarks, for example, about the 'prison' to which he expects to be confined, reveal that he does not regard his fate as unjust, so much as an instance of the providential ordering of events. 'Irrationally', he and Cordelia will be in touch with reality there, so that the prison takes on the colour of a concept opposite to one of captive servitude; it is that of Paradise, where blessing and forgiveness are freely and easily bestowed:

> We two alone will sing like birds i' th' cage;
> When thou dost ask me blessing, I'll kneel down
> And ask of thee forgiveness; so we'll live,
> And pray, and sing, and tell old tales, and laugh
> At gilded butterflies, and hear poor rogues
> Talk of court news; and we'll talk with them too –
> Who loses and who wins; who's in, who's out...
> (V, iii, 9–15)

Having achieved this kind of spiritual reality, away from the 'butterflies' of the Court, they will finally achieve the mystical and intuitive angelic vision; they will see into the secret workings of God's providence. They will

> ... take upon's the mystery of things
> As if we were God's spies...[1]
> (V, iii, 16–17)

The ending of the play reveals something of the nature of 'the mystery of things'. Cordelia's death is, of course, a very cruel event. It seems pointless by our standards, and by the same standards it seems cruel. It seems in fact 'irrational' that she should die. As Lear says,

> Why should a dog, a horse, a rat have life,
> And thou no breath at all?
> (V, iii, 306–7)

[1] I can see no satisfactory justification for Muir's emendation: 'Gods' spies', *Arden* edn., p. 200.

Yet the play, and Lear's own experiences, have answered this question already, before he asks it. We should remember the Fool's 'prophecy'. When things happen as man thinks, rationally, that they 'ought' to happen, then the result will be chaos and confusion, because the normal state of the world will have been disrupted. The world, by this argument, 'needs' sin, 'needs' corruption, 'needs' irrationality, for it is not a rational place, and it does not move in accordance with man's rationally computed 'needs'; as Lear has pointed out in his madness, the art of our necessities is 'strange', not predictable or capable of computation. The Fool's argument was against the notion of Utopias because these are rationally designed by man to fulfil his calculated 'needs'. But, if the needs are 'strange', the calculation cannot encompass them. The point of the world and the way it moves lies in its inexplicability, its incapacity for being 'reasoned' out, and this has been the burden of the argument tacitly put against all the 'reasoners' of these plays. Montaigne expresses exactly this point of view in his judgement that

> It is an occasion to induce Christians to beleeve, when they chance to meet with any incredible thing, that it is so much the more according unto reason by how much more it is against humane reason.[1]

Its basis is Tertullian's *Certum est quia impossibile est*. On the other hand, the 'reasoner' inevitably holds the reverse point of view; he requires God's world to become man's. In so doing he usurps God's authority, and suffers punishment for that. His sin becomes an aspect of the Original Sin of Pride.

This view satisfactorily explains (in Shakespeare's terms at least) the circumstances in which Cordelia's death occurs. Its whole point lies in its irrationality and, as she is a creature with 'divine' qualities, a divine irrationality destroys her. Like Christ's death, Cordelia's atones, irrationally on the level of man, for the sins of man. She must die to complete the play's argument for significantly, like Job,[2] Lear is asked finally to accept this irrational occurrence as possessed of a higher order of reason than that of the world. It constitutes the ultimately 'foolish' event with which he has to come to terms.

[1] *Op. cit.*, p. 200.
[2] Lear's resemblance to Job is fully treated by John Holloway, *op. cit.*, pp. 85 ff.

It is doubtful whether Lear does so. His repeated 'Never' is inconclusive, and he dies urging us to look at Cordelia most carefully, as if there were something in her dead body which speaks to us:

> Do you see this? Look on her. Look, her lips.
> Look there, look there!
>
> (V, iii, 310–11)

Her corpse has something to say, for it represents the price that has had to be paid for the victory of reality and intuition over appearance and reason. Albany now rules, aided by Edgar and Kent. Good has triumphed, right has been restored, and Cordelia's body has been the sacrifice with which it has been bought. The solution to the problems which the plays leading up to *King Lear* have raised lies there, as Lear perhaps realized, with her. God's world is not man's; reason destroys what it cannot encompass, and substitutes an appearance for the reality which it has destroyed. Faith, intuition, 'foolishness', on the other hand, proves insufficient by itself. The world undeniably exists, and man has to learn to live in those surroundings. Retreat from the world is no answer to the world's corruption. The world can be dealt with on its own terms, but man must draw on his own 'irrational' resources in order to match those which oppose him. The price he pays for victory in the battle he fights is a heavy one, and Cordelia's body mutely says as much, for this is what it represents. Reality has to be paid for by innocence, as Christ died, in innocence, and 'foolishly', to save the world. At the end of *King Lear* Edgar, fittingly, makes this point. Things are as they are, and they must be borne:

> The weight of this sad time we must obey;
>
> (V, iii, 323)

– but he adds that a way of dealing with life, of 'speaking' about it, exists, which is not answerable to the reason at all, but to something beyond it:

> Speak what we feel, not what we ought to say.
>
> (V, iii, 324)

He makes a statement of intuitive faith in the face of the horror that lies about him. It is a statement of victory.

CONCLUSION

'KING LEAR' is both an end and a beginning. As L. C. Knights concludes:

> . . . *King Lear* is the great central masterpiece, the great exploratory allegory to which so many of the earlier plays lead and on which the later plays depend.[1]

That 'allegory' manifests itself in many different ways, and this book has suggested that one of those may be by means of a consideration of the human faculty of reason.

It would be misleading to give the impression that this constitutes the major concern of the seven plays which have been discussed, but it remains nevertheless a discernible aspect of their diffused confrontation with fundamental and endemic problems of the human condition. To imply that those plays deal conclusively with the matter, that it ends with them, would also be misleading; *King Lear* looks forward as well as backward. In fact the play's 'centrality' results from its dual role both as a 'summing-up' of a cycle begun by *Hamlet* and as the beginning of a further cycle which *The Tempest* concludes. Accordingly, perhaps its greatest achievement lies in the fulfilment of a pattern to which it brings the final, meaningful element; completing such a pattern, *King Lear* also creates and furthers it.

So momentous a design will inevitably prove susceptible to many interpretations, as various as the particular interests of those who encounter it. Shakespeare satisfies most of our rages for order; the carpet is full of patterns. The present study has attempted to describe one of those, though it has, of necessity, involved itself in others. Its frame of reference has been two modes of cognition, conceived in Shakespeare's time as opposed mental faculties, reason and intuition, which, although anti-

---

[1] L. C. Knights, *Some Shakespearean Themes* (London, 1959), p. 158.

podean in function, had formerly been considered complementary one to another within the single faculty of *ratio*.

The dichotomy between these two seems to mirror a larger one in the culture itself. The opposition between them receives cognate manifestation in many other forms to the extent that two opposed 'ways of life' seem to align themselves in a similar oppugnancy. In effect, the conflict between reason and intuition embodies the polarities of existence; it informs and is informed by fundamental human dualities, such as that of body and spirit, to which most dichotomies are in some way analogous. Since in most societies a 'rational' way of looking at the world inevitably opposes an 'intuitive' way, just as a 'new' and 'active' view of life inevitably opposes an 'old' and 'contemplative' one, the conflict forms a basic element in human experience. Schism of such a fundamental sort furnishes the bare bones of drama, and these plays do not seem unusual in this respect; the texture of the Shakespearean carpet is that of life.

But the disposition of its pattern's constituent parts comprises a comment on life, and provides a measure of the degree of Shakespeare's commitment to one side of the opposition against the other. In so far as the plays make judgements which nominate the 'higher' reason as the faculty through which reality may be perceived, and the 'lower' reason as the faculty which can only perceive appearances, they contain moral arguments and they state a moral case. They depict a reason which looks downwards with the body, towards the world, and an intuition which looks upwards with the spirit, towards God. They argue that the values of reason, and the body, inculcate a false notion of 'manliness', whereas the values of intuition, and the spirit, inculcate a concept of the true man. Nevertheless, they also recognize man's involvement in and consequent duties towards a world which makes demands of him whose complexities will not yield to any such clear-cut arrangement of morality. On the highest level, they are realistic.

Each of the six plays which immediately precede *King Lear* contains implicit judgements in the matter, for each of them places its protagonist in a situation where aspects of that opposition impinge on him, demand his attention, and force him into a course of action which tests his moral strength or weakness in that respect. Their judgement lies in that those of the protagonists who manage to cope with the situation and to maintain a balance between the two extremes gain approbation; those who do not undergo severe punishment.

Hamlet attempts an early and tentative configuration of the entire complexity and this proves too weighty a burden for the play to bear. The prince is faced from first to last with mutually contradictory alternatives between which events force him to choose. But in endeavouring to encompass most of the ramifications of a diffused opposition, the alternatives proliferate so that they burst the bounds of the play. Choice itself, rather than one man's voice, becomes its dominant characteristic. Hamlet's personal dilemma is diminished as a result; he seems merely to dither at every turn. A contemplative from Wittenberg, events require him to act in Elsinore. A prince, he is claimed as a 'son' by two Kings, one spiritual, one very much physical, both of whom seek his allegiance. In following his real father, Hamlet opposes his apparent father. His intuitive 'madness' reveals a reality opposed to the reason of Elsinore which has substituted an appearance for it. He counters the spurious 'manliness' of the Court with the actions of a true man.

But however blurred the play's statement of the conflict may be, and however much Hamlet's release from its grip, by death, may seem to by-pass major issues, the ending contains a hint of a solution to the problem. *Hamlet* attempts too much; the burden breaks the back of the revenge-structure that carries it and reveals weaknesses in that form. But nonetheless the notion emerges of a providential design in the world, a design so vast that it overrides the limitations of the human reason. Reason, the play implies, contains the seeds of its own defeat. Knowing only the world, it knows very little of the truly real.

If *Hamlet* fails both to contain and express these matters effectively, the 'problem plays' which follow seek to remedy that failure. They experiment in the technique of presenting and commenting on the same opposition, and the 'problems' with which they deal are in part those of dramatic structure.

Thus *Troilus and Cressida* essays a sophisticated presentation of the conflict between rational and intuitive values which the Trojan war, like all great wars, eponymously suggests. Troilus, firmly on the side of Trojan intuition, finds himself trapped in a lesser version of that opposition when Cressida is handed over to the Greeks. Faced, like Hamlet, with 'new' and completely rational values, he romantically espouses their opposite, and the play exposes him to considerable, if partly sympathetic scorn as a result. Confronted by two Cressidas, one rationally, one intuitively perceived, the event finds him unable to cope with its demands. He goes under with Troy, having shown an unwillingness to distinguish between the reality of Cressida and her false appearance. 'Truth's simplicity,' if it involves simple rejection of the reason, is clearly shown to be impracticable and useless in a world whose values lie elsewhere. Intuition of itself provides no antidote to an embattled reason; it leads as far from reality in one direction as its opponent does in another.

All's Well That Ends Well replaces sophistication almost by its obverse, the traditional *naïveté* of the folk-tale. Nevertheless, Bertram faces a situation similar to that of Troilus, although the play does not subject him to such scornful treatment; as is proper in a folk-tale, the story 'ends well'. Where a conflict between reason and intuition confronted Cressida's lover, Bertram has to choose between appearance and reality, between the 'name' of honour extolled by a dealer in mere names, Parolles, and honour itself, represented by Helena, whose name means love. The play follows a simple pattern appropriate to its nature in that Bertram's initial and wrong choice resolves itself in the end. He rejects the apparent and spuriously 'manly' values of Parolles for the real and truly 'manly' values of fatherhood and marriage inherent in Helena, whose 'magic' has proved itself restorative.

Measure for Measure seems to try to combine the moods of the two plays which precede it. The sophistication of *Troilus and Cressida* informs much of the action, but it 'ends well' as a result of the Duke's benign control which oversees all its events. Like Bertram, both Angelo and Isabella learn and profit by their mistakes. Like the King in *All's Well That Ends Well*, the Duke teaches them where reality lies. It does not lie in the rigidities of 'cold' reasoning which calculates prices, punishments and rewards, but in the God-like quality of mercy, whose standards are super-rational, overriding mathematical equalities and computations.

In the problem plays, Shakespeare seems to have learned that the issues with which *Hamlet* concerned itself are best dealt with separately. Incomplete and inconclusive in themselves, they rehearse a method of dramatizing a complex idea which the three tragedies which follow practise to greater effect. Thus, where *Troilus and Cressida* treats the issue of reason opposed to intuition and *All's Well That Ends Well* concerns itself with the cognate one of appearance opposed to reality, *Measure for Measure* attempts, with some success, a combined treatment of both.

Othello begins the tragic *reprise* of these themes which reaches its climax in *King Lear*. It contains a simple and direct treatment of the opposition between reason and intuition, in which Iago's rational attack on the intuitive love between Othello and Desdemona constitutes the main theme of the play. Othello's inability to cope with that force exhibits a later and more complex version of Troilus' inadequacy. Othello's disdain for reason, his inability to meet it on its own terms, causes his tragedy.

Macbeth deals almost exclusively with the cognate opposition of appearance and reality, in which his wife's reasoning draws Macbeth from a world of honour and 'manliness' to one in which these qualities are replaced by appearances of themselves. His plight is a tragic version of Bertram's, but so much more powerfully expressed (and with such a different result) that a comparison of the play with *All's Well That Ends Well* seems almost to diminish it. There is nothing 'well' in the way *Macbeth* ends.

King Lear ends the cycle which *Hamlet* began by a triumphant combination of both themes in its dual plot. Where Lear finds himself caught in a conflict between rational and intuitive values embodied by his daughters, Gloucester is caught in the clash between appearance and reality embodied by his sons. Lear's purgative journey from reason to intuition parallels Gloucester's equally purgative journey from appearance to reality. Lear loses the reason which prevented him from perceiving reality, Gloucester loses the sight which deluded him by its appearance. Both learn to 'see' in a new way. The experiments of the problem plays have resulted in a structure which repairs and compensates for *Hamlet*'s earlier imperfection; a momentous opposition has at last been presented in its full complexity. In addition, the play completes and makes meaningful the pattern which *Hamlet* began. In fact, *Hamlet*'s ending can now be seen to have groped in the direction of that of *King Lear*. The notion of a vast providential ordering of the world which lies beyond the reason's scope has been expanded to include an acceptance of irrationality, of 'foolishness' of a sort which demands a tremendous faith in such a design. The ways of God are above reason, to be accepted, not questioned; a true 'man' must believe in a divinely 'foolish' plan of existence.

The pattern, as this brief survey shows, is kaleidoscopic, and its central elements may be variously disposed without disruption of the design. But within it, certain 'constants' may be discerned; for example, the villains of these plays could be said to share common characteristics. To a greater or lesser extent they are all 'reasoners', they speak with the same voice; they use reason to disguise reality and to create appearances in its place; they uphold and urge on others an unreal notion of 'manliness' which in fact proves more bestial than human; as a result love for them becomes mere sexuality. Their victims have to choose between that 'way of life' and another whose values lie in a different direction. These involve an intuitive way of thinking, a 'higher' kind of reality, another notion of 'manliness' which rises far above the bestial level. Love as a result takes on a spiritual, as well as a bodily quality, and it leads to the divine harmony of marriage and legitimate procreation. If the villains are all fleshly creatures whose values are those of the body and of the world, they are opposed by contrary values of the spirit and of heaven.

It has been argued that *King Lear* provides an 'answer' to the problem which these plays express, but the play contains much more than that. It comprises both a beginning and an end, and appropriately not only answers but asks a question. L. C. Knights phrases that quite simply; the play enquires of us, 'is there any escape from appearance and illusion?'[1]

In one way the dramatic formulation of such a question represents a greater achievement than the answer to it, and by the same token the most powerful experience these plays afford is that of being asked rather than told something. Shakespeare's position in time perhaps gives them that kind of power for, faced with the beginnings of a modern world, he puts to it a modern query which we, that world's inheritors, have still to answer. In

[1] *Loc. cit.*

asking the question he does so as a modern artist, perhaps the first; in answering it he speaks from an older point of view.

He seems to contend that, since the 'lower' reason proves itself untrustworthy, then it cannot be relied on, alone, as a means of knowing reality. On the other hand, he implies that the 'higher' intuitive reason alone may prove an equally disastrous basis for living in and dealing with the world. Man is a rational being whether he likes it or not. He bears the characteristic of *discursus*, and to deny that denies his humanity. To reject the reason completely invites an attack from just that quarter. The 'lower' reason is a destructive force, as Macbeth learns, and intuitive values are vulnerable to it. No victory can be won against that kind of reason on its own terms; only when the terms of a higher form of reality apply can its conclusions be rejected. Lear's victory lies in his ability to accept this principle.

Felicity consists, therefore, in a recognition of Man's true situation. Accordingly, *nosce teipsum* has a status much greater than that of a banal apothegm, it becomes a moral necessity. Virtue lies in the fulfilment of the obligations imposed by one's condition, and they should be completely fulfilled. 'Completeness' requires that Man should be *completely* rational in the 'old' sense, whereby the *ratio* exists as a unity. The activities of the 'lower' reason should complement those of its 'higher' counterpart.

When these are mutually contradictory, that is in a 'modern' situation, a man must be forced to choose between them because he cannot give credence to both. As a result his situation becomes tragic because it partakes of dis-unity, and this forms part of a characteristic pattern in the tragedies and problem plays; the protagonist's 'tragic choice' between alternatives is their 'signature'. To avoid tragedy, a man must avoid the role of chooser, and the plays which follow *King Lear* seem to make this point with increasing emphasis. They are plays in which a choice can be re-considered and so avoided, in which a 'second chance' presents itself whereby unity can be retrieved from dis-unity, and in which that which has been 'lost' can be found again.

However attractive the notion may be that such restoration is both necessary and possible, our own world has perhaps advanced too far in another direction to make it acceptable.

Conclusion

We may have lost something irretrievably, but we do not lament a loss which we do not recognize. Nor could we be said collectively to subscribe to an idea of God and His providence sufficient of itself to quicken such an idea. But if the answers no longer suit, the question remains; if the dilemma is permanent, it is ours.

We can and do reassure ourselves nevertheless by pointing to the relative nature of 'reality'. The pre-eminent achievement of anthropological investigation of human activities has been the recognition that whatever a civilization believes to be real becomes so for itself. Our solution to such a dilemma is often to deny that it exists; there is no reality beyond that which one's own culture accepts.

And yet a characteristic of the human condition lies also in the implacable nagging sense that an ultimate reality does exist which should, perhaps must, be discerned. And however much trust we now place in the 'lower' reason, we harbour undeniable suspicions about its efficacy in spite of ourselves. D. H. Lawrence speaks for these when he offers as part of his 'creed' that 'the only justice is to follow the sincere intuition of the soul, angry or gentle.'[1] The feeling that our world is fragmented and divided forms part of the modern experience, and E. M. Forster's famous plea, 'only connect', perhaps provides its most apposite epigraph because it gives the essence of a central tradition in our culture concerned with the unification of what has been disrupted rather than its acceptance. Shakespeare's tragedies and problem plays not only recognize the fact of disruption, explore its nature and point to a possible reconciliation and unity for their own culture, they also compel us to recognize, explore, and thereby attempt to reconcile a related disruption that we, in the modern world, have inherited.

[1] D. H. Lawrence, 'Benjamin Franklin', *Studies in Classic American Literature*, (London, 1924).

INDEX